GOD'S
TREASURY
OF VIRTUES

GOD'S TREASURY
OF VIRTUES

Tulsa, Oklahoma

2nd Printing
150,000 in Print

God's Treasury of Virtues
ISBN 1-56292-153-3
Copyright © 1995 by Honor Books, Inc.
Honor Books, Inc.
P.O. Box 55388
Tulsa, OK 74155

CONTENTS

INTRODUCTION

"The Virtuous Life"

What is *virtue*? Perhaps the simplest definition on which most would agree is "moral goodness." Virtue is the composite of all traits or qualities that are deemed good, right, and fitting for all persons in a particular culture.

In practice, however, virtue is an ideal. No one is completely virtuous, except perhaps in fiction. Virtue is a quality we *seek* and *pursue*, one that requires discipline and focused intent to achieve. No one is born virtuous. Virtue is acquired. And while a person may not be able to attain virtue fully, we have an innate understanding as human beings that virtue is worthy of pursuit, and that, to at least some extent, it can be gained.

Thus, virtue is linked to desire. The virtuous person must desire to be virtuous—not only to strive toward the ideal of moral goodness, but to cling fast to all aspects of goodness attained and to maintain a strong center of goodness in spite of societal turmoil, interpersonal conflict, or difficult circumstances. The virtuous person, therefore, asks two questions:

- What must I do to be a good person?
- How can I hold on to the reputation of goodness that I have won?

Both of these questions are answered best in terms of behavior. Indeed, we don't know that a person is "good" unless that person does good deeds! To BECOME a good person, one must do good things, make good choices, express good attitudes, and engage in good behavior. To MAINTAIN a reputation of goodness, one must do good things that are outwardly visible to others.

Perhaps that is why many definitions of virtue include the idea of "an inherent power." The pursuit of virtue seems to trigger a secondary activity. The more we seek to become a person marked by goodness, the more we seek to DO good. We are *compelled* in pursuit of virtue to act in certain ways that are beneficial to others, and in a cyclical fashion, bring benefit back to us.

Two broad questions, then, arise naturally.

First, what are the specific qualities that we assign to virtue? Or, what traits do we call "virtues?"

Second, what objective, outside source or criterion, is used in assigning certain traits to virtue, or of calling certain qualities "virtues?" Goodness may be defined in a number of ways. Just exactly what it is, and according to whom, is a good question.

The Source of All Virtue

In this book, these questions are answered this way.

Virtue—moral goodness—will be defined by criterion set forth in the Holy Bible. That's why this book is titled *GOD'S TREASURY OF VIRTUES.*

Jesus, the only sinless man ever to live, said of Himself when He was called good, *"Why do you call Me good? No one is good but One, that is, God"* (Matthew 19:17 NKJV). So according to the Bible, absolute goodness is a trait of God, and ultimately, a trait belonging to God alone. Anything we know of goodness, therefore, must be derived from Him and bestowed by Him.

The Bible teaches that man is not born "good," but rather with evil intent in his heart. Of man, the Lord says in (Genesis 8:21 NKJV): *"The imagination of man's heart is evil from his youth."* How then can an inherently "bad" person become a "good" person—one who reflects God's own divine nature of good?

The New Testament is clear. In it, the apostle Paul prayed for the Ephesians:

I pray that out of his glorious riches he may strengthen you with power through his Spirit in your inner being, so that Christ may dwell in your hearts through faith. And I pray that you, being rooted and established in love, may have power, together with all the saints, to grasp how wide and long and high and deep is the love of Christ, and to know this love that surpasses knowledge—that you may be filled to the measure of ALL THE FULLNESS OF GOD (Ephesians 3:16-19 NIV).

When he prayed, Paul knew this: Man becomes good when Christ dwells in his heart by faith . . . which leads to a strengthening of the inner man by the power of the Holy Spirit . . . which establishes a person in love and power (moral goodness in principle and in deed) . . . which builds in ever-increasing amounts of God's goodness until the person is *filled* with the fullness of God.

Elsewhere in the New Testament, we find very definitive lists of "goodness" inherent to the Holy Spirit that He imparts to man. One of the most comprehensive lists was given by the apostle Paul to the church in Galatia:

When the Holy Spirit controls our lives he will produce this kind of fruit in us: love, joy, peace, patience, kindness, goodness, faithfulness, gentleness, and self-control (Galatians 5:22–23 TLB).

Here, then, are the traits—or the list of specific qualities known as virtues—that will be examined in this book!

Virtue, by biblical definition, is the "fruit of the Holy Spirit" evident in our lives. We are "good" when we bear these hallmark qualities of the Spirit within us and manifest them daily to those around us. Again, the specific qualities are listed in Scripture as love, joy, peace, patience, kindness, goodness, faithfulness, gentleness, and self-control.

And for each quality, this principle holds true: these traits are not something that a person owns. They are something a person *does*.

In other words . . .

Love is not only a quality, but an action. The person who experiences love and has love in his heart, shows love through generous giving to others.

Joy manifests itself in praise and in voicing words of encouragement to others.

Peace manifests itself in calmness and an even temperament.

And so forth.

Classic Statements
About the Holy Spirit's
"Fruit" in Our Lives

Writers throughout Christian history have given us clear and varied insight into just what these traits are like, how they work in our lives, and how they are manifested to others. In this book you will find more than five hundred of these classic Christian teachings, as well as statements that are in agreement with Christian principles, that elaborate upon each trait of the Holy Spirit's "fruit." In some cases, these statements have been excerpted from longer works such as books, sermons, or plays. In other cases, they are succinct statements couched in the form of songs, poems, epitaphs and prayers. While most of the statements are nonfiction, a few segments of fiction have been included.

The male and female writers of these entries span a two-thousand-year period, reflect a diversity of doctrine and denomination, and exhibit a great variety in style; however, all of the entries have one thing in common:

> All point to God as the source of goodness
> in life, and all point to the necessity of
> doing good to others.

We suggest that you read these entries aloud—to yourself, to a friend or spouse, and to your children. This will not only enhance the meaning of these entries to you (especially those entries that are in old English or very formal style), but it will cause the teachings to become part of your very way of thinking. In this way, *GOD'S TREASURY OF VIRTUES* will not only be a reference book to you, but a means of building up virtue in your own life!

Jesus, God of peace and love,
Send Thy blessing from above,
Take, and seal us for Thine own,
Touch our hearts, and make them one.

By the sense of sin forgiven
Purge out all the former leaven,
Malice, guile, and proud offence;
Take the stone of stumbling hence.

Root up every bitter root,
Multiply the Spirit's fruit,
Love, and joy, and quiet peace,
Meek, longsuffering gentleness;

Strict and general temperance,
Boundless, pure benevolence,
Cordial firm fidelity;
All the mind which was in Thee.

Poetics: "For the Fruits of the Spirit,"
Hymn XXV (IV, 194,195)

Chapter 1

LOVE

"And above all things have fervent love for one another, for 'love will cover a multitude of sins'" (1 Peter 4:8 NKJV).

Love.
Is there any word that evokes more feeling in us?
Is there any more desired trait...more cherished quality...
or more noble virtue?

Most Christian writers seem to regard love as the epitome of virtue, the highest and most all-encompassing fruit of the Spirit:

- To some, it is the ultimate virtue toward which all other qualities point.

- To others, it is the end of a quest for virtue, a journey that is begun with self-control and which progresses upward through gentleness, faithfulness, and so forth, until it bursts through joy into the glorious infinity of God's very own nature. (See 1 John 4:8.)

- And still to others, love is the fountainhead from which all other aspects of moral goodness flow, either directly or sequentially.

All are in agreement, however, that love is the supreme characteristic of God...as the apostle John so succinctly put it, *"God is love"* (1 John 4:8 NIV).

Defined in the original Greek language of the New Testament as "agape," God's fruit of love gives itself away generously and purely, with no motive other than to express God's nature.

The First Thing

But the fruit of the Spirit is love, joy, peace, longsuffering, gentleness, goodness, faith, meekness, temperance: against such there is no law.

— *Galatians 5:22–23*
HOLY BIBLE

The fruit of the Spirit begins with love. There are nine graces spoken of, and of these nine Paul puts love at the head of the list; love is the first thing, the first in that precious cluster of fruit. Someone has said that all the other eight can be put in terms of love. Joy is love exulting; peace is love in repose; longsuffering is love on trial; gentleness is love in society; goodness is love in action; faith is love on the battlefield; meekness is love at school; and temperance is love in training. So it is love all the way; love at the top, love at the bottom, and all the way along down this list of graces. If we only just brought forth the fruit of the Spirit, what a world we would have! Men would have no desire to do evil.

— *Dwight L. Moody*

The D. L. Moody Year Book
Selected by Emma Moody Fitt
New York: Fleming H. Revell Company, 1900

The Greatest

Though I speak with the tongues of men and of angels, and have not charity, I am become as sounding brass, or a tinkling cymbal.

And though I have the gift of prophecy, and understand all mysteries, and all knowledge; and though I have all faith, so that I could remove mountains, and have not charity, I am nothing.

And though I bestow all my goods to feed the poor and though I give my body to be burned, and have not charity, it profiteth me nothing.

Charity suffereth long, and is kind; charity envieth not; charity vaunteth not itself, is not puffed up,

Doth not behave itself unseemly, seeketh not her own, is not easily provoked, thinketh no evil;

Rejoiceth not in iniquity, but rejoiceth in the truth;

Beareth all things, believeth all things, hopeth all things, endureth all things.

Charity never faileth: but whether there be prophecies, they shall fail; whether there be tongues, they shall cease; whether there be knowledge, it shall vanish away.

For we know in part, and we prophesy in part.

But when that which is perfect is come, then that which is in part shall be done away.

When I was a child, I spake as a child, I understood as a child, I thought as a child: but when I became a man, I put away childish things.

For now we see through a glass, darkly; but then face to face: now I know in part; but then shall I know even as also I am known.

And now abideth faith, hope, charity, these three; but the greatest of these is charity.

— 1 Corinthians 13
HOLY BIBLE

Two Kinds of Love

One of the puzzling questions likely to turn up sooner or later to vex the seeking Christian is how he can fulfill the Scriptural command to love God with all his heart and his neighbour as himself. He wants to, but he cannot. The delightful wells of feeling simply will not flow. How can I love by commandment?

To find our way out of the shadows and into the cheerful sunlight we need only to know that there are two kinds of love: the love of feeling and the love of willing. The one lies in the emotions, the other in the will. The love the Bible enjoins is not the love of feeling; it is the love of willing, the willed tendency of the heart. (For these two happy phrases I am indebted to another.) Religion lies in the will and so does righteousness. The will is the automatic pilot that keeps the soul on course. The will, not the feelings, determines moral direction. The root of all evil in human nature is the corruption of the will. The prodigal son took his first step upward from the pigsty when he said, "I will arise and go to my father." As he had once willed to leave his father's house, now he willed to return.

To love God with all our heart we must first of all will to do so. We should repent for our lack of love and determine from this moment on to make God the object of our devotion. We shall soon find to our great delight that our feelings are beginning to move in the direction of the "willed tendency of the heart." Our emotions will become disciplined and directed. We shall begin to taste the "piercing sweetness" of the love of Christ. The whole life, like a delicate instrument, will be tuned to sing the praises of Him who loved us and washed us from our sins in His own blood. But first of all we must will, for the will is master of the heart.

— *A. W. Tozer*

Taken from *Man: The Dwelling Place of God* by A. W. Tozer. Copyright © 1989 by A. W. Tozer. Used by permission of Christian Publications.

From Love, Of Love, For Love

Lord, my God, when Your love spilled over into creation
You thought of me.

I am
>from love,
>of love,
>for love.

Let my heart, O God, always
>recognize,
>cherish,
>and enjoy Your goodness in all of creation.

Direct all that is in me toward Your praise.
Teach me reverence for every person, all things.
Energize me in Your service.

Lord God, may nothing ever distract me from Your love. . .
>neither health nor sickness
>wealth nor poverty
>honor nor dishonor
>long life nor short life.

May I never seek nor choose to be other than You intend or wish.

Amen.

>*— Jacqueline Syrup Bergan and S. Marie Schwan*

Love, A Guide for Prayer
Winona, Minn.: Saint Mary's Press, 1985

Love in Action

This is the message you heard from the beginning: We should love one another. Do not be like Cain, who belonged to the evil one and murdered his brother. And why did he murder him? Because his own actions were evil and his brother's were righteous. Do not be surprised, my brothers, if the world hates you. We know that we have passed from death to life, because we love our brothers. Anyone who does not love remains in death. Anyone who hates his brother is a murderer and you know that no murderer has eternal life in him.

This is how we know what love is: Jesus Christ laid down his life for us. And we ought to lay down our lives for our brothers. If anyone has material possessions and sees his brother in need but has no pity on him, how can the love of God be in him? Dear children, let us not love with words or tongue but with actions and in truth. This then is how we know that we belong to the truth, and how we set our hearts at rest in his presence whenever our hearts condemn us. For God is greater than our hearts, and he knows everything.

Dear friends, if our hearts do not condemn us, we have confidence before God and receive from him anything we ask, because we obey his commands and do what pleases him. And this is his command: to believe in the name of his Son, Jesus Christ, and to love one another as he commanded us.

— *1 John 3:11-23* (NIV)
HOLY BIBLE

Unchanging

Love is not love
Which alters when it alterations finds.

— *William Shakespeare*

Sonnet CXVI
Harper's Quotations

A New Kind of Love

If God told Adam to conquer and subdue the earth, not replenish it as the old version reads, what a ministry this new creation man has in subduing selfishness, viciousness and bitterness with love, peace and joy.

A new kind of man and a new kind of love.

I can remember what Jesus said in John 13:34–35, *"A new commandment I give unto you, that ye love one another; as I have loved you, That ye also love one another. By this shall all men know that ye are my disciples, if ye have love one to another."*

A love race.

A love Covenant.

A love commander.

A love family.

The day of hardness and selfishness ends in love.

These last twenty-five years of dreadful wars have so blinded our consciousness of right and wrong, and love and joy, that we can hardly take this truth in, but the dream of the Father was that love should dominate and rule every one of us.

You see, there are two major forces in the world: selfishness and love.

Selfishness has given birth to all our sorrows, heartaches and tears. It has caused all the wars and other atrocities in which men take part.

The world is not yet acquainted with the new kind of love, Agape love.

Few have seen it in practice, and still fewer enjoy its fullness.

It absolutely eliminates selfishness.

For years I wondered what Spiritual Death was.

I knew that Spiritual Life was the Nature of the Father.

I knew that Spiritual Death must be the Nature of Satan.

Then I saw that the Nature of the Father is revealed through our conduct, our acts of love.

Like a flash I saw it, Satan's Nature is selfishness.

God so loved that He gave.

Satan was so selfish that he sought to rob God and the human race of everything worthwhile.

Selfishness is a robber.

It had reigned without a rival through the ages.

Now a mighty new Force has broken into the Sense Realm.

That mighty Force is Love.

It heads up in God.

It was unveiled in Christ.

It is becoming operative in us.

Love without the ability to use it would not be so good.

— *E. W. Kenyon*

What Happened From the Cross to the Throne
Kenyon's Gospel Publishing Society, 1969

Why God Should Be Loved

You ask me, "Why should God be loved?" I answer: the reason for loving God is God Himself. And why should God be loved for His own sake? Simply because no one could be more justly loved than God, no one deserves our love more. Some may question if God deserves our love or if they might have something to gain by loving Him. The answer to both questions is yes, but I find no other worthy reason for loving Him except Himself.

God is entitled to our love. Why? Because He gave Himself for us despite the fact that we are so undeserving. What better could He have given? If we ask why God is entitled to our love, we should answer, "Because He first loved us." God is clearly deserving of our love especially if we consider who He is that loves us, who we are that He loves, and how much He loves us.

And who is God? Is He not the one to whom every spirit bears witness: "Thou art my God?" God has no need of our worldly possessions. True love is precisely this: That it does not seek its own interests. And how much does He love us? He so loved the world that He gave His only Son; He laid down His life for us.

— *Bernard of Clairvaux*

On the Love of God
Translated by Terence L. Connolly
New England Province of the Society of Jesus, 1937

Love and God's Will

The Will as Love

Our love of God must not be gauged by the passing feelings we experience that are not controlled by the will, but rather we must judge them by the enduring quality of the will itself. For loving God means that we join our will to God's will. It means that our will consents to whatever the will of God commands. It means that we have only one reason for wishing anything, and the reason is that we know that God wills it . . . .

A Distinction Between Two Loves

Feelings are not entirely ours to command. We are attracted towards some against our will, while towards others we can never experience a spontaneous affection. If we are moved solely by our feelings, that is not love. Real love means that we are still master of our acts, and we use our inclinations and attractions simply as guides in the direction which we choose to take. And the same is true when reason tells us what direction love must take. It is not reason which impels us to love, it is we ourselves who choose to love, taking reason as our guide.

— *St. Aeired of Rievaulx*

Translation of The Mirror of Charity
by Geoffrey Webb and Adrian Walker (Mowbrays, 1962)
by permission of A. R. Mowbray & Co. Ltd.

On Love of God

"Thou shalt love the Lord thy God with thy hole heart, with thy whole soul and with thy whole mind." This is the commandment of the great God, and He cannot command the impossible. Love is a fruit in season at all times, an within reach of every hand. Anyone may gather it and no limit is set.

— *Mother Teresa*

Malcolm Muggeridge
Something Beautiful for God
San Francisco: Harper & Row, 1971

Love Thy Neighbour

"Love thy neighbour." Perhaps he rolls in riches, and thou art poor, and living in thy little cot side-by-side with his lordly mansion; thou seest every day his estates, his fine linen, and his sumptuous banquets; God has given him these gifts, covet not his wealth, and think no hard thoughts concerning him. Be content with thine own lot, if thou canst not better it, but do not look upon thy neighbour, and wish that he were as thyself. Love him, and then thou wilt not envy him.

Mayhap, on the other hand, thou art rich, and near thee reside the poor. Do not scorn to call them neighbours. Own that thou art bound to love them. The world calls them thy inferiors. In what are they inferior? They are far more thine equals than thine inferiors, for "God hath made of one blood all people that dwell upon the face of the earth." It is thy coat which is better than theirs, but thou art by no means better than they. They are men, and what art thou more than that? Take heed that thou love thy neighbour even though he be in rags, or sunken in the depths of poverty.

But, perhaps, you say, "I cannot love my neighbours, because for all I do they return ingratitude and contempt." So much the more room for the heroism of love. Wouldst thou be a feather-bed warrior, instead of bearing the rough fight of love? He who dares the most, shall win the most; and if rough be thy path of love, tread it boldly, still loving thy neighbours through thick and thin. Heap coals of fire on their heads, and if they be hard to please, seek not to please them, but to please thy Master; and remember, if they spurn thy love, thy Master hath not spurned it, and thy deed is as acceptable to Him as if it had been acceptable to them. Love thy neighbour, for in so doing thou art following the footsteps of Christ.

— *Charles H. Spurgeon*

Taken from *Morning and Evening Devotions:*
An Updated Edition of the Classic Devotional in
Today's Language by C. H. Spurgeon.
Copyright © 1987 by Thomas Nelson Publishers.
Used by permission of Thomas Nelson Publishers.

It's A Miracle

This is the miracle that happens every
time to those who really love: the more
they give, the more they possess of that
precious, nourishing love from which
flowers and children have their strength
and which could help all human beings
if they would take it without doubting.

— *Rainer Maria Rilke*

The Book of Unusual Quotations
Selected and Edited by Rudolf Flesch
New York: Harper and Brothers Publishers, 1957

God's Love of Man

God loves you. You're rebellious, you cheat, you commit
immorality, you're selfish, you sin, but God loves you with an inten-
sity beyond anything that I could describe to you. He loves you, and
He loves you so much that He gave His only Son, Jesus Christ to die
on that cross; and the thing that kept Christ on that cross was love,
not the nail.

— *Billy Graham*

The Quotable Billy Graham
Compiled and Edited by Cort R. Flint and the Staff of *Quote*
Anderson, S.C.: Droke House, 1966

God's Love . . . and Our Love

Dear friends, let us practice loving each other, for love comes from God and those who are loving and kind show that they are the children of God, and that they are getting to know him better. But if a person isn't loving and kind, it shows that he doesn't know God—for God is love.

God showed how much he loved us by sending his only Son into this wicked world to bring to us eternal life through his death. In this act we see what real love is: it is not our love for God but his love for us when he sent his Son to satisfy God's anger against our sins.

Dear friends, since God loved us as much as that, we surely ought to love each other too. For though we have never yet seen God, when we love each other God lives in us, and his love within us grows ever stronger. And he has put his own Holy Spirit into our hearts as a proof to us that we are living with him and he with us. And furthermore, we have seen with our own eyes and now tell all the world that God sent his Son to be their Savior. Anyone who believes and says that Jesus is the Son of God has God living in him, and he is living with God.

We know how much God loves us because we have felt his love and because we believe him when he tells us that he loves us dearly. God is love, and anyone who lives in love is living with God and God is living in him. And as we live with Christ, our love grows more perfect and complete; so we will not be ashamed and embarrassed at the day of judgment, but can face him with confidence and joy because he loves us and we love him too.

We need have no fear of someone who loves us perfectly; his perfect love for us eliminates all dread of what he might do to us. If we are afraid, it is for fear of what he might do to us and shows that we are not fully convinced that he really loves us. So you see, our love for him comes as a result of his loving us first.

If anyone says "I love God," but keeps on hating his brother, he is a liar; for if he doesn't love his brother who is right there in front of him, how can he love God whom he has never seen? And God himself has said that one must love not only God but his brother too.

— *1 John 4:7-21* (TLB)
HOLY BIBLE

The Sweetness of Divine Love

Jesus, how sweet is the very thought of You!
You fill my heart with joy. The sweetness of Your love
surpasses the sweetness of honey. Nothing sweeter
than You can be described; no words can express the
joy of Your love. Only those who have tasted Your love
for themselves can comprehend it. In your love You
listen to all my prayers, even when my wishes are
childish, my words confused, and my thoughts foolish.
And You answer my prayers, not according to my own
misdirected desires, which would bring only bitter
misery, but according to my real needs, which brings
me sweet joy. Thank You, Jesus, for giving Yourself for me.

— *Bernard of Clairvaux*

The Harper Collins Book of Prayers -
A Treasury of Prayers Through the Ages
Compiled by Robert Van de Weyer
San Francisco: Harper, 1993

The Love of the Lord

Believer, look back through all thine experience, and think
of the way whereby the Lord thy God has led thee in the wilderness,
and how He hath fed and clothed thee every day—how He hath borne
with thine ill manners—how He hath put up with all thy murmurings,
and all thy longings after the flesh-pots of Egypt—how He has opened
the rock to supply thee, and fed thee with manna that came down
from heaven. Think of how His grace has been sufficient for thee in
all thy troubles—how His blood has been a pardon to thee in all thy
sins—how His rod and His staff have comforted thee. When thou hast

thus looked back upon the love of the Lord, then let faith survey His love in the future, for remember that Christ's covenant and blood have something more in them than the past. He who has loved thee and pardoned thee, shall never cease to love and pardon. He is Alpha, and He shall be Omega also: He is first, and He shall be last. Therefore, bethink thee, when thou shalt pass through the valley of the shadow of death, thou needest fear no evil, for He is with thee. When thou shalt stand in the cold floods of Jordan, thou needest not fear, for death cannot separate thee from His love; and when thou shalt come into the mysteries of eternity thou needest not tremble, *"For I am persuaded that neither death; nor life, nor angels, nor principalities, nor powers, nor things present, nor things to come, nor height, nor depth, nor any other creature, shall be able to separate us from the love of God, which is in Christ Jesus our Lord."* Now, soul, is not thy love refreshed? Does not this make thee love Jesus? Doth not a flight through illimitable plains of the ether of love inflame thy heart and compel thee to delight thyself in the Lord thy God? Surely as we meditate on "the love of the Lord," our hearts burn within us, and we long to love Him more.

— *Charles H. Spurgeon*

Taken from *Morning and Evening Devotions: An Updated Edition of the Classic Devotional in Today's Language* by C. H. Spurgeon. Copyright © 1987 by Thomas Nelson Publishers. Used by permission of Thomas Nelson Publishers.

Loving Your Neighbor

Real love for one's neighbor means loving him for his own sake and not simply for the sake of God—as a matter of religious duty. Any other view is incompatible with Jesus' idea of God, Who on His part loves men for their own sakes. Likewise real love for God is something more than the sum of one's love for men; it is also the devout response of one's being to a Being of Infinite Wisdom and Love. Neither love for God nor love for man, then, is merely a derivative from its counterpart; yet each nourishes the other. When we love our fellowman for his own sake the life of God flows through us, and when we are responsive to the God of Infinite Wisdom and Love we are better able to discover and foster the moral and spiritual capacities of our fellowmen.

— *E. W. Lyman*

The Meaning and Truth of Religion
John Baillie, *And the Life Everlasting*
New York: Charles Scribner's Sons, copyright ©1933

Love Your Enemies

Jesus taught:
"But I tell you who hear me: Love your enemies, do good to those who hate you, bless those who curse you, pray for those who mistreat you. If someone strikes you on one cheek, turn to him the other also. If someone takes your cloak, do not stop him from taking your tunic. Give to everyone who asks you, and if anyone takes what belongs to you, do not demand it back. Do to others as you would have them do to you.
"If you love those who love you, what credit is that to you? Even 'sinners' love those who love them. And if you do good to those who are good to you, what credit is that to you? Even 'sinners' do that. And if you lend to those from whom you expect repayment, what credit is that to you? Even 'sinners' lend to 'sinners,' expecting to be repaid in full. But love your enemies, do good to them, and lend to them without expecting to get anything back. Then your reward will be great, and you will be sons of the Most high, because he is kind to the ungrateful and wicked. Be merciful, just as your Father is merciful."

— *Luke 6:27-36 (NIV)*
HOLY BIBLE

Three Dimensions

What then is the conclusion of the matter? Love yourself, if that means rational and healthy self-interest. You are commanded to do that. That is the length of life. Love your neighbor as you love yourself. You are commanded to do that. That is the breadth of life. But never forget that there is a first and even greater commandment: "Love the Lord thy God with all thy heart, and with all thy soul, and with all thy mind." This is the height of life. Only by a painstaking development of all three of these dimensions can you expect to live a complete life.

— *Martin Luther King, Jr.*

Taken from *Three Dimensions of a Complete Life:*
A Martin Luther King Treasury
by Martin Luther King, Jr.
Reprinted by arrangement with
The Heirs to the Estate of Martin Luther King, Jr.,
c/o Joan Daves Agency as agen⁺ for the propreitor.

Forget It

If you see a tall fellow ahead of the crowd,
A leader of music, marching fearless and proud,
And you know of a tale whose mere telling aloud
Would cause his proud head to in anguish be bowed,
　　　It's a pretty good plan to forget it.
If you know of a skeleton hidden away
In a closet, and guarded and kept from the day
In the dark; whose showing, whose sudden display
Would cause grief and sorrow and lifelong dismay,
　　　It's a pretty good plan to forget it.
If you know of a spot in the life of a friend
(We all have spots concealed, world without end)
Whose touching his heartstrings would sadden or rend,
Till the shame of its showing no grieving could mend,

It's a pretty good plan to forget it.
If you know of a thing that will darken the joy
Of a man or a woman, a girl or a boy,
That will wipe out a smile or the least way annoy
A fellow, or cause any gladness to cloy,
It's a pretty good plan to forget it.

— *Author Unknown*

from *Poems That Live Forever*
Hazel Felleman, Editor
Doubleday, 1965

Love Is Stronger Than Death

In our time, as in every age, we need to see something which is stronger than death. Death has become powerful in our time, in individual human beings, in families, in nations and in mankind as a whole. Death has become powerful—that is to say that the End, the finite, and the limitations and decay of our being have become visible. For nearly a century this was concealed in Western civilization. We had become masters in our earthly household. Our control over nature and our social planning had widened the boundaries of our being; the affirmation of life had drowned out its negation which no longer dared make itself heard, and which fled into the hidden anxiety of our hearts, becoming fainter and fainter. We forgot that we are finite, and we forgot the abyss of nothingness surrounding us. . . We kept the picture of death from our children and when here and there, in our neighborhood and in the world, mortal convulsions and the End became visible, our security was not disturbed. For us these events were merely accidental and unavoidable, but they were not enough to tear off the lid which we had fastened down over the abyss of our being.

And suddenly the lid was torn off. The picture of Death appeared, unveiled, in a thousand forms. As in the late Middle Ages the figure of Death appeared in pictures and poetry, and the Dance of Death with every living being was painted and sung, so our generation—the generation of world wars, revolutions, and mass migrations—rediscovered the reality of death. We have seen millions die in wars, hundreds of thousands in revolutions, tens of thousands in persecutions and systematic purges of minorities. . .

But who can bear to look at this picture? Only he who can look at another picture behind and beyond it—the picture of Love. For love is stronger than death. Every death means parting, separation, isolation, opposition, and not participation. So it is, too, with the death of nations, the end of generations, and the atrophy of souls. Our souls become poor and disintegrate insofar as we want to be alone, insofar as we bemoan our misfortunes, nurse our despair and enjoy our bitterness, and yet turn coldly away from the physical and spiritual needs of others. Love overcomes separation and creates participation in which there is more than that which the individuals involved can bring to it. Love is the infinite which is given to the finite. Therefore we love in others, for we do not merely love others, but we love the Love that is in them and which is more than their or our love. In mutual assistance what is most important is not the alleviation of need but the actualization of love. Of course, there is no love which does not want to make the other's need its own. But there is also no true help which does not spring from love and create love. Those who fight against death and disintegration through all kinds of relief agencies know this. Often very little external help is possible. And the gratitude of those who receive help is first and always gratitude for love and only afterwards gratitude for help. Love, not help, is stronger than death. But there is no love which does not become help. Where help is given without love, there new suffering grows from the help.

It is love, human and divine, which overcomes death in nations and generations and in all the horror of our time. Help has become almost impossible in the face of the monstrous powers which we are experiencing. Death is given power over everything finite, especially in our period of history. But death is given no power over love. Love is stronger. It creates something new out of the destruction caused by death; it bears everything and overcomes everything. It is at work where the power of death is strongest, in war and persecution and homelessness and hunger and physical death itself. It is omnipresent and here and there, in the smallest and most hidden ways as in the greatest and most visible ones, it rescues life from death. It rescues each of us, for love is stronger than death.

— *Paul Tillich*

Reprinted with the permission of Scribner,
A Division of Simon & Schuster, Inc.
from *The New Being* by Paul Tillich. Copyright 1955
Paul Tillich; copyright © 1983 Hannah Tillich

Christian Love

[A Christian's love] is in itself generous and disinterested; springing from no view of advantage to himself, from no regard to profit or praise—no, nor even the pleasure of loving. This is the daughter, not the parent, of his affection. By experience he knows that social love, if it means the love of our neighbour, is absolutely different from self-love, even of the most allowable kind—just as different as the objects at which they point. And yet it is sure that, if they are under due regulations, each will give additional force to the other till they mix together never to be divided.

— *John Wesley*

Letters: "To Dr. Conyers Middleton" (II–377)
John Wesley's Theology by Burtner and Chiles
Abingdon Press

Teach Us To Love

Lord, we thank Thee for all the love that has been given to us, for the love of family and friends, and above all for Your love poured out upon us every moment of our lives in steadfast glory. Forgive our unworthiness. Forgive the many times we have disappointed those who love us, have failed them, wearied them, saddened them. Failing them we have failed You, and hurting them we have wounded our Saviour who for love's sake died for us. Lord, have mercy on us, and forgive. You do not fail those who love You. You do not change nor vary. Teach us Your own constancy in love, Your humility, selflessness and generosity. Look in pity on our small and tarnished loving, protect, foster and strengthen it, that it may be less unworthy to be offered to You and to Your children. O Light of the world, teach us how to love.

— *Elizabeth Goudge*

The Harper Collins Book of Prayers -
A Treasury of Prayers Through the Ages
Compiled by Robert Van de Weyer
San Francisco: Harper, 1993

God Is Still Love

In the deepest heart of every man God planted a longing for Himself, as He is: a God of love. No matter what we say, our hearts cry out for God to care, to be involved with us, to love us. This is His idea. He created this longing in us. It is the longing toward the "light that lighteth every man who cometh into the world."

The human race longs for love because the human race longs for God. God and love are not similar. Love is not merely one of God's characteristics. "God is love."

No matter how it looks to us, nothing changes this. He is not dead. He is. And if we believe He is, then we can know that He is love.

Anyone can be freed to see both the truth about our world and the truth about God and come out free not only to believe in love, but to love. This does not happen overnight, but it can begin happening at any moment to anyone, and because God is growth and life as well as love, it can go on happening.

— *Eugenia Price*

Make Love Your Aim
Berkeley Press

The Everlasting Love

Too late have I loved You, O Beauty so ancient and so new, too late have I loved You! Behold, You were within me, while I was outside: it was there that I sought You, and a deformed creature, rushed headlong upon these things of beauty which You have made. You were with me, but I was not with You. They kept me far from You, those fair things which, if they were not in You, would not exist at all. You have called to me, and have cried out, and have shattered my deafness. You have blazed forth with light, and have shone upon me, and You have put my blindness to flight! You have sent forth fragrance, and I have drawn in my breath, and I pant after You. I have tasted You, and I hunger and thirst after You. You have touched me, and I have burned for Your peace.

— *St. Augustine*

From *The Confessions of St. Augustine*
by John K. Ryan. Copyright © 1960,
by Doubeday, a division of Bantam Doubleday Dell
Publishing Group, Inc. Used by permission
of Doubleday, a division of Bantam Doubleday Dell
Publishing Group, Inc.

This I Know

I know not where His islands lift
Their fronded palms in air;
I only know I cannot drift
Beyond His love and care.

— *John G. Whittier*

The Eternal Goodness, XX
The Oxford University Press
Dictionary of Quotations, 22nd edition
New York: Crescent Books, 1985

Cost of Discipleship

All that the follower of Jesus has to do is to make sure that his obedience, following and love are entirely spontaneous and unpremeditated. If you do good, you must not let your left hand know what your right hand is doing, you must be quite unconscious of it. Otherwise you are simply displaying your own virtue, and not that which has its source in Jesus Christ. Christ's virtue, the virtue of discipleship, can only be accomplished so long as you are entirely unconscious of what you are doing. The genuine work of love is always a hidden work. Take heed therefore that you know it not, for only so is it the goodness of God. If we want to know our own goodness or love, it has already ceased to be love. We must be unaware even of our love for our enemies. After all, when we love them they are no longer our enemies. This voluntary blindness in the Christian (which is really sight illuminated by Christ) is his certainty, and the fact that His life is hidden from his sight is the ground of his assurance.

— *Dietrich Bonhoeffer*

Reprinted with permission of Simon & Schuster, Inc.,
from *The Cost of Discipleship* by Dietrich Bonhoeffer,
translated from the German by R.H. Fuller.
Copyright © 1959 by SCM Press Ltd.

The Marvelous Effect of the Love of God

Love is a great and good thing, and alone makes heavy burdens light and bears in equal balance things pleasing and displeasing. Love bears a heavy burden and does not feel it, and love makes bitter things tasteful and sweet. The noble love of Jesus perfectly imprinted in man's soul makes a man do great things, and stirs him always to desire perfection and to grow more and more in grace and goodness.

Love knows no measure, but is fervent without measure. It feels no burden; it regards no labor; it desires more than it can obtain. It complains of no impossibility, for it thinks all things that can be done for its Beloved are possible and lawful. So, love does many great things and brings them to completion—things in which he who is no lover faints and fails.

Love wakes much and sleeps little and, in sleeping, does not sleep. It faints and is not weary; it is restricted in its liberty and is in great freedom. It sees reasons to fear and does not fear, but, like an ember or a spark of fire, flames always upward, by the fervor of its love, toward God, and through the special help of grace is delivered from all perils and dangers.

— *Thomas à Kempis*

The Love of Christ

Here is love, that God sent His Son, His Son who never offended, His Son who was always His delight. Herein is love, that He sent Him to save sinners; to save them by bearing their sins, by bearing their curse, by dying their death, and by carrying their sorrows.

Here is love, in that while we were yet enemies, Christ died for us; yes, here is love, in that while we were yet without strength, Christ died for the ungodly.

— *John Bunyan*

Hymns for the Family of God

For Love, For Love

Father of spirits, this my sovereign plea
I bring again and yet again to Thee.

Fulfil me now with love, that I may know
A daily inflow, daily overflow.

For love, for love, my Lord was crucified,
With cords of love He bound me to His side.

Pour through me now; I yield myself to Thee,
O Love that led my Lord to Calvary.

— Amy Carmichael

The Harper Collins Book of Prayers -
A Treasury of Prayers Through the Ages
Compiled by Robert Van de Weyer
San Francisco: Harper, 1993

O Love That Wilt Not Let Me Go

O Love that wilt not let me go,
I rest my weary soul in Thee;
I give Thee back the life I owe,
that in Thine ocean depths its flow may richer, fuller be.

O Light that followest all my way,
I yield my flickering torch to Thee;
my heart restores its borrowed ray,
that in thy sunshine's blaze its day may brighter, fairer be.

O Joy that seekest me through pain,
I cannot close my heart to Thee;
I trace the rainbow thru the rain,
and feel the promise is not vain, that morn shall tearless be.

O Cross that liftest up my head,
I dare not ask to fly from Thee;
I lay in dust life's glory dead,
and from the ground there blossoms red life that shall endless be.

— *George Matheson*

Love Begins at Home

God gives us that great strength and the great joy of loving those He has chosen. Do we use it? Where do we use it first? Jesus said love one another. He didn't say love the world, He said love one another—right here, my brother, my neighbour, my husband, my wife, my child, the old ones. Our Sisters are working around the world and I have seen all the trouble, all the misery, all the suffering. From where did it come? It has come from lack of love and lack of prayer. There is no coming together in the family, praying together, coming together, staying together. Love begins at home and we will find the poor even in our own home. We have a house in London. Our Sisters there work at night and one night they went out to pick up the people on the streets. They saw a young man there late at night, lying in the street, and they said, "You should not be here, you should be with your parents," and he said, "When I go home my mother does not want me because I have long hair. Every time I go home she pushes me out." By the time they came back he had taken an overdose and they had to take him to the hospital. I could not help thinking it was quite possible his mother was busy, with the hunger of our people of India, and there was her own child hungry for her, hungry for her love, hungry for her care and she refused it.

It is easy to love the people far away. It is not always easy to love those close to us. It is easier to give a cup of rice to relieve hunger than to relieve the loneliness and pain of someone unloved in our own home. Bring love into your home for this is where our love for each other must start.

Lord, keep us faithful to each other — in Your love. Let nothing, let nobody separate us from Your love and the love we must bear for each other. Amen.

— *Mother Teresa*

Life in the Spirit
San Francisco: Harper & Row

Second–Century Christians

They love one another. They never fail to help widows; they save orphans from those who would hurt them. If they have something they give freely to the man who has nothing; if they see a stranger, they take him home, and are happy, as though he were a real brother. They don't consider themselves brothers in the usual sense, but brothers instead through the Spirit, in God.

— *Aristides describing Christians*
to the Emperor Hadria

A Quieter, Deeper Love

Love as distinct from "being in love" is not merely a feeling. It is a deep unity, maintained by the will and deliberately strengthened by habit; reinforced by (in Christian marriages) the grace which both partners ask, and receive, from God. They can have this love for each other even at those moments when they do not like each other, as you love yourself even when you do not like yourself. They can retain this love even when each would easily, if they allowed themselves, be "in love" with someone else. "Being in love" first moved them to promise fidelity: this quieter love enables them to keep the promise. It is on this love that the engine of marriage is run: being in love was the explosion that started it.

— *C. S. Lewis*

Mere Christianity
HarperCollins, Ltd.

Best Love

Love sought is good, but giv'n unsought is better.

— *William Shakespeare*

Twelfth Night, Ib. [170]

His Command

Jesus taught:

"As the Father has loved me, so have I loved you. Now remain in my love. If you obey my commands, you will remain in my love, just as I have obeyed my Father's commands and remain in his love. I have told you this so that my joy may be in you and that your joy may be complete. My command is this: Love each other as I have loved you. Greater love has no one than this, that he lay down his life for his friends. You are my friends if you do what I command. I no longer call you servants, because a servant does not know his master's business. Instead, I have called you friends, for everything that I learned from my Father I have made known to you. You did not chose me, but I chose you and appointed you to go and bear fruit–fruit that will last. Then the Father will give you whatever you ask in my name. This is my command: Love each other."

—*John 15:9-17* (NIV)
HOLY BIBLE

Covenant Relationship

God's love is an exercise of His goodness towards individual sinners whereby, having identified Himself with their welfare, He has given His Son to be their Saviour, and now brings them to know and enjoy Him in a covenant relation . . . .It is staggering that God would love sinners; yet it is true. God loves creatures who have become unlovely and (one would have thought) unlovable. There was nothing whatever in the objects of His love to call it forth; nothing in man could attract or prompt it. Love among men is awakened by something in the beloved, but the love of God is free, spontaneous, unevoked, uncaused. God loves men because He has chosen to love them–as Charles Wesley put it, "He hath loved us, He hath loved us, because he would love"–and no reason for His love can be given save His own sovereign good pleasure.

—*J. I. Packer*

Taken from *Knowing God* by J.I. Packer.
Used by permission of InterVarsity Press,
P.O. Box 1400, Downers Grove, IL 60515.

Love Divine, All Loves Excelling

Love divine, all loves excelling,
Joy of heaven, to earth come down;
Fix in us Thy humble dwelling,
All Thy faithful mercies crown:
Jesus, Thou art all compassion,
Pure, unbounded love Thou art;
Visit us with Thy salvation,
Enter every trembling heart.

Breath, O breathe Thy loving Spirit
Into every troubled breast;
Let us all in Thee inherit,
Let us find the promised rest;
Take away the love of sinning,
Alpha and Omega be;
End of faith, as its beginning,
Set our hearts at liberty.

Come, Almighty, to deliver,
Let us all Thy life receive;
Suddenly return, and never,
Nevermore Thy temples leave.
Thee we would be always blessing,
Serve Thee as Thy hosts above,
Pray, and praise Thee without ceasing,
Glory in Thy perfect love.

Finish then Thy new creation,
Pure and spotless let us be;
Let us see Thy great salvation,
Perfectly restored in Thee;
Changed from glory into glory,
Till in heaven we take our place,
Till we cast our crowns before Thee,
Lost in wonder, love, and praise!

— *Charles Wesley*

Love Just Because

We ought to love our Maker for His own sake,
without either hope of good or fear of pain.

— Cervantes

The Book of Unusual Quotations
Selected and edited by Rudolf Flesch
New York: Harper and Brothers Publishers, 1957

It Cannot Be Stopped

If we love God and give ourselves to Him, we must give ourselves to the whole world. Otherwise we would divide off our personal experience of God from His Greatness and Infinite Presence and turn what ought to be dedication into private enjoyment.

One of the holy miracles of love is that once it is really started on its path, it cannot stop; it spreads and spreads in ever-widening circles till it embraces the whole world in God. We begin by loving those nearest to us, end by loving those who seem farthest. And as our love expands, so our whole personality will grow, slowly but truly. Every fresh soul we touch in love is going to teach us something fresh about God.

One of the mystics said: God cannot lodge in a narrow heart: our hearts are as great as our love. Let us take that into our meditation and measure our prayer and service against the unmeasured generosity of God.

— Evelyn Underhill

An Anthology of the Love of God

Knit to the Soul

So when David returned from killing the Philistine, Abner took him and brought him before Saul with the Philistine's head in his hand. And Saul said to him, "Whose son are you, young man?" And David answered, "I am the son of your servant Jesse the Bethlehemite."

Now it came about when he had finished speaking to Saul, that the soul of Jonathan was knit to the soul of David, and Jonathan loved him as himself.

And Saul took him that day and did not let him return to his father's house.

Then Jonathan made a covenant with David because he loved him as himself. And Jonathan stripped himself of the robe that was on him and gave it to David, with his armor, including his sword and his bow and his belt.

Now Saul was afraid of David, for the LORD was with him but had departed from Saul. Therefore Saul removed him from his presence, and appointed him as his commander of a thousand; and he went out and came in before the people. And David was prospering in all his ways for the LORD was with him.

Now there was an evil spirit from the LORD on Saul as he was sitting in his house with his spear in his hand, and David was playing the harp with his hand. And Saul tried to pin David to the wall with the spear, but he slipped away out of Saul's presence, so that he struck the spear into the wall. And David fled and escaped that night.

Then David fled from Naioth in Ramah, and came and said to Jonathan, "What have I done? What is my iniquity? And what is my sin before your father, that he is seeking my life?" And he said to him, "Far from it, you shall not die. Behold, my father does nothing either great or small without disclosing it to me. So why should my father hide this thing from me? It is not so!"

Yet David vowed again, saying, "Your father knows well that I have found favor in your sight, and he has said, 'Do not let Jonathan know this, lest he be grieved.' But truly as the Lord lives and as your soul lives, there is hardly a step between me and death."

Then Jonathan said to David, "The LORD, the God of Israel, be witness! When I have sounded out my father about this time tomorrow, or the third day, behold, if there is good feeling toward David, shall I not then send to you and make it known to you? If it please my father to do you harm, may the LORD do so to Jonathan and more also, if I do not make it known to you and send you away, that you may go in safety. And may the LORD be with you as He has been with my father. And if I am still alive, will you not show me the lovingkindness of the LORD that I may not die? And you shall not cut off your lovingkindness from my house forever, not even when the LORD cuts off every one of the enemies of David from the face of the earth."

So Jonathan made a covenant with the house of David, saying, "May the LORD require it at the hands of David's enemies." And Jonathan made David vow again because of his love for him, because he loved him as he loved his own life.

Then Jonathan said to him, "Tomorrow is the new moon, and you will be missed because your seat will be empty. When you have stayed for three days, you shall go down quickly and come to the place where you hid yourself on that eventful day, and you shall remain by the stone Ezel. And I will shoot three arrows to the side, as though I shot at a target. And behold, I will send the lad, saying, 'Go, find the arrows.' If I specifically say to the lad, 'Behold, the arrows are on this side of you, get them,' then come; for there is safety for you and no harm, as the LORD lives. But if I say to the youth, 'Behold, the arrows are beyond you,' go, for the LORD has sent you away. As for the agreement of which you and I have spoken, behold, the LORD is between you and me forever."

So David hid in the field; and when the new moon came, the king sat down to eat food. And it came about the . . . second day of the new moon, that David's place was empty; so Saul said to Jonathan his son, "Why has the son of Jesse not come to the meal, either yesterday or today?"

Jonathan then answered Saul, "David earnestly asked leave of me to go to Bethlehem, for he said, 'Please let me go, since our family has a sacrifice in the city, and my brother has commanded me to attend. And now, if I have found favor in your sight, please let me get away that I may see my brothers.' For this reason he has not come to the king's table."

Then Saul's anger burned against Jonathan and he said to him, "You son of a perverse, rebellious woman! Do I not know that you are choosing the son of Jesse to your own shame and to the shame of your mother's nakedness? For as long as the son of Jesse lives on the earth, neither you nor your kingdom will be established. Therefore now, send and bring him to me, for he must surely die." But Jonathan answered Saul his father and said to him, "Why should he be put to death? What has he done?"

Then Saul hurled his spear at him to strike him down; so Jonathan knew that his father had decided to put David to death. Then Jonathan arose from the table in fierce anger, and did not eat food on the second day of the new moon, for he was grieved over David because his father had dishonored him.

Now it came about in the morning that Jonathan went out into the field for the appointment with David, and a little lad was with him. And he said to his lad, "Run, find now the arrows which I am about to shoot." As the lad was running, he shot an arrow past him. When the lad reached the place of the arrow which Jonathan had shot, Jonathan called after the lad, and said, "Is not the arrow beyond you?" And Jonathan called after the lad, "Hurry, be quick, do not stay!" And Jonathan's lad picked up the arrow and came to his master. But the lad was not aware of anything; only Jonathan and David knew about the matter. Then Jonathan gave his weapons to his lad and said to him, "Go, bring them to the city."

When the lad was gone, David rose from the south side and fell on his face to the ground, and bowed three times. And they kissed each other and wept together, but David more.

And Jonathan said to David, "Go in safety, inasmuch as we have sworn to each other in the name of the LORD, saying, 'The Lord will be between me and you, and between my descendants and your descendants forever.'" Then he rose and departed, while Jonathan went into the city.

> — *1 Samuel 17:57–58; 18:1–4, 12–14;*
> *19:9–10; 20:1–3, 12–24, 27–42*
> (NASB) *HOLY BIBLE*

Let Me Walk in the Way of Love

O my God, let me walk in the way of love which knoweth not how to seek self in anything whatsoever.

But what love must it be?

It must be an ardent love,
a pure love,
a courageous love,
a love of charity,
a humble love,
and a constant love.

O Lord, give this love into my soul, that I may never more live nor breathe but out of a more pure love of Thee, my All and only God. Amen.

— Dame Gertrude More

Taken from "Let Me Walk in the Way of Love" from
Prayers From the Heart by Richard J. Foster.
Copyright © 1994 by Richard J. Foster.
Reprinted by permission of HarperCollins Publishers, Inc.

God's Great Love

I had set my feet upon the foothold of the temple and yet was held back by the worldly love which was so deeply rooted in me and thus not able to move ahead fully . . . the thought of this world still had the upper hand in me and . . . Evil was still as strong in me as a giant beside whom a child is placed.

Who is more wretched than I, had I remained in such circumstances, since I grasped heaven with one hand and the earth with the other, wished to enjoy God and the friendship of the world at the same time, or fought first against the one, then against the other, and could hold neither properly. But oh, how great is the love of God.

which He manifested to the human race in Christ Jesus! God did not cast me aside because of my deep corruption in which I stood fast, but He had patience with me and helped me in my weakness, since I could not find the courage but only always hoped that I might break through into a true light which is from God. I experienced in myself that one does not have cause to complain about God, but that He always opens door and gate where He finds a heart that honestly looks to Him and seeks His presence earnestly. God always went before me and lifted the blocks and difficulties out of the way so that I was convinced that my conversion was not mine but His work. God took me at the same time by His hand and led me as a mother leads her weak child, and so great and overpowering was His love that He always grasped me once again when I tore loose from His hand, and allowed me to sense the rod of His discipline. Finally, He heard my prayer and set me in a free and unbound state . . .

— *August Hermann Francke*

from *The Autobiography, 1692*
Pietists–Selected Writings
Edited with an Introduction by Peter C. Erb
Ramsey, N.J.: Paulist Press, 1983

Beyond Oneself

If human love does not carry a man beyond himself, it is not love. If love is always discreet, always wise, always sensible and calculating, never carried beyond itself, it is not love at all. It may be affection, it may be warmth of feeling, but it has not the true nature of love in it.

— *Oswald Chambers*

Taken from *My Utmost for His Highest*
by Oswald Chambers, edited by James Reimann,
copyright © 1992 by Oswald Chambers Publications Assn., Ltd.
Original edition copyright © 1935 by Dodd, Mead & Co.,
renewed 1963 by Oswald Chambers Publications Assn., Ltd., and is
used by permission of Discovery House Publishers, Box 3566, Grand Rapids, MI 49501.

More Love

Lord, it is my chief complaint;
That my love is weak and faint;
Yet I love thee and adore,
Oh for grace to love thee more!

— *William Cowper*

Olney Hymns, Ib
The Oxford University Press
Dictionary of Quotations, 22nd edition
New York: Crescent Books, 1985

The Stages of Love

The first stage is to believe that there is only one kind of love. The middle stage is to believe that there are many kinds of love and that the Greeks had a different word for each of them. The last stage is to believe that there is only one kind of love.

The unabashed *eros* of lovers, the sympathetic *philia* of friends, *agape* giving itself away freely no less for the murderer than for his victim (the *King James Version* translates it as *charity*)—these are all varied manifestations of a single reality. To lose yourself in another's arms, or in another's company, or in suffering for all men who suffer, including the ones who inflict suffering upon you—to lose yourself in such ways is to find yourself. Is what it's all about. Is what love is.

Of all powers, love is the most powerful and the most powerless. It is the most powerful because it alone can conquer that final and most impregnable stronghold which is the human heart. It is the most powerless because it can do nothing except by consent.

In the Christian sense, love is not primarily an emotion, but an act of the will. When Jesus tells us to love our neighbors, He is not telling us to love them in the sense of responding to them with a cozy emotional feeling. You can as easily produce a cozy emotional feeling on demand as you can a yawn or a sneeze. On the contrary, He is telling us to love our neighbors in the sense of being willing to work for their well-being even if it means sacrificing our own well-being to that end, even if it means sometimes just leaving them alone. Thus, in Jesus' terms, we can love our neighbors without necessarily liking them. In fact, liking them may stand in the way of loving them by making us overprotective sentimentalists instead of reasonably honest friends.

When Jesus talked to the Pharisees, he didn't say, "There, there. Everything's going to be all right." He said, *"You brood of vipers! how can you speak good when you are evil!"* (Matthew 12:34 NAS). And He said that to them because He loved them.

This does not mean that liking may not be a part of loving, only that it doesn't have to be. Sometimes liking follows on the heels of loving. It is hard to work for people's well-being very long without coming in the end to rather like them too.

— *Frederich Buechner*

Taken from *Wishful Thinking-A Theological ABC*
by Fredrick Buechner. Copyright © 1973
by Fredrick Buechner. Reprinted
by permission of HarperCollins Publishers, Inc.

Love Comes Back

Life may change, but it may fly not;
Hope may vanish, but can die not;
Truth be veiled, but still it burneth;
Love repulsed, but it returneth!

— *Percy Bysshe Shelley*

Hellas, l. 34
The Oxford University Press
Dictionary of Quotations, 22nd edition
New York: Crescent Books, 1985

His Love . . . Reaching

Right from the beginning God's love has reached, and from the beginning man has refused to understand. But love went on reaching, offering itself. Love offered the eternal . . . we wanted the immediate. Love offered deep joy . . . we wanted thrills. Love offered freedom . . . we wanted license. Love offered communion with God Himself . . . we wanted to worship at the shrine of our own minds. Love offered peace . . . we wanted approval for our wars. Even yet, love went on reaching. And still today, after two thousand years, patiently, lovingly, Christ is reaching out to us today. Right through the chaos of our world, through the confusion of our minds. He is reaching . . . longing to share with us . . . the very being of God.

His love still is longing, His love still is reaching, right past the shackles of my mind. And the Word of the Father became Mary's little Son. And His love reached all the way to where I was.

— *Gloria Gaither*

Love and God's Favor

As long as anyone has the means of doing good to his neighbors, and does not do so, he shall be reckoned a stranger to the love of the Lord.

— *Irenaeus*

Friendship, Human and Divine

Dear Lord, how the love of my friends toward me rejoices my heart. Who can describe the feeling in the heart that comes from knowing people's love? It is indescribable. to be aware that there are people who love me, even as the miserable sinner that I am, fills me with hope. And the source of the hope is the knowledge that my friends' love for me is a pale shadow of God's love for me. Thus, when God takes me to heaven, the present joy I have in friendship will be multiplied a thousandfold. Such bliss is worth any earthly sacrifice. Lord, Your name is Love. In Your love there is sweetness beyond words. Grant that I may always be faithful to my friends here on earth, that I may be worthy of Your faithful love for me.

— John Sergieff

The Harper Collins Book of Prayers-
A Treasury of Prayers Through the Ages
Compiled by Robert Van de Weyer
San Francisco: Harper, 1993

How Do We Know Love?

But how does man come to know that God is love? That love is because God is? That the love of God is not only available for any man to experience, it is available for any man to demonstrate? How do we come to know the true nature of love? By reading a book or embracing a particular philosophy or doctrine? Do we learn love from the Bible? From other human beings who expound it? Do we learn about the nature of love by practice? Is it an emotional or a spiritual exercise?

It is all of these to lesser and greater degrees, but it is more. . .

We can only learn of love as we learn of God. Jesus said, " . . . learn of Me."

There is no other way to learn of love.

— Eugenia Price

Make Love Your Aim
Berkeley Press

Chapter 2

JOY

*"**B**ut let all those rejoice who put their trust in You; let them ever shout for joy, because You defend them; let those also who love Your name be joyful in You" (Psalm 5:11 NKJV).*

The command that is repeated the most often in the Bible is, "Rejoice." To rejoice means not only to have joy, but to be joyful. It means to feel exceeding gladness and to express that joy. We are commanded to do it, not for God's sake, but for our sake. Joy is more than mere positive thinking or pumping oneself up with compliments and encouragement. Joy has at its root God's own nature! To rejoice is to recognize that we have a *reason* to be encouraged. God is on our side and has heartily and joyfully embraced us as His own!

The God of the Bible is a joyful God—a happy God Who delights and takes pleasure in His handiwork. He is a God Who is ever moving to bring problems to resolution, to meet needs, to bring order out of chaos and goodness out of evil. God delights in His work, and joy is His attitude!

Perhaps one of the strongest words associated with joy in the Scriptures is "delight." We are to take delight—have joy about—God's presence, Word, work and power. The more we delight in the Lord, the more fully we see Him and experience His presence. The more we see God at work, the more joy we experience. And the more joy we experience, the more likely we are to express it!

Joy is also closely linked with praise in the Scriptures. Singing and shouting, of course, naturally lead to spontaneous dancing, clapping, and general music-making. The last five psalms in the Bible each seem to burst with energy, as if the words themselves cannot contain the glory and power they desire to express. Indeed, it would seem from Scripture that there is no such thing as "a little joy." Joy comes in only one size: unspeakable hugeness of heart.

Of Joy and Faith

The joy of the Christian does not arise from any dullness or callousness of conscience. A kind of joy, it is true, may arise from this, in those whose "foolish hearts are darkened;" whose heart is callous, unfeeling, dull of sense, and, consequently, without spiritual understanding. Because of their senseless, unfeeling hearts, they may rejoice even in committing sin; and this they may probably call liberty—which is indeed mere drunkenness of soul . . . such as he could not have conceived before. He never had such a tenderness of conscience as he has had since the love of God has reigned in his heart. And this also is his glory and joy, that God has heard his daily prayer:

> Oh, that my tender soul might fly
> The first abhorr'd approach of ill;
> Quick, as the apple of an eye,
> The slightest touch of sin to feel.

Christian joy is joy in obedience; joy in loving God and keeping His commandments, and yet not in keeping them as if we were thereby to fulfill the terms of the covenant of works; as if by any works of righteousness of ours, we were to procure pardon and acceptance with God. Not so: we are already pardoned and accepted, through the mercy of God in Christ Jesus . . . We rejoice in knowing that, "being justified through his grace," we have "not received that grace of God in vain;" that God having freely (not for the sake of our willing or running, but through the blood of the Lamb) reconciled us to Himself, we run, in the strength which He has given us, the way of His commandments. He has "girded us with strength unto the war," and we gladly "fight the good fight of faith." We rejoice, through Him who lives in our hearts by faith, to "lay hold of eternal life." This is our rejoicing, that as our "Father worketh hitherto," so (not by our own might or wisdom, but through the power of His Spirit, freely given in Christ Jesus) we also work the works of God. And may He work in us whatsoever is well pleasing in His sight! To whom be the praise forever and ever!

— *John Wesley*

The John Wesley Reader
Compiled by Al Bryant
Word Books, 1983

His Blessing of Joy

O GOD, in mercy bless us; let your face beam with joy as you look down at us. Send us around the world with the news of your saving power and your eternal plan for all mankind. How everyone throughout the earth will praise the Lord! How glad the nations will be, singing for joy because you are their King and will give true justice to their people! Praise God, O world! May all the peoples of the earth give thanks to you. For the earth has yielded abundant harvests. God, even our own God, will bless us. And peoples from remotest lands will worship him.

> — *Psalm 67 (TLB)*
> HOLY BIBLE

A Necessity

Joy is an inevitable part of the Christian expression of life. And yet so few expect or enjoy it. A Roman Catholic who came into a sound experience of spiritual conversion said in surprise, "Strange, but I never associated God with joy before." But now, in an almost impossible home situation, she describes herself as "happy as a lark." She is happy *in spite of!* That is real happiness.

And happiness is not a luxury; it is a necessity. A doctor told me that he told his patients that the most dangerous disease of the world is "unhappiness." It spreads chaos not only in the mind and soul and in one's relationships, but in one's body as well. It probably causes more sickness than any other thing. There was a woman who wanted to go back to Texas to live, who was very unhappy living in Arizona. She suffered from asthma. She went to Texas and was free from asthma. Then she adjusted herself to Arizona and began to live there happily. Her asthma disappeared.

A little boy of eight was very unhappy at my leaving his home. He went upstairs, cried, and lost his dinner. His unhappiness upset his digestion.

A nurse was working in a women and children's section of a hospital. That section she said was called "The Clinic of Delinquent Husbands and Fathers." The delinquencies of the husbands and parents produced illnesses in the wives and children. Here were two daughters who had the same family problem. One reacted badly to it, was full of conflicts, wouldn't let anyone speak of her parents, and finally lost her reason. The other met it well, became a matron of a school and was loved and honored and happy. One was the center of gloom and the other of glory. The head of a trucking firm said that in tracing the cause of accidents he almost invariably ran into an unhappy home situation on the part of the truck driver. The unhappiness produced a conflict which lowered his efficiency as a driver. So the Christian redemption from unhappiness is a needed redemption. If we are not redeemed from unhappiness, we are not fully redeemed.

Many do not expect their faith to make them basically and fully joyful now. That is reserved for the hereafter. Against this, look at this passage: *"Who richly provides us with all the joys of life"* (I Timothy 6:17, Moffatt). Note: "All the joys of life." You do not have to go outside Christ to have all the joys of life fulfilled. And this in no meager, half-starved way —"who richly provides us;" it is abundant living and abundant joy in that abundant living.

A very cultured but unhappy woman said: "If I had what you have, I wouldn't be in the mess I am in." She surrendered the "mess" to Christ and was transformed. She writes: "Every day I have strength and fun to spare." Strength and fun to spare—"He provides us richly with all the joys of life." No meagerness here—strength and fun to spare! And this strength and fun are not because she is not meeting difficulties and opposition. She has both, but she writes: "I grow best under the lash." Her joy is *in spite of!* The Christian position and privilege is this: *"Rejoice at all times"* (I Thessalonians 5:16, Moffatt). Note "at all times." The Christian can rejoice "at all times," for if nothing else is the cause of his rejoicing, he can find a cause for rejoicing in his own growth. He grows under the lash. So even the lash contributes.

Another verse: *"In everything give thanks . . ."* (I Thessalonians 5:18, Moffatt). For everything furthers the Christian if he knows how to use it. But if you thank God for everything, you must see God in everything. Not in its genesis, but in its exodus. It may have begun with the devil, but by the time it gets to you and through you it has a divine destiny running though it. An old lady was praying for bread. Some boys, hearing her, decided to play a trick on her. They threw some loaves down the chimney. The old lady began to shout. The boys said, "But we threw it down, not God." She replied, "The devil may have fetched it, but God sent it."

So wherever an event may come from, by the time it gets to you it has passed the will of God for you and is a source of blessing.

— E. Stanley Jones

Growing Spiritually
Nashville: Abingdon Press

The Joy of It All

O Thou Creator of all things that are, I lift up
my heart in gratitude to Thee for this day's happiness:
For the mere joy of living:
For all the sights and sounds around me:
For the sweet peace of the country and the pleasant
bustle of the town:
For all things bright and beautiful and gay:
For friendship and good company:
For work to perform and the skill and strength
to perform it:
For a time to play when the day's work was done,
and for health and a glad heart to enjoy it.

— *John Baillie*

A Diary of Private Prayer, 1949

Happiness or Joy?

The service of the Holy Spirit is that He helps us to distinguish pleasure from happiness and develop real joy. There are many experiences which give us temporary pleasure but do not add up to abiding satisfaction. Their thrills pass quickly, and sometimes leave a trail of regret and remorse. Some of our sense pleasures are like lightning flashes, while true joy is like the sunlight.

— *Ralph W. Sockman, D.D.*

On Joy

Joy is prayer—joy is strength—joy is love—joy is a net of love by which you can catch souls. God loves a cheerful giver. He gives most who gives with joy. The best way to show our gratitude to God and the people is to accept everything with joy. A joyful heart is the normal result of a heart burning with love. Never let anything so fill you with sorrow as to make you forget the joy of Christ Risen.

We all long for heaven where God is, but we have it in our power to be in heaven with Him right now—to be happy with Him at this very moment. But being happy with Him now means:

> loving as He loves,
> helping as He helps,
> giving as He gives,
> serving as He serves,
> rescuing as He rescues,
> being with Him twenty-four hours,
> touching Him in His distressing
> disguise.

— *Mother Teresa*

Malcolm Muggeridge
Something Beautiful for God
San Francisco: Harper & Row, 1971

Joyful Generosity

Thoughts disentangle themselves . . . over the lips and through the fingertips.

I learned that saying over thirty years ago, and just about every time I put it to the test, it works! Whenever I have difficulty comprehending the complicated or clarifying the complex, I talk it out or write it out. This is especially helpful when it comes to scriptural truth. For some strange reason the human brain seems reluctant to retain divine information simply by hearing it.

Take the importance of joy, for example—or, more specifically, giving joyful to God. Second Corinthians 9:7 (NASB) says, *"Let each one to do just as he has purposed in his heart; not grudgingly or under compulsion; for God loves a cheerful giver."*

Look again at those final five words: *"God loves a cheerful giver."* The original meaning of the word translated here as "cheerful" is *hilarious*, and this is the only time it is found in the New Testament. It's the hilarious giver God prizes.

I can think of a couple more examples of hilarious givers in the New Testament: a man named Onesiphorus who "often refreshed" Paul (2 Timothy 1:16-18); and a church—the Philippians—who contributed generously to Paul's needs (Phillipians 4:14-16).

Now, how does all this translate into daily life? How do these thoughts disentangle themselves to become meaningful parts of our lives? I'd like to make the following four suggestions for ways we can bring joy into our giving:

Reflect on God's gifts to you.

Hasn't He been good? He certainly has to me. Better than I deserve! My list includes good health, harmonious family, sufficient food, clothing, and shelter. Friends. Great job. In light of God's magnificent grace, a cheerful heart and openhanded generosity seem the most natural responses.

Remind yourself of His promises regarding generosity.

Call to mind a few biblical principles that promise a bountiful harvest to those who sow bountifully. Jesus Himself spoke of how much more blessed it is to give than to receive. Bumper crops are God's specialties, so we have nothing to restrain us from dropping maximum seed. He's honored by such faith.

Examine your hearts.

This is something no one else can do for you. Nobody knows the combination to your private vault. Only you can probe its contents by asking the hard questions: Do I really believe God's promise on giving generously? Am I responding as I do because I care or because I feel guilty? Is my giving proportionate to my income? Have I prayed, or is my giving impulsive? Am I a consistent giver or more hot 'n' cold?

Glorify God by becoming generous.

He prizes generosity, especially joyful generosity. Perhaps we need to break the habit of being so conservative, so careful. Maybe we even need to "scare" ourselves with acts of generosity . . . going out on a limb, as it were, and genuinely trusting God to honor our financial faith.

Well, that's it. Just a little lips-and-fingertips clarification. It has helped me to review this. I hope it's helped you, too. Goodness knows, all of us would be wise to address our reluctance to sacrifice financially for the cause of Christ. After all, our goal is joyful generosity, isn't it?

— *Charles R. Swindoll*

The Finishing Touch
Dallas: Word Publishing, 1994

Joy–Full

Jesus said to His disciples:

"If you keep My commandments, you will abide in My love, just as I have kept My Father's commandments and abide in His love. These things I have spoken to you, that My joy may remain in you, and that your joy may be full."

> — *John 15:10–11* (NKJV)
> HOLY BIBLE

Some Divine Attributes of Joy

Joy seems to have a necessity to it, as God does. God not only is but could not be otherwise, could not change. We change, so we are not always in joy, nor joy in us; but joy itself is unchangeable, eternal, and necessary. When it comes, though it appears new to us, a surprise, it also seems old, ancient, having existed "before the beginning of time." . . . Pleasure and happiness have nothing of that air of eternity about them that joy does. . . .

Yet the joy in our spirit does not stay there, bottled up and stagnant. Spirit is essentially dynamic, and its joy flows out in three directions: back to God in gratitude and rejoicing, out to others like a watering fountain, and into our own soul and body as a sort of overspill. Joyful feelings and thoughts, even pleasure and health, result from joy; and this is a foretaste of heaven.

> — *Peter J. Kreeft*

Full of Joy

My dear child, I want to tell you how much I rejoice in you. It grieves Me that so many of My children do not believe I enjoy them. They are constantly distracted by their inadequacies. They imagine I look at them with a frown instead of a smile.

Think of the joy a father and mother have when their child is born. What great joy I had when you were born again! I caused all heaven to rejoice.

I want My joy to be in you and your joy to be full. Many of your inhibitions have gone, haven't they? I love to break through all that stuff. It's great when you want to skip and dance and rejoice with Me. This is My joy in you. Don't you realize I was already rejoicing before it even occurred to you?

Joy is not an emotional response to situations. I am not an emotion; I am spirit. Joy is a fruit of My Spirit in your life. I don't want to see that joy suffocated by problems and cares that concern you.

I never take My joy away from you. It is always within you and can always be expressed in your life.

— *Colin Urquhart*

My Dear Child
Lake Mary, Fla.: Creation House, 1991

Joy at His Life

Jesus said to His disciples:

"Most assuredly, I say to you that you will weep and lament, but the world will rejoice; and you will be sorrowful, but your sorrow will be turned into joy. A woman, when she is in labor, has sorrow because her hour has come; but as soon as she has given birth to the child, she no longer remembers the anguish, for joy that a human being has been born into the world. Therefore you now have sorrow; but I will see you again and your heart will rejoice, and your joy no one will take from you."

— *John 16:20-22* (NKJV)
  HOLY BIBLE

Joy Is the Word

Today, whatever may annoy,
The word for me is Joy, just simple joy;
The joy of life;
The joy of children and of wife;
The joy of bright, blue skies;
The joy of rain; the glad surprise
Of twinkling stars that shine at night;
The joy of winged things upon their flight;
The joy of noonday, and the tried
True joyousness of eventide;
The joy of labor, and of mirth;
The joy of air, and sea, and earth—
The countless joys that ever flow from Him
Whose vast beneficence doth dim
The lustrous light of day,
And lavish gifts divine upon our way,
Whate'er there be of Sorrow
I'll put off till Tomorrow,
And when Tomorrow comes, why then
'Twill be Today and Joy again!

— John Kendrick Bangs

A Treasury of Contentment
Compiled and Edited by Ralph L. Woods
New York: Trident Press, 1969
A Division of Simon and Schuster

Better Than Wine

Nothing gives the believer so much joy as fellowship with Christ. He has enjoyment as others have in the common mercies of life, he can be glad both in God's gifts and God's works; but in all these separately, yea, and in all of them added together, he doth not find such substantial delight as in the matchless person of his Lord Jesus. He has wine which no vineyard on earth ever yielded; he has bread which all the cornfields of Egypt could never bring forth. Where can such sweetness be found as we have tasted in communion with our Beloved? In our esteem, the joys of earth are little better than husks for swine compared with Jesus, the heavenly manna. We would rather have one mouthful of Christ's love, and a sip of His fellowship, than a whole world full of carnal delights. What is the chaff to the wheat? What is the sparkling paste to the true diamond? What is a dream to the glorious reality? What is time's mirth, in its best trim, compared to our Lord Jesus in His most despised estate? If you know anything of the inner life, you will confess that our highest, purest, and most enduring joys must be the fruit of the tree of life which is in the midst of the Paradise of God. No spring yields such sweet water as that well of God which was digged with the soldier's spear. All earthly bliss is of the earth earthy, but the comforts of Christ's presence are like Himself, heavenly. We can review our communion with Jesus, and find no regrets of emptiness therein; there are no dregs in this wine, no dead flies in this ointment. The joy of the Lord is solid and enduring. Vanity hath not looked upon it, but discretion and prudence testify that it abideth the test of years, and is in time and in eternity worthy to be called "the only true delight." For nourishment, consolation, exhilaration, and refreshment, no wine can rival the love of Jesus.

— *Charles H. Spurgeon*

Taken from *Morning and Evening Devotions: An Updated Edition of the Classical Devotional in Today's Language* by C. H. Spurgeon. Copyright © 1987 by Thomas Nelson Publishers. Used by permission of Thomas Nelson Publishers.

Joy No One Can Take Away

In the second century, they brought a martyr before a king, and the king wanted him to recant and give up Christ, but the man spurned the thought. The king said: "If you don't do it, I will banish you." The man smiled and answered: "You can't banish me from Christ. He says He will never leave me nor forsake me." The king got angry, and said: "Well, I will confiscate your property and take it all from you." And the man replied: "My treasures are laid up on high; you cannot get them." The king became still more angry, and said: "I will kill you." "Why," the man answered, "I have been dead forty years; I have been dead with Christ; dead to the world. My life is hid with Christ in God, and you cannot touch it." And so we can rejoice, because we are resurrection ground, having risen with Christ. Let persecution and opposition come. "Your joy no man taketh from you."

— Dwight L. Moody

The D. L. Moody Year Book
Selected by Emma Moody Fitt
New York: Fleming H. Revell Co., 1900

At All Times

We must recognize that there is all the difference in the world between rejoicing and feeling happy. The Scripture tells us that we should always rejoice. Take the lyrical Epistle of Paul to the Philippians where he says: "Rejoice in the Lord always: and again I say, Rejoice." He goes on saying it. To rejoice is a command, yes, but there is all the difference in the world between rejoicing and being happy. You cannot make yourself happy, but you can make yourself rejoice, in the sense that you will always rejoice in the Lord. Happiness is something within ourselves, rejoice is "in the Lord." How important it is then, to draw the distinction between rejoicing in the Lord and feeling happy. Take the fourth chapter of the Second Epistle to the Corinthians. There you will find that the great Apostle puts it all very plainly and clearly in that series of extraordinary contrasts which he makes: "We are troubled on every side (I don't think he felt very happy at the moment) yet not distressed," "we are perplexed (he wasn't feeling happy at all at that point) but not in despair," "persecuted but not forsaken," "cast down, but not destroyed"—and so on. In other words the Apostle does not suggest a kind of happy person in a carnal sense, but he was still rejoicing. That is the difference between the two conditions.

— *Martin Lloyd-Jones*

Reprinted from *Hymns for the Family of God* by Dr. Martin Lloyd-Jones. Copyright © 1976 by Dr. Martin Lloyd-Jones. Used by permission of William B. Eerdmans Publishing Company.

Bitter to Sweet

The joy of life is living it and doing things of worth,
In making bright and fruitful all the barren spots of earth.
In facing odds and mastering them and rising from defeat,
And making true what once was false, and what was bitter, sweet.
For only he knows perfectly joy whose little bit of soil
Is richer ground than what it was when he began to toil.

— *Anonymous*

A Treasury of Contentment
Compiled and Edited by Ralph L. Woods
New York: Trident Press, 1969
A Division of Simon and Schuster

This Is Joy

O to share the great, sunny, joyous life of the earth! to be as
happy as the birds are! as contented as the cattle on the hills! as the
leaves of the trees that dance and rustle in the wind! as the waters that
murmur and sparkle to the sea! To be able to see that the sin and
sorrow and suffering of the world are a necessary part of the natural
course of things, a phase of the law of growth and development that
runs through the universe, bitter in its personal application, but
illuminating when we look upon life as a whole!

— *John Burroughs*

A Treasury of Contentment
Compiled and edited by Ralph L. Woods
New York: Trident Press, 1969
A Division of Simon and Schuster

Preacher of Joy

"The Spirit of the L<small>ORD</small> G<small>OD</small> is upon Me,
Because the L<small>ORD</small> has anointed Me
To preach good tidings to the poor;
He has sent Me to heal the brokenhearted,
To proclaim liberty to the captives,
And the opening of the prison to those who are bound;
To proclaim the acceptable year of the L<small>ORD</small>,
And the day of vengeance of our God;
To comfort all who mourn,
To console those who mourn in Zion,
To give them beauty for ashes,
The oil of joy for mourning,
The garment of praise for the spirit of heaviness;
That they may be called trees of righteousness,
The planting of the L<small>ORD</small>, that He may be glorified."

And they shall rebuild the old ruins,
They shall raise up the former desolations,
And they shall repair the ruined cities,
The desolations of many generations.
Strangers shall stand and feed your flocks,
And the sons of the foreigner
Shall be your plowmen and your vinedressers.
But you shall be named the priests of the L<small>ORD</small>,
They shall call you the servants of our God.
You shall eat the riches of the Gentiles,
And in their glory you shall boast.
Instead of your shame you shall have double honor,
And instead of confusion they shall rejoice in their portion.
Therefore in their land they shall possess double;
Everlasting joy shall be theirs.

— ***Isaiah 61:1-7*** *(NKJV)*
HOLY BIBLE

Joy Is the Christian Word

There is something deeper than happiness, and that is joy. Happiness comes from happenings, but joy may be within in spite of happenings. "Happiness" is the world's word; "joy" is the Christian's word. The New Testament does not use the word "happiness" or promise it—it uses the word "joy." And for a reason.

Many people are expecting happiness from following the Christian faith—that God will arrange the things that happen to me so they will all add up to happiness. When the things that happen to them do not mean happiness, such people are dismayed and feel God has let them down. Why should this happen to me? They expect to be protected from happenings that make them unhappy. This is a false view and leads to a lot of disillusionment. For the Christian is not necessarily protected from things that make people unhappy. Was Jesus protected from things that make people unhappy? Was Paul? Their Christian faith got them into opposition, into persecution, into death. How could a faith that has a cross at its center promise exemption from happenings that ordinarily bring unhappiness? Then what is the answer? The Christian faith offers joy in the midst of happenings which make people with that faith unhappy. When the Christian doesn't find joy on account of his happenings, he can always find joy in spite of them.

The Christian is taught not merely to accept limitations, but to use them. Take what you have and make something out of it. You must learn to live *in spite of*. Carlyle once said: "You may hear it said of me that I am cross-grained and disagreeable. Don't believe it. Only let me have my own way exactly in everything with all about me precisely as I wish, and a sunnier or pleasanter creature does not exist." But Carlyle was being satirical here. We must make our happiness not dependent upon happenings. We can make everything into something else. Use everything.

— *E. Stanley Jones*

Christian Maturity
Nashville: Abingdon Press, 1957

Work for Joy

There is a strange elusive joy that comes into life at times. We may call it the satisfaction of making things or the joy of creation. It must come in very real measure to all real artists, who paint pictures, make statues, design buildings, write music or poetry, or fine prose. They have to pay for it by going through hours of agonizing fumbling, when things will not cease to be clouded and the spiritual something they are feeling will not come clear. And they pay for it, too, through long hours of dogged labor, and even then are seldom satisfied. They are creators and they experience birth pangs. Nonetheless, the joy they exprience is due to the fact that they are in tune with the Creator. The inspiration that started and sustained them came from Him.

— A. H. Gray

A Treasury of Contentment
Compiled and edited by Ralph L. Woods
New York: Trident Press, 1969
A Division of Simon and Schuster

Joyful Praise

HALLELUJAH! YES, PRAISE THE LORD!

Praise him in his Temple and in the heavens he made with mighty power. Praise him for his mighty works. Praise his unequaled greatness. Praise him with the trumpet and with lute and harp. Praise him with the drums and dancing. Praise him with stringed instruments and horns. Praise him with the cymbals, yes, loud clanging cymbals.

Let everything alive give praises to the Lord! You praise him!

Hallelujah!

— Psalm 150 (TLB)
HOLY BIBLE

Reaping in Joy

When the Lord turned again the captivity of Zion, we were like them that dream.

Then was our mouth filled with laughter, and our tongue with singing: then said they among the heathen, The LORD hath done great things for them.

The LORD hath done great things for us; whereof we are glad.

Turn again our captivity, O LORD, as the streams in the south.

They that sow in tears shall reap in joy.

He that goeth forth and weepeth, bearing precious seed, shall doubtless come again with rejoicing, bringing his sheaves with him.

— Psalm 126
HOLY BIBLE

Dancing with Joy

So the priests and the Levites underwent the ceremonies of sanctification in preparation for bringing home the Ark of Jehovah, the God of Israel. Then the Levites carried the Ark on their shoulders with its carrying poles, just as the Lord had instructed Moses.

King David also ordered the Levite leaders to organize the singers into an orchestra, and they played loudly and joyously upon psaltries, harps, and cymbals. . . [Priests] formed a bugle corps to march at the head of the procession . . .

Then David and the elders of Israel and the high officers of the army went with great joy to the home of Obed-edom to take the Ark to Jerusalem . . . David, the Levites carrying the Ark, the singers, and Chenaniah the song leader were all dressed in linen robes. David also wore a linen ephod. So the leaders of Israel took the Ark to Jerusalem with shouts of joy, the blowing of horns and trumpets, the crashing of cymbals, and loud playing on the harps and zithers. (But as the Ark arrived in Jerusalem, David's wife Michal, the daughter of King Saul, felt a deep disgust for David as she watched from the window and saw him dancing like a madman.)

So they brought the Ark of God into the special tent that David had prepared for it, and the leaders of Israel sacrificed burnt offerings and peace offerings before God. At the conclusion of these offerings David blessed the people in the name of the Lord; then he gave every person present (men and women alike) a loaf of bread, some wine, and a cake of raisins.

He appointed certain of the Levites to minister before the Ark by giving constant praise and thanks to the Lord God of Israel and by asking for his blessings upon his people.

— *1 Chronicles 15:14-16, 24-25, 27-29; 16:1-4 (TLB)*
HOLY BIBLE

Deep-down Joy

Joy is distinctly a Christian word and a Christian thing. It is the reverse of happiness. Happiness is the result of what happens of an agreeable sort. Joy has its springs deep down inside. And that spring never runs dry, no matter what happens. Only Jesus gives that joy. He had joy, singing its music within, even under the shadow of the cross. It is an unknown word and thing except as He has sway within.

— *Samuel Dickey Gordon*

The Encyclopedia of Religious Quotations
Compiled and Edited by Frank S. Mead
Fleming H. Revell Co., 1965

Joy

Every night and every morn
Some to misery are born;
Every morn and every night
Some are born to sweet delight;
Some are born to sweet delight,
Some are born to endless night.
Joy and woe are woven fine,
A clothing for the soul divine;
Under every grief and pine
Runs a joy with silken twine.
It is right it should be so;
Man was made for joy and woe;
And when this we rightly know
Safely through the world we go.

— *William Blake*

Freedom, Love and Truth
William Inge
London: Longman, Green and Co., Inc., 1936

The Joy of the Spirit

The selfless love to which God calls you and me produces a deep joy in our hearts. This joy or happiness of the Spirit has three dimensions.

Joy is the assurance of faith that we are acceptable to God and that God's good providences are working on our behalf. This joy is an inner calm produced by confidence in God. It is untouched by outward circumstances and is not diminished by pain and sorrow.

Sometimes this joy gives us a sense of satisfaction and comfort.

The highest level of joy is a kind of ecstasy or overflowing happiness. There is no way of describing this—no more than we can say what it is like to be in love. It is simply a graced moment, and may last only a short time. We are cautioned by spiritual leaders not to seek this experience. God gives it when it pleases Him—it is always a by-product of faith.

— *Jerry L. Mercer*

Reprinted from *Cry Joy!*
by Jerry L. Mercer
Published by Victor Books, Copyright © 1987,
Scripture Press Publications, Inc., Wheaton, Il. 60189

Unconditional Joy

I know not how God will dispose of me. I am always happy. All the world suffers; and I, who deserve the severest discipline, feel joys so continual and so great that I can scarce contain them.

— *Brother Lawrence*

Taken from *The Practice of the Presence of God* by Brother Lawrence of the Resurrection. Copyright © 1963 by Peter Pauper Press. Used by permission of Peter Pauper Press, Inc.

Joy's Source

Joy is like a well containing sweet water. It is not enough to know the water is there or even to drill the well. If the well is to be useful, the water must be brought to the surface. Those who know Christ have found the source of joy.

— *Charles R. Hembree*

Fruits of the Spirit Grand Rapids, Mich.: Baker Book House, 1969

Joyful, Joyful, We Adore Thee

Joyful, joyful, we adore Thee,
God of glory, Lord of love;
Hearts unfold like flowers before Thee,
Hail Thee as the sun above.
Melt the clouds of sin and sadness;
Drive the dark of doubt away;
Giver of immortal gladness,
Fill us with the light of day!

All Thy works with joy surround Thee,
Earth and heaven reflect Thy rays,
Stars and angels sing around Thee,
Center of unbroken praise:
Field and forest, vale and mountain,
Blossoming meadow, flashing sea,
Chanting bird and flowing fountain,
Call us to rejoice in Thee.

Thou art giving and forgiving,
Ever blessing, ever blest,
Well-spring of the joy of living,
Ocean-depth of happy rest!
Thou our Father, Christ our Brother,—
All who live in love are Thine:
Teach us how to love each other,
Lift us to the Joy Divine.

Mortals join the mighty chorus,
Which the morning stars began;
Father-love is reigning o'er us
Brother-love binds man to man.
Ever singing march we onward,
Victors in the midst of strife;
Joyful music lifts us sunward
In the triumph song of life.

— *Henry Van Dyke*

Henry Van Dyke, Charles Scribner's Sons
Joyful, Joyful, We Adore Thee
Copyright © 1920

Am I Convinced by Christ?

"Notwithstanding in this rejoice not . . ., but rather rejoice because your names are written in heaven" (Luke 10:20).

Jesus Christ says, in effect, Don't rejoice in successful service, but rejoice because you are rightly related to Me. The snare in Christian work is to rejoice in successful service, to rejoice in the fact that God has used you. You never can measure what God will do through you if you are rightly related to Jesus Christ. Keep your relationship right with Him, then whatever circumstances you are in, and whoever you meet day by day, He is pouring rivers of living water through you, and it is of His mercy that He does not let you know it. When once you are rightly related to God by salvation and sanctification, remember that wherever you are, you are put there by God; and by the reaction of your life on the circumstances around you, you will fulfil God's purpose, as long as you keep in the light as God is in the light.

The tendency today is to put the emphasis on service. Beware of the people who make usefulness their ground of appeal. If you make usefulness the test, then Jesus Christ was the greatest failure that ever lived. The lodestar of the saint is God Himself, not estimated usefulness. It is the work that God does through us that counts, not what we do for Him. All that Our Lord heeds in a man's life is the relationship of worth to His Father. Jesus is bringing many sons to glory.

— Oswald Chambers

Taken from *My Utmost for His Highest*
by Oswald Chambers, edited by James Reimann,
Copyright © 1992 by Oswald Chambers Publications Assn., Ltd.
Original edition Copyright © 1935 by Dodd, Mead & Co.,
Renewed 1963 by Oswald Chambers Publications Assn., Ltd., and is
used by permission of Discovery House Publishers, Box 3566, Grand Rapids, MI 49501.
All rights reserved.

Better To Give

God gives us joy that we may give;
He gives us joy that we may share;
Sometimes He gives us loads to lift
That we may learn to bear.
For life is gladder when we give,
And love is sweeter when we share,
And heavy loads rest lightly too
When we have learned to bear.

— *Anonymous*

A Treasury of Contentment
Compiled and edited by Ralph L. Woods
New York: Trident Press, 1969
A Division of Simon and Schuster

The Lost Is Found

Jesus taught:

"If you had a hundred sheep and one of them strayed away and was lost in the wilderness, wouldn't you leave the ninety-nine others to go and search for the lost one until you found it? And then you would joyfully carry it home on your shoulders. When you arrived you would call together your friends and neighbors to rejoice with you because your lost sheep was found.

"Well, in the same way heaven will be happier over one lost sinner who returns to God than over ninety-nine others who haven't strayed away!

"Or take another illustration: A woman has ten valuable silver coins

and loses one. Won't she light a lamp and look in every corner of the house
and sweep every nook and cranny until she finds it? And then won't she call
in her friends and neighbors to rejoice with her? In the same way there is joy
in the presence of the angels of God when one sinner repents."

To further illustrate the point, he told them this story:

"A man had two sons. When the younger told his father, 'I want
my share of your estate now, instead of waiting until you die!' his father
agreed to divide his wealth between his sons.

"A few days later this younger son packed all his belongings and
took a trip to a distant land, and there wasted all his money on parties
and prostitutes. About the time his money was gone a great famine swept
over the land, and he began to starve. He persuaded a local farmer to hire
him to feed his pigs. The boy became so hungry that even the pods he was
feeding the swine looked good to him. And no one gave him anything.

"When he finally came to his senses, he said to himself, 'At home
even the hired men have food enough and to spare, and here I am, dying
of hunger! I will go home to my father and say, "Father, I have sinned
against both heaven and you, and am no longer worthy of being called
your son. Please take me on as a hired man."'

"So he returned home to his father. And while he was still a long
distance away, his father saw him coming, and was filled with loving pity
and ran and embraced him and kissed him.

"His son said to him, 'Father, I have sinned against heaven and
you, and am no worthy of being called your son'—

"But his father said to the slaves, 'Quick! Bring the finest robe in
the house and put it on him. And a jeweled ring for his finger; and shoes!
And kill the calf we have in the fattening pen. We must celebrate with a
feast, for this son of mine was dead and has returned to life. He was lost and
is found.'" So the party began.

"Meanwhile, the older son was in the fields working; when he
returned home, he heard dance music coming from the house, and he asked
one of the servants what was going on.

'Your brother is back,' he was told, 'and your father has killed the
calf we were fattening and has prepared a great feast to celebrate his coming
home again unharmed.'

"The older brother was angry and wouldn't go in. His father came out and begged him, but he replied, 'All these years I've worked hard for you and never once refused to do a single thing you told me to; and in all that time you never gave me even one young goat for a feast with my friends.

"'Yet when this son of yours comes back after spending your money on prostitutes, you celebrate by killing the finest calf we have on the place.'

"'Look, dear son,' his father said to him, 'you and I are very close, and everything I have is yours. But it is right to celebrate. For he is your brother; and he was dead and has come back to life! He was lost and is found!'"

— *Luke 15:3-32* (TLB)
HOLY BIBLE

Set the Right Goal

Joy is the effect which comes when we use our powers. Joy, rather than happiness, is the goal of life, for joy is the emotion which accompanies our fulfilling our natures as human beings. It is based on the experience of one's identity as a being of worth and dignity . . .

— *Rollo May*

Choose Life
Bernard Mandelbaum
Random House, NY, 1968

Remembered Joy

There are men who suffer terrible distress and are unable to tell what they feel in their hearts, and they go their way and suffer and suffer. But if they meet one with a laughing face, he can revive them with his joy. And to revive a man is no slight thing.

— *Hasidic*

Choose Life
Bernard Mandelbaum
New York: Random House, 1968

The Goal Is Joy

Dance and game are frivolous, unimportant down here; for "down here" is not their natural place. Here, they are a moment's rest from the life we were placed here to live. But in this world everything is upside down. That which, if it could be prolonged here, would be a truancy, is likest that which in a better country is the End of Ends. Joy is the serious business of Heaven.

— *C. S. Lewis*

The Joyful Christian
127 Readings From C. S. Lewis
New York: Macmillan Publishing Co., 1977

Joy and Triumph

Joy and triumph everlasting
Hath the heav'nly Church on high;
For that pure immortal gladness
All our feast-days mourn and sigh:
Yet in death's dark desert wild
Doth the mother aid her child;
Guards celestial thence attend us,
Stand in combat to defend us.

Here the world's perpetual warfare
Holds from heav'n the soul apart;
Legioned foes in shadowy terror
Vex the Sabbath of the heart.
O how happy that estate
Where delight doth not abate!
For that home the spirit yearneth,
Where none languisheth nor mourneth.

There the body hath no torment,
There the mind is free from care,
There is ev'ry voice rejoicing,
Ev'ry heart is loving there.
Angels in that city dwell;
Them their King delighteth well:
Still they joy and weary never,
More and more deserving ever.

There the seers and fathers holy,
There the prophets glorified,
All their doubts and darkness ended,
In the Light of Light abide.
There the saints, whose memories old
We in faithful hymns uphold,
Have forgot their bitter story
In the joy of Jesus' glory.

— *Adam of St. Victory, 12th Century*

Enter Laughing

There is, above all, the laughter that comes from the eternal joy of creation, the joy of making the world anew, the joy of expressing the inner riches of the soul—laughter from triumphs over pain and hardship in the passion for an enduring ideal, the joy of bringing the light of happiness, of truth and beauty into a dark world. This is divine laughter par excellence.

— *J. E. Boodin*

A Treasury of Contentment
Compiled and Edited by Ralph L. Woods
New York: Trident Press, 1969
A Division of Simon and Schuster

Grace Brings Joy

See, this kingdom of God is now found within us. The grace of the Holy Spirit shines forth and warms us, and, overflowing with many and varied scents into the air around us, regales our senses with heavenly delight, as it fills our hearts with joy inexpressible.

— *St. Seraphim of Sarov*

Man and God
Victor Gollancz
Boston: Houghton Mifflin Co., 1951

Restore Unto Me the Joy of Thy Salvation

See, Lord, I am but the least of Thy disciples: I have not much intelligence, I am not versed in the things of heaven, but I love Thee.

No doubt I have been too busy attending to the affairs of my material life, and that is why it is so difficult for Thy life to be born in me!

It seems that I am made of a heavier clay than other men. How does it happen that my soul so rarely knows joy, when others more unfortunate than myself I hear laugh and sing? Without joy, Lord, even the faith of Thy saints would be an earth without a sun, and their charity would have no perfume. They are like the birds of the air, like the flowers of the field, counting on Thee to feed and clothe them, but thou givest them besides that overflowing of the heart that is like the song of birds and the scent of flowers.

It is for lack of this that Thou seest me every day dejected. It seems that Thou respondest so rarely to my call! So rarely does there sound in my heart that bell of joy that peals in the carillon of the gospel!

And yet Thou didst say: "Blessed are they that mourn." Do I not grieve enough? "Blessed are they which do hunger and thirst." Knowest Thou how I hunger to share the joy of Thine elect?

Lord, I am ready to bless Thee in spite of Thy silences, and in spite of loneliness, but at least rekindle my soul! Give me something, even if it be only the joyous heart of a vagabond whistling along the road, or the song of the nightingale!

I would love Thee as one who rejoices, and not as one who carries a crushing burden!

— *Philippe Vernier*

With the Master
Translated by Edith Lovejoy Pierce
Fellowship Publications

More Than You Ask For

Fulness of joy can be understood in two ways. First, on the part of the thing rejoiced in, so that one rejoices in it as much as it is fitting that one should rejoice in it, and thus God's joy alone in Himself is filled, because it is infinite, and this is wholly fitting to the infinite goodness of God; but the joy of any creatures must be finite. Secondly, fulness of joy may be understood on the part of the one who rejoices. Now joy is compared to desire as rest to movement . . . and rest is full when there is no more movement. Hence joy is full, when there remains nothing to be desired. But as long as we are in this world, the movement of desire does not cease in us, because it still remains possible for us to approach nearer to God by grace . . . When once, however, perfect happiness has been attained, nothing will remain to be desired because then there will be full enjoyment of God, in which man will obtain whatever he had desired, even with regard to other goods. . . . Hence, desire will be at rest, not only our desire for God, but all our desires, that the joy of the blessed is full to perfection,—indeed over-full, since they will obtain more than they were capable of desiring.

— *Thomas Aquinas*

Summa Theologica, II-II, 28, 3
Great Treasury of Western Thought
Edited by Mortimer J. Adler and Charles Van Doren
New York: R. R. Bowker Co., 1977

Joyful Abandon

Joy, not grit, is the hallmark of holy obedience. We need to be lighthearted in what we do to avoid taking ourselves too seriously. It is a cheerful revolt against self and pride. Our work is jubilant, carefree, merry. Utter abandonment to God is done freely and with celebration.

— *Richard J. Foster*

Taken from "Joyful Abandon" from
Freedom of Simplicity by Richard J. Foster.
Copyright © 1981 by Richard J. Foster.
Reprinted by permission of HarperCollins Publishers, Inc.

Supernaturally Joyous

George Mueller would not preach until his heart was happy in the grace of God; Jan Ruysbroeck would not write while his feelings were low, but would retire to a quiet place and wait on God till he felt the spirit of inspiration. It is well known that the elevated spirits of a group of Moravians convinced John Wesley of the reality of their religion, and helped to bring him a short time later to a state of true conversion.

The Christian owes it to the world to be supernaturally joyful.

— *A. W. Tozer*

Alliance Weekly

Shout for Joy!

Shout for joy to the LORD, all the earth.
Worship the LORD with gladness;
    come before him with joyful songs.
Know that the LORD is God.
It is he who made us, and we are his;
    we are his people, the sheep of his pasture.
Enter his gates with thanksgiving
    and his courts with praise;
    give thanks to him and praise his name.
For the LORD is good and his love endures forever;
    his faithfulness continues through all generations.

    — Psalm 100 (NIV)
      HOLY BIBLE

Joy Is the Flag Flown High Over My Heart

Joy is the flag flown high from the castle of my heart,
from the castle of my heart,
from the castle of my heart.

Joy is the flag flown high from the castle of my heart
when the King is in residence there.

So let it fly in the sky, let the whole world know,
let the whole world know, let the whole world know.
So let it fly in the sky, let the whole world know
that the King is in residence there.

— Chorus of unknown origin

Joy in Giving

Then the leaders of families, the officers of the tribes of Israel, the commanders of thousands and commanders of hundreds, and the officials in charge of the king's work gave willingly. They gave toward the work on the temple of God five thousand talents and ten thousand darics of gold, ten thousand talents of silver, eighteen thousand talents of bronze and a hundred thousand talents of iron. Any who had precious stones gave them to the treasury of the temple of the LORD in the custody of Jehiel the Gershonite. The people rejoiced at the willing response of their leaders, for they had given freely and wholeheartedly to the LORD. David the king also rejoiced greatly.

— 1 Chronicles 29:6-9 (NIV)
HOLY BIBLE

Remember this: Whoever sows sparingly will also reap sparingly, and whoever sows generously will also reap generously. Each man should give what he has decided in his heart to give, not reluctantly or under compulsion, for God loves a cheerful giver.

— **2 Corinthians 9:6–7**(NIV)
HOLY BIBLE

When the builders laid the foundation of the temple of the LORD, the priests stood in their apparel with trumpets, and the Levites, the sons of Asaph, with cymbals, to praise the LORD, according to the ordinance of David king of Israel. And they sang responsively, praising and giving thanks to the LORD:
"For He is good,
For His mercy endures forever toward Israel."
Then all the people shouted with a great shout, when they praised the LORD, because the foundation of the house of the Lord was laid.
But many of the priests and Levites and heads of the fathers' houses, old men who had seen the first temple, wept with a loud voice when the foundation of this temple was laid before their eyes. Yet many shouted aloud for joy, so that the people could not discern the noise of the shout of joy from the noise of the weeping of the people, for the people shouted with a loud shout, and the sound was heard afar off.

— *Ezra 3:10-13* (NKJV)
HOLY BIBLE

Selfless Delight

Real love always heals fear and neutralizes egotism, and so, as love grows up in us, we shall worry about ourselves less and less, and admire and delight in God and His other children more and more, and this is the secret of joy.

Its [joy] very being is lost in the great tide of selfless delight — creation's response to the infinite loving of God. But, of course, the point for us is that this selfless joy has got to go on at times when we ourselves are in the dark, obsessed by the sorrow of life, so that we feel no joy because we cannot gaze at the beauty. Joy is a fruit of the Spirit, not of our gratified emotions. "Ye that by night stand in the House of the Lord, lift up your hands in the sanctuary and praise the Lord!"

— *Evelyn Underhill*

The Fruits of the Spirit
London: Longmans, Green and Co. Ltd., 1949

Transformed

When people are merry and dance, it sometimes happens that they catch hold of someone who is sitting outside and grieving, pull him into the round, and make him rejoice with them. The same happens in the heart of one who rejoices: grief and sorrow draw away from him, but it is a special virtue to pursue them with courage and to draw grief into gladness, so that all the strength of sorrow may be transformed into joy.

— *Hasidic*

Choose Life
Bernard Mandelbaum
Random House, NY, 1968

Joy in the Morning

*Sing praise to the L*ORD*, you saints of His,*
And give thanks at the remembrance of His holy name.
For His anger is but for a moment,
His favor is for life;
Weeping may endure for a night,
But joy comes in the morning.

> *— Psalm 30:4–5 (*NKJV*)*
> *HOLY BIBLE*

Heavenly Mirth

Give me, O Lord, a heart of grace,
A voice of joy, a shining face,
That I may show where'er I turn
Thy love within my soul doth burn!

A tenderness for all that stray,
With strength to help them on the way
A cheerfulness, a heavenly mirth,
Brightening my steps along the earth!

> *— Lady Gilbert*

Joy and Strength
Mary Wilder Tileston
World Wide Publications
1901, 1929, 1986

Our Joy Is God

Great art Thou, O Lord, and greatly to be praised; great is Thy power, and of Thy wisdom there is no number. And man desires to praise Thee. He is but a tiny part of all that Thou hast created. He bears about him his mortality, the evidence of his sinfulness, and the evidence that Thou dost resist the proud: yet this tiny part of all that Thou hast created desires to praise Thee.

Thou dost so excite him that to praise Thee is his joy. For Thou hast made us for Thyself and our hearts are restless till they rest in Thee.

For there is a joy which is not given to the ungodly but only to those who love Thee for Thy own sake, whose joy is Thyself. And this is happiness, to be joyful in Thee and for Thee and because of Thee, this and no other. Those who think happiness is any other, pursue a joy that is apart from Thee and is no true joy.

— St. Augustine

Taken from *The Confessions of St. Augustine*, trans. by F. J. Sheed. Copyright © 1942, renewed © 1970 by Sheed and Ward. Used by permission of Sheed and Ward Publishers.

Joy Is Grace

> Take joy home,
> And make a place in thy great heart for her,
> And give her time to grow, and cherish her!
> Then will she come and often sing to thee
> When thou art working in the furrows; ay,
> Or weeding in the sacred hour of dawn.
> It is a comely fashion to be glad.
> Joy is the grace we say to God.

— Jean Ingelow

A Treasury of Contentment
Compiled and edited by Ralph L. Woods
New York: Trident Press, 1969
A Division of Simon and Schuster

Share It

Grief can take care of itself, but to get the full value of joy you must have somebody to divide it with.

— Mark Twain

The Book of Unusual Quotations
Selected and Edited by Rudolf Flesch
New York: Harper and Brothers Publishers, 1957

Joyful Journey

Let me but live from year to year,
With forward face and unreluctant soul.
Not hastening to, nor turning from the goal;
Not mourning for the things that disappear
In the dim past, nor holding back in fear
    From what the future veils; but with a whole
    And happy heart, that pays its toll
To youth and age, and travels on with cheer.
So let the way wind up the hill or down,
    Though rough or smooth, the journey will be joy,
    Still seeking what I sought when but a boy,
New friendship, high adventure, and a crown,
    I shall grow old, but never lose life's zest,
    Because the road's last turn will be the best.

— *Henry Van Dyke*

A Treasury of Contentment
Compiled and edited by Ralph L. Woods
New York: Trident Press, 1969
A Division of Simon and Schuster

Joy to the World

Joy to the world! the Lord is come:
Let earth receive her King;
Let ev'ry heart prepare Him room,
And heav'n and nature sing.

Joy to the world! the Saviour reigns:
Let men their songs employ,
While fields and floods, rocks, hills, and plains,
Repeat the sounding joy.

No more let sins and sorrows grow,
Nor thorns infest the gound;
He comes to make His blessings flow
Far as the curse is found.

He rules the world with truth and grace,
And makes the nations prove
The glories of His righteousness,
And wonders of His love.

— Isaac Watts, 1719

*Amazing Grace: 366 Inspiring
Hymn Stories for Daily Devotions*
Kenneth Osbeck
Grand Rapids, Mich.: Kregel Publications, 1990

Chapter 3

PEACE

"Peace I leave with you, My peace I give to you; not as the world gives do I give to you. Let not your heart be troubled, neither let it be afraid" (John 14:27 NKJV).

It is difficult to conceive that a person who truly has experienced the unconditional and generous love and joy of God in his or her heart could feel anything other than deep and abiding peace. Peace seems the automatic outcome of a life filled with God's love and joy.

And yet, peace is distinguished among the fruit of the Spirit as a separate and desirable trait.

The word peace in Scripture is not merely that brought forth by the word "shalom"—a standard greeting of "peace" exchanged liberally among people in Bible times. The peace of the New Testament, "eirene," (pronounced i-ray'-nay), denotes the absence or end of all strife. It speaks of a state of untroubled, undisturbed well-being and the utmost of security. Eirene is not simply a matter of feeling safe and secure from one's enemies for the moment. It speaks of a feeling that one's enemies have been utterly destroyed and that safety and security are an everlasting possession.

Ultimately, peace comes as the result of reconciliation—the new relationship between man and God brought about by the atonement of Christ on the cross. Because of this human-divine reconciliation, a new relationship between man and man can exist. Indeed, eirene bears within it the concept of being "at one" or of being "set at one" again.

Peace be with you.

In God's Hand

At the heart of the cyclone tearing the sky
And flinging the clouds and the towers by,
    Is a place of central calm;
So here in the roar of mortal things,
I have a place where my spirit sings,
    In the hollow of God's palm.

— Edwin Markham

A Treasury of Contentment
Compiled and Edited by Ralph L. Woods
New York: Trident Press, 1969
A Division of Simon and Schuster

Peace—Fruit of a Living Faith

Another fruit of living faith is peace. For, *"being justified by faith,"* having all our sins blotted out, *"we have peace with God through our Lord Jesus Christ"* (Romans 5:1). This indeed our Lord Himself, the night before His death, solemnly bequeathed to all His followers: *"Peace,"* said He, *"I leave with you;"* (you who "believe in God," and "believe also in Me") *"my peace I give unto you: not as the world giveth, give I unto you. Let not your heart be troubled, neither let it be afraid"* (John 14:27). And again, *"These things have I spoken unto you, that in Me ye might have peace"* (John 16:33). This is that "peace of God which passeth all understanding," that serenity of soul which it has not entered into the heart of a natural man to conceive, and which it is not possible for even the spiritual man to utter. And it is a peace which all the powers of earth and hell are unable to take from him. Waves and storms beat upon it, but they shake it not; for it is founded upon a rock. It keeps the hearts and minds of the children of God, at all times and in all places. Whether they are in ease or in pain, in sickness or health, in abundance or want, they are happy in God. In every state they have learned to be content, yea, to give thanks unto God through Christ Jesus; being well assured that "whatsoever is, is best," because it is His will concerning them: so that in all the vicissitudes of life their "heart standeth fast, believing in the Lord."

— *John Wesley*

The John Wesley Reader
Compiled by Al Bryant
Word Books, 1983

Called To Live in Peace

If it is possible, as much as depends on you, live peaceably with all men.

— *Romans 12:18* (NKJV)
HOLY BIBLE

God has called us to peace.

— *1 Corinthians 7:15* (NKJV)
HOLY BIBLE

And let the peace of God rule in your hearts, to which also you were called in one body; and be thankful.

— *Colossians 3:15* (NKJV)
HOLY BIBLE

Are You Ever Disturbed?

There are times when our peace is based upon ignorance, but when we awaken to the facts of life, inner peace is impossible unless it is received from Jesus. When our Lord speaks peace, He makes peace, His words are ever "spirit and life." Have I ever received what Jesus speaks? "My peace I give unto you"—it is a peace which comes from looking into His face and realizing His undisturbedness.

Are you painfully disturbed just now, distracted by the waves and billows of God's providential permission, and having, as it were, turned over the boulders of your belief, are you still finding no well of peace or joy or comfort; is all barren? Then look up and receive the undisturbedness of the Lord Jesus. Reflected peace is the proof that you are right with God because you are at liberty to turn your mind to Him. If you are not right with God, you can never turn your mind anywhere but on yourself. If you allow anything to hide the face of Jesus Christ from you, you are either disturbed or you have a false security.

Are you looking unto Jesus now, in the immediate matter that is pressing and receiving from Him peace? If so, He will be a gracious benediction of peace in and through you. But if you try to worry it out, you obliterate Him and deserve all you get. We get disturbed because we have not been considering Him. When one confers with Jesus Christ the perplexity goes, because He has no perplexity, and our only concern is to abide in Him. Lay it all out before Him, and in the face of difficulty, bereavement and sorrow, hear Him say, "Let not your heart be troubled."

— Oswald Chambers

Peace at Last

In summing up the superiority of the Christian life over all other ways of living we cannot overlook the advantage that the Christian will have for all eternity. Job said, *"If a man die, shall he live again?"* (Job 14:14). He answered his own question when he said, *"For I know that my redeemer liveth, and that he shall stand at the latter day upon the earth"* (Job 19:25).

What a prospect! What a future! What a hope! What a life! I would not change places with the wealthiest and most influential person in the world. I would rather be a child of the King, a joint-heir with Christ, a member of the Royal Family of heaven!

I know where I've come from, I know why I'm here, I know where I'm going—and I have peace in my heart. His peace floods my heart and overwhelms my soul!

The storm was raging. The sea was beating against the rocks in huge, dashing waves. The lightning was flashing, the thunder was roaring, the wind was blowing; but the little bird was asleep in the crevice of the rock, its head serenely under its wing, sound asleep. That is peace: to be able to rest serenely in the storm!

In Christ we are relaxed and at peace in the midst of the confusions, bewilderments, and perplexities of this life. The storm rages, but our hearts are at rest. We have found peace—at last!

— Billy Graham

Peace With God
Grason, 1953

Prince of Peace Proclaimed!

Now there were in the same country shepherds living out in the fields, keeping watch over their flock by night. And behold, an angel of the LORD stood before them. . . And suddenly there was with the angel a multitude of the heavenly host praising God and saying:

> *"Glory to God in the highest,*
> *And on earth peace, goodwill toward men!"*

Then, as He [Jesus] was now drawing near the descent of the Mount of Olives, the whole multitude of the disciples began to rejoice and praise God with a loud voice for all the mighty works they had seen, saying:

> *"Blessed is the King who comes in the name*
> *of the LORD!"*
> *Peace in heaven and glory in the highest!"*

> — *Luke 2:8-9a, 13-14; 19:37-38* (NKJV)
> *HOLY BIBLE*

Give Me Peace

> With eager heart and will on fire,
> I strove to win my great desire.
> "Peace shall be mine," I said; but life
> Grew bitter in the barren strife.
>
> My soul was weary, and my pride
> Was wounded deep; to Heaven I cried,
> "God grant me peace or I must die;"
> The dumb stars glittered no reply.

Broken at last, I bowed my head,
Forgetting all myself, and said,
"Whatever comes, His will be done;"
And in that moment peace was won.

— *Henry van Dyke*

Masterpieces of Religious Verse
Edited by James Dalton Morrison
Harper and Brothers Publishers, 1948

The Prince of Peace

For unto us a child is born, unto us a son is given; and the government shall be upon his shoulder. And his name will be called Wonderful, Counselor, the mighty God, the everlasting Father, Prince of Peace.

Of the increase of his government and peace there will be no end, upon the throne of David, and over his kingdom, to order it, and establish it with judgment and justice from that time forward even forever. The zeal of the Lord of hosts will perform this.

— *Isaiah 9:6-7 (NKJV)*
HOLY BIBLE

Key To Peace

Who is the best cared for in every household? Is it not the little children? And does not the least of all, the helpless baby, receive the largest share? We all know that the baby toils not, neither does it spin; and yet it is fed, and clothed, and loved, and rejoiced in more tenderly than the hardest worker of them all.

This life of faith, then, about which I am writing, consists in just this—being a child in the Father's house. And when this is said, enough is said to transform every weary, burdened life into one of blessedness and rest.

Let the ways of childish confidence and freedom from care, which so please you and win your hearts in your own little ones, teach you what should be your ways with God; and, leaving yourselves in His hands, learn to be literally "careful for nothing;" and you shall find it to be a fact that the peace of God, which passeth all understanding, shall keep (as with a garrison) your hearts and minds through Christ Jesus.

"Thou wilt keep him in perfect peace, whose mind is stayed on thee: because he trusteth in thee." This is the divine description of the life of faith about which I am writing. It is no speculative theory, neither is it a dream of romance. There is such a thing as having one's soul kept in perfect peace, now and here in this life; and childlike trust in God is the key to its attainment.

— Hannah Whitall Smith

The Christian's Secret of a Happy Life
Old Tappan, N.J.: Spire Books, Fleming H. Revell Co.,
1942, 1970, 1978

His Peace

Jesus said:
Peace I leave with you, my peace I give unto you: not as the world giveth, give I unto you. Let not your heart be troubled, neither let it be afraid.

— John 14:27
HOLY BIBLE

Peace Is Flowing

> Peace is flowing like a river;
> flowing out of you and me.
> Flowing out into the desert,
> setting all the captives free.

— Chorus by Carey Landry

The Comforter—

Giver of Peace

"I will ask the Father and he will give you another Comforter, and he will never leave you. He is the Holy Spirit, the Spirit who leads into all truth. The world at large cannot receive him, for it isn't looking for him and doesn't recognize him. But you do, for he lives with you now and some day shall be in you. No, I will not abandon you or leave you as orphans in the storm—I will come to you. In just a little while I will be gone from the world, but I will still be present with you. For I will live again—and you will too.

"I am leaving you with a gift—peace of mind and heart! And the peace I give isn't fragile like the peace the world gives. So don't be troubled or afraid. Remember what I told you—I am going away, but I will come back to you again."

—John 14:15-19, 27-28 (TLB)
HOLY BIBLE

Calm and Still

I take Thee for my Peace, O Lord,
　　My heart to keep and fill;
Thine own great calm, amid earth's storms,
　　Shall keep me always still,
And as Thy Kingdom doth increase,
So shall Thine ever-deepening peace.

— Annie W. Marston

Joy and Strength
Mary Wilder Tileston
Minnesota: World Wide Publications,
1901, 1929, 1986

Perfect Peace

Thou wilt keep him in perfect peace, whose mind is stayed on thee: because he trusteth in thee. Trust ye in the LORD for ever: for in the LORD JEHOVAH is everlasting strength.

— Isaiah 26:3-4
HOLY BIBLE

As long as our mind is stayed on our dear selves, we will never have peace. Some people think more of themselves than of all the rest of the world. It is self in the morning, self at noon, and self at night. It is self when they wake up, and self when they go to bed. They are all the time looking at themselves and thinking about themselves, instead of "looking unto Jesus." Faith is an outward look. Faith does not look within; it looks without. It is not what I think, or what I feel, or what I have done, but it is what Jesus Christ is and has done, that is the important thing for us to dwell upon.

— Dwight L. Moody

The D. L. Moody Year Book
Selected by Emma Moody Fitt
New York: Fleming H. Revell Co., 1900

Peace, Perfect Peace

Peace, perfect peace, in this dark world of sin?
The blood of Jesus whispers peace within.

Peace, perfect peace, by thronging duties pressed?
To do the will of Jesus, this is rest.

Peace, perfect peace, with sorrows surging round?
On Jesus' bosom naught but calm if found.

Peace, perfect peace, our future all unknown?
Jesus we know, and He is on the throne.

Peace, perfect peace, death shadowing us and ours?
Jesus has vanquished death and all its powers.

It is enough; earth's struggles soon shall cease,
And Jesus, call us to heav'n' perfect peace.

— Edward T. Bickersteth

Hymns of Faith
Tabernacle Publishing, 1980

Finding Rest in God

In comparison with this big world, the human heart is only a small thing. Though the world is so large, it is utterly unable to satisfy this tiny heart. The ever-growing soul and its capacity can be satisfied only in the infinite God. As water is restless until it reaches its level, so the soul has no peace until it rests in God.

— Sundar Singh

The Cross is Heaven:
The Life and Writings of Sadhu Sundar, 1957
Association Press

God's Gift of Peace

Let us thank God for His gift of peace that reminds us that we have been created to live that peace, and that Jesus became man in all things like us except in sin, and He proclaimed very clearly that He had come to give the good news. The news was peace to all men of goodwill and this is something that we all want—peace of heart.

Let us preach the peace of Christ as He did. He went about doing good. He did not stop His works of charity because the Pharisees and others hated Him or tried to spoil His Father's work. He just went about doing good. Cardinal Newman wrote: "Help me to spread Thy fragrance everywhere I go—let me preach Thee without preaching, not by words but by my example." Our works of love are nothing but the works of peace.

Let us not use bombs and guns to overcome the world. Let us use love and compassion. Peace begins with a smile—smile five times a day at someone you don't really want to smile at, at all—do it for peace. So let us radiate the peace of God and so light his light and extinguish in the world and in the hearts of all men all hatred and love for power.

— Mother Teresa

Life in the Spirit
San Francisco: Harper & Row

Pax

All that matters is to be at one with the living God
to be a creature in the house of the God of Life.

Like a cat asleep on a chair
at peace, in peace
and at one with the master of the house, with the mistress,
at home, at home in the house of the living,
sleeping on the hearth, and yawning before the fire.

Sleeping on the hearth of the living world
yawning at home before the fire of life
feeling the presence of the living God
like a great reassurance
a deep calm in the heart
a presence
as of a master sitting at the board
in his own and greater being,
in the house of life.

— Dwight H. Lawrence

The English Spirit
Nashville: Abingdon Press, 1987

Pray for Peace

Do not be anxious about anything, but in everything, by prayer and petition, with thanksgiving, present your requests to God. And the peace of God, which transcends all understanding, will guard your hearts and your minds in Christ Jesus.

— Philippians 4:6-7 (NIV)
HOLY BIBLE

Peace

Father eternal, ruler of creation,
> Spirit of life, which moved ere form was made,
Through the thick darkness covering every nation,
> Light to man's blindness, O be thou our aid:
Thy kingdom come, O Lord, Thy will be done.

Races and peoples, lo, we stand divided,
> And, sharing not our griefs, no joy can share.
By wars and tumults love is mocked, derided;
> His conquering cross no kingdom wills to bear.
Thy kingdom come, O Lord, Thy will be done.

Envious of heart, blind-eyed with tongues confounded,
> Nation by nation still goes unforgiven,
In wrath and fear, by jealousies surrounded,
> Building proud towers which shall not reach to
> heaven:
Thy kingdom come, O Lord, Thy will be done.

Lust of possession worketh desolations;
> There is no meekness in the sons of earth;
Led by no star, the rulers of the nations
> Still fail to bring us to the blissful birth:
Thy kingdom come, O Lord, Thy will be done.

How shall we love thee, holy hidden Being,
> If we love not the world which thou hast made?
O give us brother-love for better seeing
> Thy Word made flesh, and in a manger laid:
Thy kingdom come, O Lord, Thy will be done.

— *Laurence Housman*

Freedom, Love and Truth
William Inge
London: Longman, Green & Co., Inc., 1936

Peace

Were half the power that fills the world with terror,
     Were half the wealth bestowed on camps and courts,
Given to redeem the human mind from error,
     There were no need of arsenals or forts.

The warrior's name would be a name abhorr-d!
     And every nation that should lift again
Its hand against a brother, on its forehead
     Would wear for evermore the curse of Cain!

Down the dark future, through long generations,
     The echoing sounds grow fainter, and then cease;
And like a bell, with solemn, sweet vibrations,
     I hear once more the voice of Christ say 'Peace!'

Peace! and no longer from its brazen portals
     The blast of War's great organ shakes the skies!
But beautiful as songs of the immortals,
     The holy melodies of love arise.

— Henry W. Longfellow

Freedom, Love and Truth
William Inge
London: Longman, Green & Co., Inc., 1936

Constantly Abiding

There's a peace in my heart that the world never gave,
A peace it cannot take away;
Tho' the trials of life may surround like a cloud,
I've a peace that has come there to stay!

All the world seemed to sing of a Savior and King,
When peace sweetly came to my heart;
Troubles all fled away and my night turned to day,
Blessed Jesus, how glorious Thou art!

This treasure I have in a temple of clay,
While here on His footstool I roam;
But He's coming to take me some glorious day,
Over there to my heavenly home!

Constantly abiding, Jesus is mine;
Constantly abiding, rapture divine;
He never leaves me lonely, whispers, O so kind:—
"I will never leave thee," Jesus is mine.

— *Mrs. Will L. Murphy*

Melodies of Praise
Gospel Publishing House

We Seek Peace

From his cradle to his grave a man never does a single thing
which has any first and foremost object save one—to secure peace of
mind, spiritual comfort, for himself.

— *Mark Twain*

The Book of Unusual Quotations
Selected and Edited by Rudolph Flesch
New York: Harper and Brothers Publishers, 1957

Collect for Peace

Most holy God, the source of all good desires, all right judgments, and all just works, give to us, Your servants, that peace which the world cannot give, so that our minds may be fixed on the doing of Your will, and that we, being delivered from the fear of all enemies, may live in peace and quietness; through the mercies of Christ Jesus our Savior. *Amen.*

— *Daily Evening Prayer*

The Book of Common Prayer

Living by Grace

All men who live with any degree of serenity live by some assurance of grace. In every life there must at least be times and seasons when the good is felt as a present possession and not as a far-off goal.

— *Reinhold Niebuhr*

A Treasury of Contentment
Compiled and Edited by Ralph L. Woods
New York: Trident Press, 1969
A Division of Simon and Schuster

Fall Silently

With that deep hush subduing all
Our words and works that drown
The tender whisper of Thy call,
As noiseless let Thy blessing fall
As fell the manna down.

— *John G. Whittier*

Joy and Strength
Mary Wilder Tileston
Minnesota: World Wide Publications
1901, 1929, 1986

Foundation for a True Inner Peace

As it was formerly, so it is now; there are many who corrupt the Word of God and deal deceitfully with it. It was so in a special manner in the prophet Jeremiah's time; and he, faithful to his Lord, faithful to that God who employed him, did not fail from time to time to open his mouth against them, and to bear a noble testimony to the honor of that God in whose name he from time to time spake. If you will read his prophecy, you will find that none spake more against such ministers than Jeremiah. . . . says he, *"They have healed also the hurt of the daughter of my people slightly, saying, Peace, peace; when there is no peace"* (Jeremiah 6:14). *"Therefore,"* says he, in the eleventh and twelfth verses, *"I am full of the fury of the Lord; I am weary with holding in: I will pour it out upon the children abroad, and upon the assembly of young men together: for even the husband with the wife shall be taken, the aged with him that is full of days. And their houses shall be turned unto others, with their fields and wives together: for I will stretch out my hand upon the inhabitants of the land, saith the Lord."*

. . . How many of us cry, Peace, peace, to our souls, when there is no peace! How many are there who are now settled upon their lees, that now think they are Christians, that now flatter themselves that they have an interest in Jesus Christ; whereas if we come to examine their experiences we shall find that their peace is but a peace of the devil's making—it is not a peace of God's giving—it is not a peace that passeth human understanding.

It is a matter, therefore, of great importance, my dear hearers, to know whether we may speak peace to our hearts. We are all desirous of peace; peace is an unspeakable blessing; how can we live without peace? And, therefore, people from time to time must be taught how far they must go and what must be wrought in them before they can speak peace to their hearts.

Before you can speak peace to your hearts, you must be made to see, made to feel, made to weep over, made to bewail your actual transgressions against the law of God. According to the covenant of works, "The soul that sinneth it shall die"; cursed is that man, be he what he may, be he who he may, that continueth not in all things that are written in the book of the law to do them.

We are not only to do some things, but we are to do all things, and we are to continue so to do, so that the least deviation from the moral law, according to the covenant of works, whether in thought, word, or deed, deserves eternal death at the hand of God. And if one evil thought, if one evil word, if one evil action deserves eternal damnation, how many hells, my friend, do every one of us deserve whose whole lives have been one continued rebellion against God! Before ever, therefore, you can speak peace to your hearts, you must be brought to see, brought to believe, what a dreadful thing it is to depart from the living God.

And now, my dear friends, examine your hearts, for I hope you came hither with a design to have your souls made better. Give me leave to ask you, in the presence of God, whether you know the time, and if you do not know exactly the time, do you know there was a time when God wrote bitter things against you, when the arrows of the Almighty were within you? Was ever the remembrance of your sins grievous to you? Was the burden of your sins intolerable to your thoughts? Did you ever see that God's wrath might justly fall upon you, on account of your actual transgressions against God? Were you ever in all your life sorry for your sins? Could you ever say, My sins are gone over my head as a burden too heavy for me to bear? Did you ever experience any such thing as this? Did ever any such thing as this pass between God and your soul? If not, for Jesus Christ's sake, do not call yourselves Christians; you may speak peace to your hearts, but there is no peace. May the Lord awaken you, may the Lord convert you, may the Lord give you peace, before you go home!

Before you can speak peace to your heart you must not only be sick of your original and actual sin, but you must be made sick of your righteousness, of all your duties and performances. There must be a deep conviction before you can be brought out of your self-righteousness; it is the last idol taken out of our heart. The pride of our heart will not let us submit to the righteousness of Jesus Christ. But if you never felt that you had no righteousness of your own, if you never felt the deficiency of your own righteousness, you cannot come to Jesus Christ.

But then, before you can speak peace to your souls, there is one particular sin you must be greatly troubled for, and yet I fear there are few of you think what it is; it is the reigning, the damning sin of the Christian world, and yet the Christian world seldom or never thinks of it.

And pray what is that? It is what most of you think you are not guilty of—and that is, the sin of unbelief. Before you can speak peace to your heart, you must be troubled for the unbelief of your heart.

My dear friends, there must be a principle wrought in the heart by the Spirit of the living God. Did I ask you how long it is since you believed in Jesus Christ, I suppose most of you would tell me you believed in Jesus Christ as long as ever you remember—you never did misbelieve. Then, you could not give me a better proof that you never yet believed in Jesus Christ, unless you were sanctified early, as from the womb; for they that otherwise believe in Christ know there was a time when they did not believe in Jesus Christ.

You say you love God with all your heart, soul, and strength. If I were to ask you how long it is since you loved God, you would say, as long as you can remember; you never hated God, you know no time when there was enmity in your heart against God. Then, unless you were sanctified very early, you never loved God in your life.

. . . I am not talking of the invisible realities of another world, of inward religion, of the work of God upon a poor sinner's heart. I am not talking of a matter of great importance, my dear hearers; you are all concerned in it, your souls are concerned in it, your eternal salvation is concerned in it. You may be all at peace, but perhaps the devil has lulled you asleep into a carnal lethargy and security, and will endeavor to keep you there till he get you to hell, and there you will be awakened; but it will be dreadful to be awakened and find ourselves so fearfully mistaken, when the great gulf is fixed, when you will be calling to all eternity for a drop of water to cool your tongue and shall not obtain it.

— John Whitefield from his sermon
"On the Method of Grace"

The World's Famous Orations
Edited by William Jennings Bryan
Funk & Wagnalls, 1906

Peace Is . . .

Peace is not an absence of war, it is a virtue, a state of mind, a disposition for benevolence, confidence, justice.

— *Benedict Spinoza*

Harper's Quotations

God's Peace

My peace I give in times of deepest grief,
Imparting calm and trust and My relief.

My peace I give when prayer seems lost, unheard;
Know that My promises are ever in My Word.

My peace I give when thou art left alone—
The nightingale at night has sweetest tone.

My peace I give in time of utter loss,
The way of glory leads right to the cross.

My peace I give when enemies will blame,
Thy fellowship is sweet through cruel shame.

My peace I give in agony and sweat,
For mine own brow with bloody drops was wet.

My peace I give when nearest friend betrays—
Peace that is merged in love, and for them prays.

My peace I give when there's but death for thee—
The gateway is the cross to get to Me.

—*L. S. P.*

Streams in the Desert
Compiled by Mrs. Charles E. Cowman
Los Angeles: Cowman Publications, Inc., 1959

The Subconscious at Peace

When we are "in Christ," we are secure. I saw a bird's nest hollowed out of a prickly cactus tree in the deserts of Arizona. It was surrounded by thorns, but among these thorns it had hollowed out a place of security and peace. I said to myself: "In the midst of a thorny world I can find a place of peace in the very heart of God."

And that peace is available in the hour of crisis. There was a woman who put up with a drunken husband when he used to lock her out of her house for days. He came home one day and in a drunken fit choked her until she was getting blue in the face, when the Inner Voice said: "Relax." She did, and as she did so, she slumped out of his grasp and sank upon the floor—saved.

Her subconscious mind was at peace and could be spoken to in a crisis. For the subconscious is included in this peace, and included especially. If the subconscious is not redeemed from clash and chaos, then that unpeace of the subconscious will spill over into the conscious and will trouble it. A research scientist was showing me around a raja's palace now converted into a science laboratory. He said: "I can convert the upper stories into an All-India Drug Research Laboratory, but the cellar with its many subterranean passages seems impossible to convert." The subconscious mind is like that cellar—difficult to convert from old ways. But not impossible. For Christ can save to the uttermost, and the uttermost means the deepmost.

If we have unsurrendered fears and anxieties and conflicts down in the subconscious, then there is not much use in our trying to mop them up in the conscious by various expedients. The subconscious is the place of peace or unpeace. Tackle it there at the source, and then the stream will run peace. And how do we tackle it there? By the one real remedy—surrender! Turn over all you know—the conscious— and all you don't know—the subconscious, and the Holy Spirit will take over the subconscious and will cleanse and coordinate and make it peaceful and calm with His presence and His power.

Father, I thank Thee that there can be a total redemption from unpeace. Heal me at the depths, and then I shall be healed. Amen.

Affirmation for the day: My depths are held by peace. The surface may be disturbed; it's the depths that count.

— E. Stanley Jones

Growing Spiritually
Nashville: Abingdon Press

Prayer for Peace

Eternal God, in whose perfect kingdom no sword is drawn but the sword of righteousness, no strength known but the strength of love: So mightily spread abroad Your Spirit, that all peoples may be gathered under the banner of the Prince of Peace, as children of one Father; to whom be dominion and glory, now and forever. *Amen.*

The Book of Common Prayer

God Is Always There

Your faith has met unusual trials, and . . . you ask for thoughts which may strengthen you. Your experience of life and of God's goodness is a far better teacher than any suggestions of a fellow being. The thought on which I delight to dwell, as I advance in life, is that God is within me—always present to my soul, to teach, to rebuke, to aid, to bless—that He truly desires my salvation from all inward evils, that He is ever ready to give His Spirit, that there is no part of my lot which may not carry me forward to perfection, and that outward things are of little or no moment, provided this great work of God goes on within. The body and the world vanish more and more, and the soul, the immortal principle, made to bear God's image, to partake of his truth, goodness, purity, and happiness, comes out of my consciousness more and more distinctly; and in feeling God's intimate presence with this, to enlighten, quicken, and save, I find strength, and hope, and peace.

— *William Ellery Channing*

A Treasury of Contentment
Compiled and Edited by Ralph L. Woods
New York: Trident Press, 1969
A Division of Simon and Schuster

Peace in the Midst

Two painters each painted a picture to illustrate his conception of rest. The first chose for his scene a still, lone lake among the far-off mountains.

The second threw on his canvas a thundering waterfall, with a fragile birch tree bending over the foam; and at the fork of the branch, almost wet with the cataract's spray, sat a robin on its nest.

The first was only *stagnation*; the last was *rest*.

Christ's life outwardly was one of the most troubled lives that ever lived: tempest and tumult, tumult and tempest, the waves breaking over it all the time until the worn body was laid in the grave. But the inner life was a sea of glass. The great calm was always there.

At any moment you might have gone to Him and found rest. And even when the human bloodhounds were dogging Him in the streets of Jerusalem, He turned to His disciples and offered them, as a last legacy, "My peace."

Rest is not a hallowed feeling that comes over us in church; it is the repose of a heart set deep in God.

— *Drummond*

Streams in the Desert
Compiled by Mrs. Charles E. Cowman
Los Angeles: Cowman Publications, Inc., 1959

How Good It Is for a Man To Be Peaceful

First put yourself at peace, and then you may the better make others be at peace. A peaceful and patient man is of more profit to himself and to others, too, than a learned man who has no peace. A man who is passionate often turns good into evil, and easily believes the worst. But a good, peaceful man turns all things to the best, and suspects no man.

He who is not content is often troubled with many suspicions, and is neither quiet himself nor allows others to be quiet. He often speaks what he should not, and fails to speak what it would be more expedient to say. He considers seriously what others are bound to do, but he grandly neglects that to which he himself is bound.

First, therefore, have a zealous regard to yourself and to your own soul, and then you may more righteously and with better ordered charity have zeal for your neighbor's soul. You are at once ready to excuse your own defects, but you will not hear the excuses of your brethren. Truly, it would be more charitable and more profitable to you to accuse yourself and excuse your brothers, for, if you will be borne, bear with others. Consider how far you yet are from the perfect humility and charity of Christian people, who cannot be angry with any except themselves.

It is no great thing to get on well with good and docile men, for that is naturally pleasant to all people, and all men gladly have peace with those and most love those who are agreeable. But to live peacefully with evil men and with impertinent men who lack good manners and are illiterate and rub us the wrong way–that is a great grace, and manly deed, and much to be praised, for it cannot be done save through great spiritual strength. Some people can be quiet themselves, and live quietly with others, and some cannot be quiet themselves, nor permit others to be quiet; they are grievous to others—they are more grievous to themselves. And some can keep themselves in good peace, and can also bring others to live in peace. Nevertheless, all our peace, while we are in this mortal life, rests more in the humble endurance of troubles and of things that are irksome to us than in not feeling them at all. For no man is here without some trouble. Therefore, he who can suffer best will have most peace, and he who is the true conqueror of himself is the true lord of the world, the friend of Christ, and the true inheritor of the kingdom of heaven.

— *Thomas à Kempis*

From *The Imitation of Christ* by Thomas à Kempis.
Copyright © 1955 by Doubleday, a division of Bantam,
Doubleday, Dell Publishing Group, Inc.
Used by permission of Doubleday,
A Division of Bantam Doubleday Dell Publishing Group, Inc.

The Light of Day

An old rabbi once asked his pupils how they could tell when the night had ended and the day had begun.

"Could it be," asked one of the students, "when you can see an animal in the distance and tell whether it's a sheep or a dog?"

"No," answered the rabbi.

Another asked, "Is it when you can look at a tree in the distance and tell whether it's a fig tree or a peach tree?"

"No," answered the rabbi.

"Then when is it?" the pupils demanded.

"It is when you can look on the face of any man or woman and see that it is your sister or brother. Because if you cannot see this, it is still night."

— *Tales of the Hasidim*

Live Peaceably With All Men

May those who hold in their hands the fate of the nations take care to avoid anything that might make the situation in which we now find ourselves still more difficult and might still further endanger us. May they take to heart the wonderful word of the Apostle Paul: *"As much as lieth in you, live peaceably with all men"* (Romans *12:18*). This is true not only for individuals but also for nations. May they go to the utmost limit of possibility in their effort to preserve the peace with each other, so that there may be time for the human spirit to grow strong and to act.

— Albert Schweitzer

Taken from *Albert Schweitzer: Genius in the Jungle*
by Joseph Gollomb. Copyright © 1949
by Vanguard Press.

Peacemakers

Peacemaking is a noble vocation. But you can no more make peace in your own strength than a mason can build a wall without a trowel, a carpenter build a house without a hammer, or an artist paint a picture without a brush. You must have the proper equipment. To be a peacemaker, you must know the Peace Giver. To make peace on earth, you must know the peace of heaven. You must know Him who "is our peace."

— Billy Graham

The Quotable Billy Graham
Compiled and Edited by Cort R. Flint and the Staff of *Quote*
Anderson, S.C.: Droke House, 1966

How Beautiful!

"How beautiful on the mountains
are the feet of those who bring good news,
who proclaim peace,
who bring good tidings,
who proclaim salvation,
who say to Zion,
Your God reigns!
Listen! Your watchmen lift up their voices;
together they shout for joy.
When the Lord returns to Zion,
they will see it with their own eyes.
Burst into songs of joy together,
you ruins of Jerusalem,
for the Lord has comforted his people,
he has redeemed Jerusalem.
The Lord will lay bare his holy arm
in the sight of all the nations,
and all the ends of the earth will see
the salvation of our God."

— Isaiah 52:7-10 (NIV)
HOLY BIBLE

Instrument of His Peace

Lord, make me an instrument of your peace;
Where there is hatred, let me sow love;
Where there is injury, pardon;
Where there is doubt, faith;
Where there is despair, hope;
Where there is darkness, light;
Where there is sadness, joy.

O Divine Master,
grant that I may not so much seek
to be consoled, as to console;
To be understood, as to understand;
To be loved, as to love.
For it is in giving that we receive;
It is in pardoning that we are pardoned;
It is in dying that we are born to eternal life.

— *Attributed to St. Francis of Assisi*

Prayer for All Peoples

O God, who hast made of one blood all nations of men for to
dwell on the face of the earth, and didst send Thy blessed Son, Jesus
Christ, to preach peace to them who are afar off, and to them that
are nigh: Grant that all the peoples of the world may feel after Thee
and find Thee; and hasten, O heavenly Father, the fulfillment of
Thy promise to pour out Thy Spirit upon all flesh, through Jesus
Christ our Saviour.

— *Bishop George Cotton, 1813-1866*

The Oxford Book of Prayer
Edited by George Appleton
Oxford: Oxford University Press, 1985

Four Things That Bring Peace to the Soul

My son, now I shall teach you the truest way of peace and of perfect liberty.

O Lord Jesus, do as You say, for it is very joyous for me to hear.

Study, my son, to fulfill another man's will rather than your own. Choose always to have little worldly riches rather than much. Seek, also, the lowest place, and desire to be under others rather than above them; desire always and pray that the will of God be wholly done in you. Lo, such a person enters surely into the very true way of peace and inward quiet.

O Lord, this short lesson You have taught me contains in itself much high perfection. It is short in words, but it is full of wisdom and fruitful in virtue. If I observed it well and faithfully, disquiet would not so easily spring up in me as it has.

For, as often as I feel myself restless and discontent, I find that I have departed from this lesson and from this good doctrine. But You, Lord Jesus, who have all things under Your governance, and who always love the health of man's soul, increase Your grace in me still more, so that I may from now on fulfill these teachings and always do what will be to Your honor and to the salvation of my soul.

— *Thomas à Kempis*

Fulfill vs. Fill

Not every driving purpose is permanent enough to give us lasting peace. Hence the Holy Spirit gives another factor, namely, the peace that comes through fulfillment.

We greedy grown-up children still follow the false principle that peace comes through filling.

Through the Holy Spirit we learn that the peace of God comes not by trying to fill ourselves but by trying to fulfill ourselves.

And since we are made in the image of God and God is a Spirit, we find the peace of fulfillment through giving ourselves to godly and spiritual things. We cannot be content on the animal level. As Saint Augustine said, "Thou hast made us for Thyself, O God, and we are restless till we find rest in Thee."

— Ralph W. Sockman, D.D.

From *How To Believe* by Ralph W. Sockman, D.D.
Copyright © 1953 by Ralph W. Sockman.
Used by permission of Doubleday, a division of
Bantam Doubleday Dell Publishing Group, Inc.

Woven Together

Peace is the result of grace. It literally means, "to bind together." In other words, the peace which comes from unmerited, unearned love can weave and bind our fragmented lives into wholeness. And the civil war of divergent drives, which makes us feel like rubber bands stretched in all directions, is ended. The Lord is in control. He has forgiven the past, He is in charge of now, and shows the way for each new day.

— Lloyd John Ogilvie

Let God Love You
Word Books, 1974

False Peace

We have our peace movements, and all we want is peace--abroad and at home. But if by peace we mean appeasing tyranny, compromising with gangsters and being silent because we haven't the moral fortitude to speak out against injustice, then this is not real peace. It is a false peace. It is a farce and it is a hoax.

— Billy Graham

The Quotable Billy Graham
Compiled and Edited by Cort R. Flint and the Staff of *Quote*
Anderson, S.C.: Droke House, 1966

Peace and Tranquillity

Keep your heart in peace; let nothing in this world disturb it: all things have an end.

In all circumstances, however hard they may be, we should rejoice, rather than be cast down, that we may not lose the greatest good, the peace and tranquillity of our souls.

If the whole world and all that is in it were thrown into confusion, disquietude on that account would be vanity, because that disquietude would do more harm than good.

To endure all things with an equable and peaceful mind, not only brings with it many blessings to the soul, but also enables us, in the midst of our difficulties, to have a clear judgment about them, and to minister the fitting remedy for them.

— *St. John of the Cross*

Mnd and God
Victor Gollancz
Boston: Houghton Mifflin Co., 1951

Inward Quiet

Consider that it was not during His ministry in Galilee, but when He drew near the crisis and agony of the Passion and the tension of His own life was great, that Christ more and more emphasized peace. "Peace I give unto you, not as the world giveth give I unto you"—I give the deep, enduring, tranquil peace, the inward quiet of acceptance, the mind stayed on God ready for anything because anchored on His eternal Reality—indifferent to its own risks, comforts or achievements, sunk in the great movement of His life.

That sounds all right and sometimes in prayer we seem to draw near it; but the test comes later on, when this peace and joy must be matched against the troubles and assaults, the evils, cruelties and contradictions of the world. Then we shall see whether our peace is just a feeling or a fact — a true fruit which exists and endures, grows and ripens in the sun and wind of experience. For the peace of God does not mean apathy in respect of the world's sorrows and sins. It can co-exist with the sharpest pain, the utmost bewilderment, the agony of compassion which feels the whole awful weight of evil and suffering. We see this so clearly in the saints who bore the whole weight of redemptive suffering with a tranquil joy — for this peace of God is linked with the Altar and the Cross.

— *Evelyn Underhill*

The Fruits of the Spirit
London: Longmans, Green and Co., Ltd., 1949

He Sustains Us

We are conformed to Him in proportion as our lives grow in quietness, His peace spreading within our souls. Even amid all that outwardly disturbs us we have, if we have Him, the same peace, because He is our peace, sustaining our whole being.

— *T. T. Carter*

Joy and Strength
Mary Wilder Tileston
Minnesota: World Wide Publications
1901, 1929, 1986

What's in Your Heart?

When God is in the midst of a kingdom or city He makes it as firm as Mount Zion, that cannot be removed. When He is in the midst of a soul, though calamities throng about it on all hands, and roar like the billows of the sea, yet there is a constant calm within, such a peace as the world can neither give nor take away. What is it but want of lodging God in the soul, and that in His stead the world is in men's hearts, that makes them shake like leaves at every blast of danger?

— Archbishop Leighton

Streams in the Desert
Compiled by Mrs. Charles E. Cowman
Los Angeles: Cowman Publications, Inc., 1959

It Is Well with My Soul

When peace, like a river, attendeth my way,
when sorrows like sea billows roll;
whatever my lot, Thou hast taught me to say,
It is well, it is well with my soul.

Though Satan should buffet, though trials should come,
let this blest assurance control,
that Christ has regarded my helpless estate,
and hath shed His own blood for my soul.

My sin, oh, the bliss of this glorious thought!
My sin, not in part but the whole,
is nailed to the cross, and I bear it no more,
praise the Lord, praise the Lord, O my soul!

And, Lord, haste the day when my faith shall be sight,
the clouds be rolled back as a scroll;
the trump shall resound, and the Lord shall descend,
even so, it is well with my soul.

It is well with my soul,
it is well, it is well with my soul.

— Horatio G. Spafford

United Methodist Hymnal

Rejoicing Peace

Rejoice in the Lord always. I will say it again: Rejoice! Let your gentleness be evident to all. The Lord is near. Do not be anxious about anything, but in everything, by prayer and petition, with thanksgiving, present your requests to God. And the peace of God, which transcends all understanding, will guard your hearts and your minds in Christ Jesus.

— Philippians 4:4-9 (NIV)
HOLY BIBLE

The Root of Peace

The habit of resignation is the root of peace.

A godly child had a ring given him by his mother, and he greatly prized it, but on one occasion he unhappily lost his ring and he cried bitterly. But recapturing his composure, he stepped aside and prayed, after which his sister laughingly said to him, "Brother, what is the good of praying about a ring—will praying bring back your ring?" "Perhaps not," said he, "but praying has done this for me; it has made me quite willing to do without the ring if it is God's will; and is not that almost as good as having it?"

Thus faith quiets us by resignation, as a babe is hushed in his mother's bosom. Faith makes us quite willing to do without the mercy which once we prized; and when the heart is content to be without the outward blessing, it is as happy as it would be with it; for it is at rest.

— *Charles H. Spurgeon*

Devotions and Prayers of Charles H. Spurgeon
Edited by Donald E. Demaray
Grand Rapids, Mich.: Baker Book House, 1960

Correction Brings Peace

"Behold, happy is the man whom God corrects;
Therefore do not despise the chastening of the Almighty.
For He bruises, but He binds up;
He wounds, but His hands make whole.
He shall deliver you in six troubles,
Yes, in seven no evil shall touch you.
In famine He shall redeem you from death,
And in war from the power of the sword.
You shall be hidden from the scourge of the tongue,
And you shall not be afraid of destruction when it comes.
You shall laugh at destruction and famine,
And you shall not be afraid of the beasts of the earth.
For you shall have a covenant with the stones of the field,
And the beasts of the field shall be at peace with you.
You shall know that your tent is in peace;
You shall visit your dwelling and find nothing amiss.
You shall also know that your descendants shall be many,

And your offspring like the grass of the earth.
You shall come to the grave at a full age,
As a sheaf of grain ripens in its season."

— *Job 5:17-26* (NKJV)
HOLY BIBLE

God's Commandments Are for Peace

'If you walk in My statues and keep My commandments,
and perform them,
then I will give you rain in its season, the land shall yield
its produce, and the trees of the field shall yield their fruit.
Your threshing shall last till the time of vintage, and the vintage
shall last till the time of sowing; you shall eat your bread to the full, and
dwell in your land safely.
I will give peace in the land, and you shall lie down, and none will
make you afraid;
I will rid the land of evil beasts,
and the sword will not go through your land.
You will chase your enemies,
and they shall fall by the sword before you.
Five of you shall chase a hundred, and a hundred of you shall put
ten thousand to flight; your enemies shall fall by the sword before you.
For I will look on you favorably and make you fruitful,
multiply you and confirm My covenant with you.
You shall eat the old harvest, and clear out the old because
of the new.
I will set My tabernacle among you, and My soul shall not
abhor you.
I will walk among you and be your God, and you shall be
My people.

*I am the LORD your God, who brought you out of the land
of Egypt, that you should not be their slaves;*

I have broken the bands of your yoke and made you walk upright.

*But if you do not obey Me, and do not observe all these
commandments, and if you despise My statutes, or if your soul abhors My
judgments, so that you do not perform all My commandments, but break
My covenant, I also will do this to you:*

*I will even appoint terror over you, wasting disease and fever which
shall consume the eyes and cause sorrow of heart.*

And you shall sow your seed in vain, for your enemies shall eat it.

*I will set My face against you, and you shall be defeated by
your enemies.*

*Those who hate you shall reign over you, and you shall flee
when no one pursues you.'*

— Leviticus 26:3-17 (NKJV)
HOLY BIBLE

Aaron's Blessing

*And the Lord spoke to Moses, saying: "Speak to Aaron and his sons,
saying, 'This is the way you shall bless the children of Israel. Say to them:*

"The Lord bless you and keep you;
The Lord make His face shine upon you,
And be gracious to you;
The Lord lift up His countenance upon you,
And give you peace."'

"So they shall put My name on the children of Israel, and I will bless them."

— Numbers 6:22-27 (NKJV)
HOLY BIBLE

Psalm of Peace

The Lord is my shepherd; I shall not want.
He maketh me to lie down in green pastures:
he leadeth me beside the still waters.
He restoreth my soul: he leadeth me in the paths
of righteousness for his name's sake.
Yea, though I walk through the valley of the
shadow of death, I will fear no evil:
for thou art with me; thy rod and thy
staff they comfort me.
Thou preparest a table before me in the presence
of mine enemies: thou anointest my head
with oil; my cup runneth over.
Surely goodness and mercy shall follow me all
the days of my life: and I will dwell in the
house of the Lord for ever.

— Psalm 23 (KJV)
HOLY BIBLE

Divine Peace

Joy is like restless day; but peace divine
Like quiet night:
Lead me, O Lord—till perfect Day shall shine,
Through Peace to Light.

— Adelaide Ann Procter

A Chaplet of Verses
The Oxford University Press Dictionary of Quotations 2nd edition
New York: Crescent Books, 1985

Love Can Conquer Hate

The oceans of history are made turbulent by the ever-rising tides of revenge. Man has never risen above the injunction of the *lex talionis* "Life for life, eye for eye, tooth for tooth, hand for hand, foot for foot." In spite of the fact that the law of revenge solves no social problems, men continue to follow its disastrous leading. History is cluttered with the wreckage of nations and individuals that pursued this self-defeating path.

Jesus eloquently affirmed from the cross a higher law. He knew that the old eye-for-an-eye philosophy would leave everyone blind. He did not seek to overcome evil with evil. He overcame evil with good. Although crucified by hate, He responded with aggressive love.

What a magnificent lesson! Generations will rise and fall; men will continue to worship the god of revenge and bow before the altar of retaliation; but ever and again this noble lesson of Calvary will be a nagging reminder that only goodness can drive out evil and only love can conquer hate.

— Martin Luther King, Jr.

Diary of a Young Girl

I keep my ideals because in spite of everything I still believe that people are really good at heart. I simply can't build up my hopes on a foundation consisting of confusion, misery and death. I can feel the sufferings of millions, and yet, if I look up into the heavens, I think that it will come right, that this cruelty too will end, and that peace and tranquility will return again.

— Anne Frank
(Jewish teenager who died in a Nazi concentration camp)

Coming Day of Peace

"For thus says the Lord of hosts: 'Once more (it is a little while) I will shake heaven and earth, the sea and dry land; and I will shake all nations, and they shall come to the Desire of All Nations, and I will fill this temple with glory,' says the Lord of hosts. 'The silver is Mine, and the gold is Mine,' says the Lord of hosts. 'The glory of this latter temple shall be greater than the former,' says the Lord of hosts. 'And in this place I will give peace,' says the Lord of hosts."

— *Haggai 2:6-9* (NKJV)
HOLY BIBLE

Interview with Billy Graham

Sojourners: How does your commitment to the lordship of Christ shape your response to the nuclear threat?

Graham: I am not sure I have thought through all the implications of Christ's lordship for this issue—I have to be honest about that. But for the Christian there is—or at least should be—only one question: What is the will of God? What is His will both for this world and for me in regard to this issue?

Let me suggest several things. First, the lordship of Christ reminds me that we live in a sinful world. The cross teaches me that. Like a drop of ink in a glass of water, sin has permeated everything—the individual, society, creation. That is one reason why the nuclear issue is not just a political issue—it is a moral issue and spiritual issue as well. And because we live in a sinful world it means we have to take something like nuclear armaments seriously. We know the terrible violence of which the human heart is capable.

Secondly, the lordship of Jesus Christ tells me that God is not interested in destruction, but in redemption. Christ came to seek and to save that which was lost. He came to reverse the effects of the Fall.

Now I know there are mysteries to the workings of God. I know God is sovereign and sometimes He permits things to happen which are evil, and He even causes the wrath of man to praise him. But I cannot see any way in which nuclear war could be branded as being God's will. Such warfare, if it ever happens, will come because of the greed and pride and covetousness of the human heart. But God's will is to establish His kingdom, in which Christ is Lord.

Third, of course, Christ calls us to love, and that is the critical test of discipleship. Love is not a vague feeling or an abstract idea. When I love someone, I seek what is best for them. If I begin to take the love of Christ seriously, then I will work toward what is best for my neighbor. I will seek to bind up the wounds and bring about healing, no matter what the cost may be.

Therefore, I believe that the Christian especially has a responsibility to work for peace in our world. Christians may well find themselves working and agreeing with non-believers on an issue like peace. But our motives will not be identical.

The issues are not simple, and we are always tempted to grasp any program which promises easy answers. Or, on the other side, we are tempted to say that the issues are too complex, and we cannot do anything of significance anyway. We must resist both temptations.

Peacemakers
Edited by Jim Wallis
San Francisco: Harper & Row, 1983

Blessed Are the Peacemakers

Peacemaking is a divine work. For peace means reconciliation, and God is the author of peace and of reconciliation . . . It is hardly surprising, therefore, that the particular blessing which attaches to peacemakers is that "they shall be called sons of God." For they are seeking to do what their Father has done, loving people with His love . . . It is the devil who is a troublemaker; it is God who loves reconciliation and who now through his children, as formerly through His only begotten Son, is bent on making peace.

— *John Stott*

Reprinted from *Christian Counter-Culture* by
John R. W. Stott. Copyright © 1978 by
John R. W. Stott. Used by permission of InterVarsity Press,
P. O. Box 1400, Downers Grove, IL 60515.

No Anxiety

Just think of having His wonderful peace guarding one's heart and one's thoughts all day long. But it is only on condition that we fulfill the sixth verse, *"In nothing be anxious,"*—this is a distinct command, and, if we fail to fulfill it, we shall not get the blessing. Sorrow even is anxiety, and should be laid upon our blessed Lord. Then in prayer and supplication we must not forget that thanksgiving is also distinctly commanded; we must praise God for His dealings with us, even though we cannot make them out at times. Pray God to make you cease from anxiety about yourself and your plans; just be willing to do the work our dear Father gives you at the time.

— *John Kenneth Mackenzie*

Joy and Strength
Mary Wilder Tileston
Minnesota: World Wide Publications
1901, 1929, 1986

No Fear

Hallowed be Thy name,
 not mine,
Thy kingdom come,
 not mine,
Thy will be done,
 not mine,
Give us peace with Thee
Peace with men
Peace with ourselves,
And free us from all fear.

— *Dag Hammarskjöld*

Reprinted from *Dag Hammarskjöld's White Book*
by Gustaf Aulen, Copyright © 1969 Fortress Press.
Used by permission of Augsburg Fortress.

Heavenly Peace

My soul, there is a country
    Far beyond the stars,
Where stands a winged sentry
    All skillful in the wars;
There above noise and danger
    Sweet Peace sits crowned with smiles,
And one born in a manger
    Commands the beauteous files;
He is thy gracious friend,
    And (O my soul, awake!)
Did in pure love descend
    To die here for thy sake;
If thou canst get but thither,
    There grows the flower of peace,
The rose that cannot wither,
    Thy fortress, and thy ease;
Leave then thy foolish ranges;
    For none can thee secure,
But One, who never changes,
    Thy God, thy life, thy cure.

— Henry Vaughan

Beginning With Poems—An Anthology
Edited by Reuben A. Brower, Anne D. Ferry, and David Kalstone
W. W. Norton & Co., Inc., 1966

Chapter 4

PATIENCE

"Longsuffering, bearing with one another in love"
(Ephesians 4:2 NKJV)

A frequent prayer heard in today's world is this: "Lord, give me patience, and give it to me right away." What we fail to recognize is that the Lord has been patiently waiting to give us His patience long before we asked for it!

In the King James Version of the Bible, patience is translated as *"longsuffering."*

The patient person is one who "suffers long"—who, even in the most difficult times and with the most trying person, remains in relationship.

God doesn't try to be patient. He simply is. He doesn't bite His tongue, or hold Himself in check, or restrain His emotions until He reaches the bursting point. On the contrary, God doesn't even recognize His own patience. He simply bears with His children through thick and thin. He keeps no running scoreboard of His relationship with any one of us. There's virtually nothing we can do to separate ourselves from His love. (See Romans 8:35.)

This is the quality that God desires to bestow upon us. We are in relationship with our brothers and sisters in Christ Jesus as if we were true blood relations. As such, we are to love, defend, honor, stand by, prefer, encourage, edify, and uphold one another, even covering one another's sins with our love . . . no matter what circumstances, or trials, or difficulties might assail us.

The Character of Patience

Patience is the transcendent radiance of a loving and tender heart which, in its dealings with those around it, looks kindly and graciously upon them. Patience graciously, compassionately, and with understanding judges the faults of others without unjust criticism. Patience also includes perseverance—the ability to bear up under weariness, strain, and persecution when doing the work of the Lord.

— *Billy Graham*

The Faithful Christian: An Anthology of Billy Graham
Compiled by William Griffin and Ruth Graham Dienert
New York, McCracken Press, 1994

Patience

I would submit to all Thy will,
　　For Thou art good and wise;
Let every anxious thought be still,
　　Nor one faint murmur rise.

Thy love can cheer the darksome gloom,
　　And bid me wait serene,
Till hopes and joys immortal bloom
　　And brighten all the scene.

Lincoln's Devotional
Greatneck, N.Y.: Channel Press, 1951

The Nature of Patience

Patience is the guardian of faith, the preserver of peace, the cherisher of love, the teacher of humility. Patience governs the flesh, strengthens the spirit, sweetens the temper, stifles anger, extinguishes envy, subdues pride: she bridles the tongue, restrains the hand, tramples upon temptations, endures persecutions, consummates martyrdom. Patience produces unity in the church, loyalty in the state, harmony in families and society; she comforts the poor, and moderates the rich; she makes us humble in prosperity, cheerful in adversity, unmoved by calumny and reproach; she teaches us to forgive those who have injured us, and to be the first in asking forgiveness of those whom we have injured; she delights the faithful, and invites the unbelieving; she adorns the woman, and approves the man; she is beautiful in either sex and every age. Behold her appearance and her attire! Her countenance is calm and serene as the face of heaven unspotted by the shadow of a cloud; and no wrinkle of grief or anger is seen in her forehead. Her eyes are as the eyes of doves for meekness, and on her eyebrows sit cheerfulness and joy. Her mouth is lovely in silence; her complexion and color that of innocence and security; while, like the virgin, the daughter of Sion, she shakes her head at the adversary, despising, and laughing him to scorn. She is clothed in the robes of the martyrs, and in her hand she holds a sceptre in the form of a cross. She rides not in the whirlwind and stormy tempest of passion, but her throne is the humble and contrite heart, and her kingdom is the kingdom of peace.

— *Bishop Horne*

6000 Sermon Illustrations
Baker Book House, 1956

Life's Hardest Lesson

Perhaps the hardest lesson to learn in life is patience. To wait unperturbed while the child in the high chair does everything with his food except eat it. Quietly to hear out the interminable tales and complaints of the harried neighbor, the long-winded friend, or the very old. To give earnest attention to a son or daughter as he or she describes in minute detail the movie, or an episode at school.

Not to interrupt. Not to cut the other off. Not to explode. To curb the forces within us that would hurry, hurry, hurry. To hush the frenzied voices of rebellion. To still the frantic and usually futile impulses that would result only in hurt feelings and unnecessary distress . . . .

Withdraw the emotions, practice detachment, kindly interest, self-control. With the conscious effort comes a strange calm, a sense of being not the prey of outer forces, but in command of some subtle yet significant inner forces of one's own.

— *Marjorie Holmes*

From *Love and Laughter* by Marjorie Holmes.
Copyright © 1967 by Marjorie Holmes Mighell.
Used by permission of Doubleday, a division
of Bantam Doubleday Dell Publishing Group, Inc.

What's Happening When Nothing Seems To Be

How many times have you prayed, knowing full well that you have put the matter before God in faith, resting upon His Word . . . and then nothing happens?

Before long, a rash of possible explanations or procedures tempt you:

– Doubt—"Maybe God hasn't heard me."

– Fear—"Maybe He has heard me, but doesn't want to do anything about it."

– Uncertainty—"Perhaps it isn't God's will (except I was so sure when I prayed)."

– Condemnation—"It's probably because I don't deserve an answer. I've failed often enough that I can't blame God for turning away from me occasionally."

– Haste—"I've waited long enough, I guess God just wants me to be the answer. I'll just barge into the situation on my own and do my best."

– Presumption—"The key is to demonstrate my faith, so I'll act like everything has changed and treat the situation as though it were accomplished."

We live in an instant credit, get-everything-now economy. We eat add-water-and-mix foods or drive by fast-food outlets which poke our palates with immediate delicacies ranging from burgers and burritos to fried chicken and fish 'n' chips. All of this trains us to want what we want now on the basis of something that requires little or nothing of us. We don't grow trees in our yards, we buy them potted and several years advanced in their growth—or move to another house where they're already grown.

Waiting is not in style, and patience has never been a forte of the flesh.

But the Word of God has a great deal to say about "waiting." Sample some of the truth . . .

> *Indeed, let no one who waits on You be ashamed;*
> *Let those be ashamed who deal treacherously without cause . . .*
> *Lead me in Your truth and teach me,*
> *For You are the God of my salvation;*
> *On You I wait all the day . . .*
> *Let integrity and uprightness preserve me,*
> *For I wait for You . . .*
> *Wait on the Lord;*
> *Be of good courage,*
> *And He shall strengthen your heart;*
> *Wait, I say, on the Lord! . . .*

I will praise You forever,
Because You have done it;
And in the presence of Your saints
I will wait on Your name, for it is good . . .

I will wait for You, O You his Strength;
For God is my defense . . .

My soul, wait silently for God alone,
For my expectation is from Him.

(Psalm 25:3,5,21; 27:14; 52:9; 59:9; 62:5 NKJV)

These verses represent but a simple start on the theme—and only from one book in the Bible. Try Psalm 69 for size. Read of a heart crying for a long-awaited answer . . . and how faith eventually rises in the face of fear, doubt, impatience, and questioning.

If God weren't growing sons and daughters, things would not take nearly as long. But since He is more interested in our growth than He is in our getting, waiting becomes a very essential and useful means toward that end. He doesn't traffic in add-water-and-mix saints, or in freezer-to-microwave-to-table kids. He builds with neither plastic nor papier-mache.

What do you do, then, while you're waiting?

Know that He isn't teasing you.

Be confident that He takes no delight in compelling you to wait. He is, rather, patiently overseeing your life. He doesn't want you to drown while you're still learning to swim.

Rest . . . for He wants you to trust Him.

When nothing seems to be happening, something really is! You're facing a new opportunity for learning faith—the kind that grows, not just "gets."

— Jack Hayford

Moments With Majesty
Portland, Ore.: Multnomah Press, 1990

Surviving the Storm

There is no such thing as preaching patience into people unless the sermon is so long that they have to practice it while they hear. No man can learn patience except by going out into the hurly-burly world, and taking life just as it blows. Patience is but lying to and riding out the gale.

— *Henry Ward Beecher*

The New Dictionary of Thoughts
Originally Compiled by Tryon Edwards D. D.
Revised and Enlarged by C. N. Catrevas A. B.,
Jonathan Edwards A. M., & Ralph
Emerson Browns A. M.
Standard Book Co., 1961

On Missing One's Train

There is a story of a man who prayed earnestly one morning for grace to overcome his besetting sin of impatience. A little later he missed a train by half a minute and spent an hour stamping up and down the station platform in furious vexation. Five minutes before the next train came in he suddenly realized that here had been the answer to his prayer. He had been given an hour to practice the virtue of patience; he had missed the opportunity and wasted the hour. There are also many stories of men who have similarly missed trains which have been wrecked, and who ascribe their escape to Providence. If they are combining the thought of God as the celestial chess-player with the thought of God as preeminently concerned in their enjoyment of earthly life at the expense of others, there is not much to be said for their point of view. But if they are humbly acknowledging a call to further service on earth before they pass beyond, they are rightly interpreting their escape. In all probability all the events which led up to all these men missing their various trains could be adequately accounted for in terms of the interaction of natural law, human freedom, and divine grace. But at every point within the interaction God sees what are its possibilities for good, and the man who shares His enlightenment and His power and gives himself to make that good come true, has found the meaning of that moment and his 'special providence.' The gates of the future are indeed open, the universe is in the making. But only if made aright can the making stand. . . . The end is sure, for He who at every moment in the process sees its possibilities for good is God omnipotent—omnipotent to turn all circumstances to good account, to turn today's defeat into tomorrow's victory. But this omnipotence will never be so exercised as to substitute the external compulsion of men for the internal eliciting of their freedom.

— *Leonard Hodgson*

A Diary of Readings
John Baillie
New York: Collier Books/Macmillan, 1955, 1986

Patience with Yourself

Patience with ourselves is a duty for Christians and the only real humility. For it means patience with a growing creature whom God has taken in hand and whose completion He will effect in His own time and His own way. "Rest in the Lord, wait patiently on Him and He shall give thee thy heart's desire." The more central this thought becomes, the less difficult you will find its outward expression, that is to say, longsuffering and gentleness in all the encounters of everyday life. It is not always easy to entertain that pair of heavenly twins properly—in fact, we can hardly manage it at all without the help of the Spirit and constant resort to prayer. Yet even from the most practical point of view, longsuffering is as essential a factor in the art of living as in the art of prayer. The constant tension of resisting this, grasping that, pressing forward, never relaxing, never lying quiet on the waves, destroys the strongest in the end and wastes precious energy all the time. On every level of life from housework to heights of prayer, in all judgment and all forts to get things done, hurry and impatience are sure marks of the amateur. A great artist treats his material with gentleness and reverence and is always ready to wait; the great teacher never drives or hustles the pupil; the great climber waits till conditions are suitable before trying the awkward traverse. All these accept conditions and conform to them; and so too must we do in the spiritual life. It is God Who gives the conditions. Our part is to accept them with humility and cultivate the quiet spirit of acceptance; to adjust our will to His great rhythm, and not waste the strength he has given us in fighting against the stream. "In the midst of the waters I shall be with thee."

— *Evelyn Underhill*

The Fruits of the Spirit
London: Longman's House, 1949

I Waited for the Lord

I waited for the Lord my God,
And patiently did bear;
At length to me He did incline
My voice and cry to hear.

He took me from a fearful pit,
And from the miry clay,
And on a rock He set my feet,
Establishing my way.

He put a new song in my mouth,
Our God to magnify:
Many shall see it, and shall fear,
And on the Lord rely.

O blessed is the man whose trust
Upon the Lord relies;
Respecting not the proud, nor such
As turn aside to lies.

O Lord my God, full many are
The wonders Thou hast done;
Thy gracious thoughts to usward far
Above all thoughts are gone.

— *Psalm XL*

Scottish Psalter, 1650

Keeping On—Anyway

We are not on the walk of faith long before we encounter frustrations, obstacles, and obstructions. Then what? Then it's time to hang on to one powerful, positive word—endure!

To endure means: "Inch by inch, anything is a cinch."

To endure means: "There is no gain without pain."

To endure means: "When faced with a mountain, I will not quit. I will keep on striving until I climb over, find a pass through, tunnel underneath . . . or simply stay and turn the mountain into a gold mine, with God's help!"

To endure means: "I have to look at what I have, not at what I've lost."

So you are unemployed? To endure means you're going to keep on living a meaningful life anyway.

So you have people problems and are frustrated with regulations and roadblocks and negative forces? You are so tired of fighting you'd like to throw in the towel and quit?

What does it mean to endure? It means to remember that when you face problems, you keep this point in the forefront of your mind: people, problems, and pressures are constantly changing, so don't split. You'll run into the same basic frustrations no matter where you go.

So you are grieving over the loss of your wife? Your husband? To endure means you keep on being positive about life—anyway!

Never forget this wise warning: *Never make a negative decision in a down time.*

This is only a phase that you are going through. It will pass. When it is over, you'll be glad you hung in there!

— *Robert Schuller*

Tough-Minded Faith for Tender-Hearted People
1983, Crystal Cathedral Minstries, Anaheim, Ca.

Locust Years

There are years in South Africa when locust swarm the land and eat the crops. They come in hordes, blocking out the sun. The crops are lost and a hard winter follows. The "years that the locusts eat" are feared and dreaded. But the year after the locusts, South Africa reaps its greatest crops, for the dead bodies of the locust serve as fertilizer for the new seed. And the locust year is restored as great crops swell the land.

This is a parable of our lives. There are seasons of deep distress and afflictions that sometimes eat all the usefulness of our lives away. Yet, the promise is that God will restore those locust years if we endure. We will reap if we faint not. Although now we do not know all the 'whys,' we can be assured our times are in His hands.

— *Charles R. Hembree*

Fruits of the Spirit
Grand Rapids, Mich.: Baker Book House, 1969

Life's Lessons

I learn, as the years roll onward
    And leave the past behind,
That much I had counted sorrow
    But proves that God is kind;
That many a flower I had longed for
    Had hidden a thorn of pain,
And many a rugged bypath
    Led to fields of ripened grain.

The clouds that cover the sunshine
    They cannot banish the sun;
And the earth shines out the brighter
    When the weary rain is done.
We must stand in the deepest shadow
    To see the clearest light;
And often through wrong's own darkness
    Comes the very strength of light.

The sweetest rest is at even,
    After a wearisome day,
When the heavy burden of labor
    Has borne from our hearts away;
And those who have never known sorrow
    Cannot know the infinite peace
That falls on the troubled spirit
    When it sees at last release.

We must live through the dreary winter
    If we would value the spring;
And the woods must be cold and silent
    Before the robins sing.
The flowers must be buried in darkness
    Before they can bud and bloom,
And the sweetest, warmest sunshine
    Comes after the storm and gloom.

— *Unknown*

Poems That Live Forever
Selected by Hazel Felleman
Doubleday, 1965

Endure to the End

Jesus taught:

"I am sending you out as sheep among wolves. Be as wary as serpents and harmless as doves. But beware! For you will be arrested and tried, and whipped in the synagogues. Yes, and you must stand trial before governors and kings for my sake. This will give you the opportunity to tell them about me, yes, to witness to the world.

"When you are arrested, don't worry about what to say at your trial, for you will be given the right words at the right time. For it won't be you doing the talking—it will be the Spirit of your heavenly Father speaking through you!

"Brother shall betray brother to death, and fathers shall betray their own children. And children shall rise against their parents and cause their deaths. Everyone shall hate you because you belong to me. But all of you who endure to the end shall be saved."

— *Matthew 10:16-22* (TLB)
  HOLY BIBLE

Holy Patience

He that with steadfast humility and patience suffereth and endureth tribulation, through fervent love of God, soon shall attain to great grace and virtues, and shall be lord of this world, and shall have a foretaste of the next and glorious world. Everything that a man doeth, good or evil, he doeth it unto himself; therefore, be not offended with him that doeth thee an injury, for rather oughtest thou to have humble patience with him, and only grieve within thee for his sin, taking compassion on him and praying God earnestly for him. The stronger a man is to endure and suffer patiently injuries and tribulations, for love of God, the greater is he in the sight of God, and no more; and the weaker a man is to endure pain and adversity, for love of God, the less is he in the sight of God. . . .

Therefore, my brother, believe of a surety, the straight way of salvation is the way to perdition. But when we are not good bearers of tribulation, then we cannot be seekers after everlasting consolations. Much greater consolation and a more worthy thing it is to suffer injuries and revilings patiently, without murmuring, for love of God, than to feed a hundred poor folk and fast continually every day. But how shall it profit a man, or what shall it avail him, to despise himself and afflict his body with great fastings and vigils and scourgings, if he be unable to endure a small injury from his neighbour? For which thing, a man shall receive a much greater reward and greater merit than for all the afflictions a man can give to himself of his own will; because to endure the revilings and injuries of one's neighbour, with humble patience and without murmuring, purgeth sin away much more quickly than doth a fount of many tears. . . .

— *St. Francis of Assisi*

The Little Flowers of St. Francis
Everyman's Library
Translated by Thomas Okey
E. P. Dutton & Co.

Waiting for God's Will

December 11, 1850—The special burden of my prayer is that God would be pleased to teach me His will. My mind had also been especially pondering how I could know His will satisfactorily concerning this particular. Sure I am that I will be taught. I therefore desire patiently to wait for the Lord's time, when He shall be pleased to shine on my path concerning this point.

December 26—Fifteen days have elapsed since I wrote the preceding paragraph. Every day since then I have continued to pray about this matter, and that with a goodly measure of earnestness, by the help of God. There has passed scarcely an hour during these days, in which, while awake, this matter has not been more or less before me. But all without a shadow of excitement. I converse with no one about it. Hitherto have I not even done so with my dear wife. From this I refrain still and deal with God alone about the matter, in order that no outward influence and no outward excitement may keep me from attaining unto a clear discovery of His will. I have the fullest and most peaceful assurance that He will clearly show me His will.

This evening I have had again an especially solemn season for prayer, to seek to know the will of God. But while I continue to entreat and beseech the Lord, that He would not allow me to be deluded in this business, I may say I have scarcely any doubt remaining on my mind as to what will be the result, even that I should go forward in this matter.

Since this, however, is one of the great momentous steps that I have ever taken, I judge that I cannot go about this matter with too much caution, prayerfulness, and deliberation. I am in no hurry about it. I could wait for years, by God's grace, were this His will, before even taking one single step toward this thing, or even speaking to any-one about it; and on the other hand, I would set to work tomorrow, were the Lord to bid me so.

The calmness of mind, this having no will of my own in the matter, this only wishing to please my heavenly Father in it—this state of heart, I say, is the fullest assurance to me that my heart is not under a fleshly excitement and that, if I am helped thus to go on, I shall know the will of God to the full.

— *George Miller*

They Walked With God
Compiled by James S. Bell, Jr.
Chicago: Moody Press, 1993

Taking the Long View

Thousands of Christians have learned the secret of contentment and joy in trial. Some of the happiest Christians I have met have drunk the full cup of trial and misfortune. Some have been lifelong sufferers.

They have had every reason to sigh and complain, being denied so many privileges and pleasures that they see others enjoy, yet, they have found greater cause for gratitude and joy than many who are prosperous, vigorous, and strong.

They have learned to give thanks "always . . . in the name of our Lord Jesus Christ to God the Father" (Ephesians 5:20 RSV).

Christians can rejoice in tribulation because they have eternity's values in view. When the pressures are on, they look beyond their present predicament to the glories of heaven. The thoughts of the future life with its prerogatives and joys help to make the trials of the present seem light and transient.

— *Billy Graham*

Unto the Hills
Billy Graham , 1986
Word Inc., Dallas, Texas.

Its Perfect Work

My brethren, count it all joy when you fall into various trials, knowing that the testing of your faith produces patience. But let patience have its perfect work, that you may be perfect and complete, lacking nothing.

Therefore be patient, brethren, until the coming of the Lord. See how the farmer waits for the precious fruit of the earth, waiting patiently for it until it receives the early and latter rain. You also be patient. Establish your hearts, for the coming of the Lord is at hand.

My brethren, take the prophets, who spoke in the name of the Lord, as an example of suffering and patience. Indeed we count them blessed who endure. You have heard of the perseverance of Job and seen the end intended by the Lord that the Lord is very compassionate and merciful.

—*James 1:2-4, 5:7-8, 10-11 (NKJV)*
HOLY BIBLE

God's Stretching

Patience is more than endurance. A saint's life is in the hands of God like a bow and arrow in the hands of an archer. God is aiming at something the saint cannot see, and He stretches and strains, and every now and again the saint says—"I cannot stand anymore." God does not heed, He goes on stretching till His purpose is in sight, then He lets fly. Trust yourself in God's hands. For what have you need of patience just now? Maintain your relationship to Jesus Christ by the patience of faith. "Though He slay me, yet will I wait for Him."

Faith is not a pathetic sentiment, but robust, vigorous confidence built on the fact that God is holy love. You cannot see Him just now, you cannot understand what He is doing, but you know Him. Shipwreck occurs where there is not that mental poise which comes from being established on the eternal truth that God is holy love. Faith is the heroic effort of your life, you fling yourself in reckless confidence on God.

God has ventured all in Jesus Christ to save us, now He wants us to venture our all in abandoned confidence in Him. There are spots where that faith has not worked in us as yet, places untouched by the life of God. There were none of those spots in Jesus Christ's life, and there are to be none in ours. "This is life eternal, that they might know Thee." The real meaning of eternal life is a life that can face anything it has to face without wavering. If we take this view, life becomes one great romance, a glorious opportunity for seeing marvelous things all the time. God is disciplining us to get us into this central place of power.

— *Oswald Chambers*

Taken from *My Utmost for His Highest*
by Oswald Chambers, edited by James Reimann,
Copyright © 1992 by Oswald Chambers Publications Assn., Ltd.
Original edition Copyright © 1935 by Dodd, Mead & Co.,
Renewed 1963 by Oswald Chambers Publications Assn., Ltd., and is
used by permission of Discovery House Publishers, Box 3566, Grand Rapids, MI 49501.

Increased Hope

Patience is not passive: on the contrary it is active; it is concentrated strength.

There is one form of hope which is never unwise, and which certainly does not diminish with the increase of knowledge. In that form it changes its name, and we call it patience.

— *Bulwer*

The New Dictionary of Thoughts
Originally Compiled by Tryon Edwards D.D.
Revised and Enlarged by C. N. Catrevas A. B.,
Jonathan Edwards A. M., & Ralph
Emerson Browns A. M.
Standard Book Co., 1961

Waiting on Jesus

Waiting on Jesus when I am weak,
Claiming His promise to those who seek;
Waiting on Jesus when I am strong,
Trusting Him only all the day long.

Waiting on Jesus when I'm opprest,
Finding in Him sweet comfort and rest;
Trusting Him fully, whate'er befall,
Jesus my Saviour, Jesus my all.

Waiting on Jesus lest I despair,
Knowing He ever heareth my prayer;
How can I doubt Him when He is near?
No one so loving, no one so dear.

Refrain:
Waiting on Jesus, rapture divine!
Wonder of wonders, Jesus is mine;
Trusting and praying, whate'er betide,
Walking each moment close by His side.

— *Oswald J. Smith*

The Heavenly Footman

It is an easy matter for a man to run hard for a spurt, for a furlong, for a mile or two: Oh, but to hold out for a hundred, for a thousand, for ten thousand miles!—that man that doth this, he must look to meet with cross, pain, and wearisomeness to the flesh, especially if, as he goeth, he meeteth with briers and quagmires, and other encumbrances that make his journey so much the more painful.

Nay, do you not see with your eyes daily, that perseverance is a very great part of the Cross? Why else do men so soon grow weary? I could point out a man, that after they had followed the ways of God about a twelvemonth, often it may be two, three, or four (some more, and some less) years, they have been beat out of wind, have taken up their lodging and rest before they have gotten halfway to heaven, some in this, some in that sin, and have secretly, nay, sometimes openly, said that the way is too straight, the race too long, the religion too holy—I cannot hold out, I can go no further.

One of the great reasons why men and women do so little regard the other world is because they see so little of it . . . When men do come to see the things of another world, what a God, what a Christ, what a heaven, and what an eternal glory there is to be enjoyed; also, when they see that it is possible for them to have a share in it, I tell you it will make them run through thick and thin to enjoy it . . . .

O this blessed inflamed will for heaven! What is it like? If a man be willing, then any argument shall be matter of encouragement; but if unwilling, then any argument shall give discouragement. This is seen both in saints and sinners; in them that are the children of God, and also those that are the children of the devil. As:

1. The saints of old, they being willing and resolved for heaven, what could stop them? Could fire and fagot, sword or halter, stinking dungeons, whips, bears, bulls, lions, cruel rackings, stoning, starving, nakedness? *"And in all these things they were more than conquerors, through Him that loved them."*

2. See again, on the other side, the children of the devil, because they are not willing, how many shifts and starting-holes they will have. I have married a wife; I have a farm; I shall offend my landlord; I shall offend my master; I shall lose my trading; I shall lose my pride, my pleasures; I shall be mocked and scoffed; therefore I dare not come. I, saith another, will stay till I am older, till my children are out, till I am gotten a little aforehand in the world, till I have done this and that, and the other business: but, alas! the thing is, they are not willing; for were they but soundly willing, these, and a thousand such as these, would hold them no faster than the cords held Samson, when he broke them like burnt flax.

I tell you the will is all; that is one of the chief things which turns the wheel either backward or forward; and God knoweth that full well, and so likewise doth the devil, and therefore they both endeavor very much to strengthen the will of their servants. God, He is for making of His a willing people to serve Him; and the devil, he doth what he can to possess the will and affection of those who are his with love to sin; and therefore when Christ comes close to the matter, indeed, saith He, "You will not come to Me. How often would I have gathered you as a hen doth her chickens, but you would not." The devil had possessed their wills, and so long he was sure enough of them. Oh, therefore, cry hard to God to inflame thy will for heaven and Christ; thy will, I say, if that be rightly set for heaven, thou wilt not be beat off with discouragements. . . .

Get thy will tipped with heavenly grace, and resolution against all discouragements, and then thou goest full speed for heaven; but if thou falter in thy will, and be not found there, thou wilt run hobbling and halting all the way thou runnest, and also to be sure thou wilt fall short at last. The Lord give thee a will and a courage.

— Bunyan, excerpts from sermon

Titled "The Heavenly Footman" first delivered in 1698
The World's Famous Orations
Edited by William Jennings Bryan
Funk and Wagnalls Co., 1906

Waiting Isn't Easy

It may seem an easy thing to wait, but it is one of the postures which a Christian soldier learns not without years of teaching. Marching and quick-marching are much easier to God's warriors than standing still. There are hours of perplexity when the most willing spirit, anxiously desirous to serve the Lord, knows not what part to take. Then what shall it do? Vex itself by despair? Fly back in cowardice, turn to the right hand in fear, or rush forward in presumption? No, but simply wait. Wait in prayer, however. Call upon God, and spread the case before Him; tell Him your difficulty, and plead His promise of aid. In dilemmas between one duty and another, it is sweet to be humble as a child, and wait with simplicity of soul upon the Lord. It is sure to be well with us when we feel and know our own folly, and are heartily willing to be guided by the will of God. But wait in faith. Express your unstaggering confidence in Him; for unfaithful, untrusting waiting, is but an insult to the Lord. Believe that if He keep you tarrying even till midnight, yet He will come at the right time; the vision shall come and shall not tarry. Wait in quiet patience, not rebelling because you are under the affliction, but blessing your God for it. Never murmur against the second cause, as the children of Israel did against Moses; never wish you could go back to the world again, but accept the case as it is, and put it as it stands, simply and with your whole heart, without any self-will, into the hand of your covenant God, saying, "Now, Lord, not my will, but Thine be done. I know not what to do; I am brought to extremities, but I will wait until Thou shalt cleave the floods, or drive back my foes. I will wait, if Thou keep me many a day, for my heart is fixed upon Thee alone, O God, and my spirit waiteth for Thee in the full conviction that Thou wilt yet be my joy and my salvation, my refuge and my strong tower."

— Charles H. Spurgeon

Taken from *Morning and Evening Devotions:*
An Updated Edition of the Classic Devotional in
Today's Language by C. H. Spurgeon.
Copyright © 1987 by Thomas Nelson Publishers.
Used by permission of Thomas Nelson Publishers.

Bundle Up

Patience serves as a protection against wrongs as clothes do against cold. For if you put on more clothes, as the cold increases it will have no power to hurt you. So in like manner you must grow in patience when you meet with great wrongs, and they will then be powerless to vex your mind.

— Leonardo da Vinci

The Book of Unusual Quotations
Selected and Edited by Rudolf Flesch
New York: Harper and Brothers Publishers, 1957

Let Patience Have Her Perfect Work:
Cooperate With Her

Of all the virtues Patience is the least dramatic. Perhaps that is why it is today the least popular. We feel that it is hurry which gets things done. The worse things get, the less we wish to think why; the more we believe we must get a move on. But if we would wait a moment we could not fail to see that the jam we are in is due to our determination to push everything at breakneck speed. Now, however, the concept of growth as being the essence of life, is coming back. Man is master of all the beasts precisely because he takes longer to grow up, to get ready, than any of them; because he takes more time to learn. Man will master himself only when he takes as long to understand himself as he has taken to understand his surroundings. For patience is not just hanging about. Patience is cooperating. We have learned that with nature. You cannot force natural forces. If you go with them, they will carry you. Thwart them and they will break you. Even in pure thought we have learned the value of patience. From the proved value of second thoughts up to the danger of those premature syntheses which have had equally tragic results in science and theology, we are taught the vital value of the suspended judgment, the danger of the closed mind. Indeed, it is always the sign of a fool, a symptom of oncoming failure, to attempt to force things. Shakespeare's point of view is often pessimistic, but he seems to have concluded that "ripeness is all."

St. James says, "Let Patience have her perfect work." For God's work is never hurried, and indeed has in it no element of the climax or the drama because He is an inexhaustible fount of growth, being eternal. We must learn His notion of time. It is certainly very alien to anything we call up-to-date. Certainly our impatience with nature, with our fellows, with ourselves, is always spoiling the beauty of design God would otherwise show us every moment. God means us to have long, patient, beautiful lives, when after each day has been lived fully, without remorse or anxiety, we should come to the full physical ripeness of a glad and healthy death. *"Wait upon the Lord, and He shall renew thy strength as an eagle's."* If we wait rightly, we shall be able to rest; if we rest we shall be renewed and reborn: by patience to work, by sleep to a new day, by death to the life eternal.

Prayers and Meditations
Edited by Gerald Heard
New York: Harper and Brothers Publishers, 1949

A Trait We Admire

Longsuffering: we admire that quality a great deal more than we practice it. We admire longsuffering in other folks. We admire longsuffering in the schoolmaster, in the regent mother, in the creditor to whom we owe a debt. It inspires almost the dignity of perfect beauty. A man who will let you abuse him, a man who will let you cheat him even, a man who forgets today what you said or did yesterday—his longsuffering, oh, how beautiful it is! It is a patience that is not easily provoked and thinketh no evil. Yet look at that matron who through the years of early life inherited bereavements and sorrows, the thinning out of the precious flock, the dishonoured name of the husband, the death, the rolling upon her of the responsibility of rearing the whole flock, the unwearied fidelity, the inexhaustible patience, furrow after furrow that experience is ploughing upon her brow; at last the children had come to ripeness, and they in their turn are lifting her out of trouble, and she sits serene at the close of life more beautiful than the going down of the sun. Is there any object in life that a man can look upon that is more beautiful than longsuffering?

— *Henry Ward Beecher*

Summer in England
New York: Fords, Howard, and Hulbert, 1887

Between the Doing and the Fulfilling

"For ye have need of patience, that, after ye have done the will of God, ye might receive the promise" (Hebrews 10:36).

The implication is, that many of those to whom the apostle wrote, consciously having performed their duty in the Lord, had not received any token or evidence of the fruit of the performance of duty, and were discouraged, and thought it perhaps a vain thing to attempt a religious life—reasoning in this way: "If we attempt any secular improvement we see that the work which we are performing grows under our hands. If I be a husbandman, I perceive, on sowing the seed, that there is use in it; for it springs up, and I have my harvests. If I am a vintner, I perceive in my vines, and in the fruitage, that for which I labour. And even when I do not perceive at once the full fruit, I see the tokens of its coming, and all the steps by which it comes."

"Now," says the apostle, *"ye that are spiritual husbandmen, as it were, have need of patience, after ye have done the will of God and nothing comes, until you receive the promise."* It is recognized that there is a long space between the doing and the fulfilling, as there often is, and that is the point where men specially need patience, and patience for the purpose of keeping up their faith in the reality of personal religion. For the context is this:

"Cast not away therefore your confidence, which hath great recompense of reward. For ye have need of patience, that, after ye have done the will of God, ye might receive the promise. For yet a little while, and he that shall come will come, and will not tarry. Now the just shall live by faith; but if any man draw back, my soul shall have no pleasure in him" (Hebrews 10:35-38).

Patience is not one of those stupid experiences which have been sometimes in vogue. It is not the grace of indifference or of laziness. Neither is it a kind of dogged obstinacy under difficulties. It is the sequence of enterprise and of endeavour, and is an act of self-control. It is the control of one's desires, either when he longs for gratification and has it not, or when he is under the pressure of suffering. It is the power of holding one's self calmly and contentedly under deprivations or under difficulties.

It is another name, then, for self-control, and self-control under circumstances of suffering.

In the text, the teacher points to a very common experience—namely, impatience because labour does not bring forth its results immediately. Divine providence is conducting a double system in this world, or rather a single system with two developments. Constantly these two elements in it are clashing, by reason of men's misunderstandings; but they are co-operative and harmonious in the plan of God. There is a physical life in this world. We are grounded in that. We begin in that. It is the root of all our life. But out of that is to spring a still higher life; and the problem of living in this world is the development of that other and higher manhood out of that lower or physical manhood.

While this development is going on, we are the subjects of material laws. We are living in societies, under occupations, under governments; and we are obliged to carry ourselves with a wisdom which is adapted to the physical senses. Yet while we are doing this (we learn this first, and it is very apt to be the strongest impulse in us)—while we are doing this there is, at the same time, to be carried on another development to which this is auxiliary, and for which this has been originally constituted—the unfolding of the higher spiritual life, which is so different from this lower one, that it is called a "new life" created by the spirit of God in man.

And although he that is living in the highest development of his spiritual life is living in a way which harmonizes him with all physical influences; on the other hand, a man may live so as to be in harmony with all physical laws, and yet not be developing his true spiritual life.

These two elements, which are going on together, induce a conflict and a misapprehension and a jar; and men are sacrificing their higher life for the sake of gaining this lower and physical life.

Thus we have this duality recognized all the way through—the life of the body and the life of the soul.

Now, our Father is conducting a providence which recognizes both of them, but subordinates them, keeping the lower low, and the higher supreme. He administers all the time among the infinite choices that are to be made in adapting His providence to His subjects. He is perpetually administering His government as we who are wise parents administer ours in the family. We take care of our children's bodies; of their food; of their dress; of their physical comfort. At the same time it is with reference to an ulterior manhood. And in every instance, if there is a choice in reference to truth-telling, purity, delicacy of mind and generosity of love, we teach the child to sacrifice the lower for the sake of keeping the higher. We are in our households carrying on a duplex education, which is at its base physical, and in its higher developments moral and social. And that which we are doing in the small, God is doing in the large sphere. And the human race is being developed at the bottom physically, and at the top spiritually.

We find a recognition of this matter in the Second Epistle to the Corinthians by a relative valuation of the two systems:

"We look not at the things which are seen (not at the sense-life), *but at the things which are not seen* (at the invisible, spiritual, immortal life): *for the things which are seen are temporal; but the things which are not seen are eternal"* (2 Corinthians 4:18).

— Henry Ward Beecher

Sermons, Preached in Plymouth Church, Brooklyn, New York
London: Richard D. Dickinson, 1875

Willing To Work, Willing To Wait

Lord, what he said was,
"You can have instant coffee, and instant tea, and instant
potatoes, but you can't have instant relationships."
And he was right.
We can't measure out a portion of ourselves to
each other, and stir once, and be friends.
> Or measure out an instant prayer, and beat with a
> fork until fluffy.
For "instant" never quite satisfies like the real.
And a depth relationship has a mutual history of
> shared joy and anguish.
> It is a mellowed blend of caring and being cared
> for—
> of listening—
> of removing masks (which is seldom easy)—
> of openness and honesty . . . without which
> no relationship is valid.
Not with him . . . nor with them . . . nor with thee.
> All of this takes time. And effort.
> And expenditure of self.
So, Lord, why do I keep asking for instant communion?
Why am I not willing to put the same effort—the same
care—into my relationship with Thee, that I have found necessary in
my relationships with others?
Why am I so unwilling to wait?
So unwilling to apprentice my soul?
So reluctant to do my part?
> Ah, Lord. I come . . . in joys and in anguish . . .in my
moments of peace, and in my times of quiet desperation—
> to sing,
> to listen,
> to pour out my humanness, to remove my masks. Amen.

— *Jo Carr and Imogene Sorley*

From *Mockingbirds and Angel Songs*
By Jo Carr and Imogene Sorley.
Copyright © 1975 by Abingdon Press.
Used by permission

Impatience

As I write this I'm at 35,000 feet. It's 5:45 p.m., Saturday. It should be 4:15. The airliner was an hour and a half late. People are grumpy. Some are downright mad. Stewardesses are apologizing, promising extra booze to take off the edge. To complicate matters, a Japanese man across the aisle from me has a rather severe nosebleed and they're trying to instruct the poor chap . . . *but he doesn't speak a word of English!*

So now the meal is late. The lady on my left has a cold and makes an enormous sound when she sneezes (about every ninety seconds—I've timed her). It's something like a dying calf in a hailstorm or a bull moose with one leg in a trap. Oh, one more thing. The sports film on golf just broke down and so did the nervous systems of half the men on board. It's a zoo!

It all started with the *delay.* "Mechanical trouble," they said. "Inexcusable," responded a couple of passengers. Frankly, I'd rather they fix it before we leave than decide to do something about it en route. But we Americans don't like to wait. Delays are irritating. Aggravating. Nerve-jangling. With impatient predictability we are consistently—and I might add obnoxiously— demanding. We want what we want when we want it. Not a one of us finds a delay easy to accept.

Do you question that? Put yourself into these situations:

• You're at the grocery store. Busy evening ahead. Long lines. Shopping cart has a wheel that drags. You finally finish and choose a stall with only two ahead of you. The checker is new on the job . . . her hands tremble . . . beads of perspiration dot her brow. Slowly she gets to you. Her cash register tape runs out. She isn't sure how to change it. You're delayed. How's your response?

• It's dinner-out-with-the-family night. That special place. You've fasted most of the day so you can gorge tonight. You're given a booth and a menu, but the place is terribly busy and two waitresses short. So there you sit, hungry as a buffalo in winter with a glass of water and a menu you've begun to gnaw on. You're delayed. How's your response?

• You're a little late to work. The freeway's full so you decide to slip through traffic using a rarely known shortcut only Daniel Boone could have figured out. You hit all green lights as you slide around trucks and slow drivers. Just about the time you start feeling foxy, an ominous clang, clang, clang strikes your ears. A train! You're delayed. How's your response?

The rubber of Christianity meets the road of proof at just such intersections in life. As the expression goes, our faith is "fleshed out" at times like that. The best test of my Christian growth occurs in the mainstream of life, not in the quietness of my study. Anybody can walk "in victory" when surrounded by books, silence, and the warm waves of sunshine splashing through the window. But those late takeoffs, those grocery lines, those busy restaurants, those trains! That's where faith is usually "flushed out."

The stewardess on this plane couldn't care less that I'm a "pretribulation rapturist." Your waitress will not likely be impressed that you can prove the authorship of the Pentateuch. Nor will the gal at the checkstand stare in awe as you inform her of the distinctive characteristics of biblical infallibility which you embrace.

One quality, however—a single, rare virtue scarce as diamonds and twice as precious—will immediately attract them to you and soften their spirits. That quality? The ability to accept delay graciously. Calmly. Quietly. Understandingly. With a smile. If the robe of purity is far above rubies, the garment of patience is even beyond that. Why? Because its threads of unselfishness and kindness are woven on the Lord's loom, guided within our lives by the Spirit of God. But, alas, the garment seldom clothes us!

Remember the verse? *"But the fruit of the Spirit is love, joy, peace, . . ."*

And what else? The first three are the necessary style along with the buttons and zipper of the garment. The rest give it color and beauty:

". . . patience, kindness, goodness, faithfulness, gentleness, self-control . . . (Galatians 5:22,23)."

The ability to accept delay. Or disappointment. To smile back at setbacks and respond with a pleasant, understanding spirit. To cool it while others around you curse it. For a change, I refused to be hassled by today's delay. I asked God to keep me calm and cheerful, relaxed and refreshed. Know what? He did. He really did! No pills. No booze. No hocus-pocus. Just relaxing in the power of Jesus.

I can't promise you that others will understand. You see, I've got another problem now. Ever since takeoff I've been smiling at the stewardesses, hoping to encourage them. Just now I overheard one of them say to the other, "Watch that guy wearing glasses. I think he's had too much to drink."

— Charles Swindoll

Taken from *Growing Strong in the Seasons of Life* by Chuck Swindoll. Copyright © 1983 by Charles R. Swindoll, Inc. Used by permission of Zondervan Publishing House.

Teach Me, Lord, To Wait

Lord, to wait down on my knees
Till in Your own good time You answer my pleas;
Teach me not to rely on what others do,
But to wait in prayer for an answer from You.

They that wait upon the Lord shall renew their strength,
They shall mount up with wings as eagles;
They shall run and not be weary,
They shall walk and not faint.
Teach me, Lord, teach me, Lord, to wait.

— Stuart Hamblen

God Doesn't Hurry

Consider the longsuffering of God, the longsuffering and gentleness of Absolute Perfection and Absolute Power, and how the further we press into the deeps of spiritual experience, the more those qualities are seen. How God looks past the imperfections of men (as we look past those of children), with what unexacting love He accepts and uses the faulty. See how Christ deliberately chooses Peter; while completely realizing Peter, his unreliable qualities, his boasting and cocksureness, his prompt capitulation to fear. Peter's family must have thought, "Thank heaven! a chance for the tiresome creature now" when he joined the Apostolic band. But Christ did not just put up with him. He offered him a continual and special friendship, knowing what was in the man. He took Peter into the inner fastness of Gethsemane and asked for his prayer and did not get it. (Is that the way we handle our tiresome and unreliable friends? Because it is with personal contacts we have always got to begin.) It was to Peter Christ addressed his rare approach, "What! Could you not watch one hour?" and it was from this that Peter went to the denial. Yet in spite of all, the longsuffering love and trust of Christ won in the end and made Peter the chief of the apostles—the Rock—what irony!—on which He built the Church.

He was right, for here the Church is now. In Peter's care and Peter's love Christ left the feeding of the sheep: a remarkable sequel. Who shines in that series of events? Christ or Peter? Christ shines—but Peter is transformed. Christ's attitude and action are only possible to holiness, and they are justified by results. Here is a standard set for us in our dealing with the faulty. The fruit of the Spirit is never rigorism but always longsuffering. No startling high standard. No all or nothing demands, but gentleness and tolerance in spiritual, moral, emotional, intellectual judgements and claims. No hurry and no exactingness. That is not easy when we are keen, and see the work we love imperiled by someone else's fault. But God, says St. Paul, is a God of patience. He works in tranquility, and tranquility seldom goes into partnership with speed. God breaks few records, but He always arrives in the end. One of the best things we can do for souls is to wait, and one of the worst things we can is to force the issue. God lets the plant grow at its own pace. That is why He can bring forth supernatural beauty in and through imperfect instructions.

All of us need this grace of longsuffering in respect to our own life of prayer. There, too, we must learn to wait, realizing the degree in which it depends on God's quiet, creative action, the profound nature of the changes it demands in our whole being. We have got to become a "new creature," as the New Testament says, a creature living towards God. If it takes nine months to make a natural baby, would it be very surprising if it took nine years to make a supernatural baby? Tarry though the Lord's leisure. . . .

— *Evelyn Underhill*

The Fruits of the Spirit
London: Longmans House, 1949

A Prayer of Patience

O blessed Lord, lead me whither Thou pleasest, I will follow Thee without complaint. I submit to Thy orders: I reverance Thy wisdom: I trust myself with Thy goodness; I depend upon Thy almighty power: I rely on Thy promises; beseeching Thee to support me, till patience having its perfect working in me, I may be perfect, and entire, wanting nothing. I know the time is but short, and that Thou hast prepared long joys to recompense our momentary sorrows; help me, therefore, always to possess my soul in patience at present (giving thanks for the hope we have as an anchor of the soul both sure and steadfast) that so I may at last, after I have done Thy will, O God, inherit the promise. Amen.

— *Evelyn Underhill*

An Anthology of Devotional Literature
Compiled by Thomas S. Kepler
Grand Rapids, Mich.: Baker Book House, 1947

After the Power

And friends, though you may have tested of the power and been convinced and have felt the light, yet afterwards you may feel winter storms, tempests, and hail, and be frozen, in frost and cold and a wilderness and temptations. Be patient and still in the power and still in the light that doth convinc you, to keep your minds to God; in that be quiet, that you may come to the summer, that your flight be not in the winter. For if you sit still in the patience which overcomes in the power of God, there will be no flying. For the husbandman, after he hath sown in his seed, he is patient. For by the power and by the light you will come to see through and feel over winter storms, tempests, and all the coldness, barrenness, emptiness. And the same light and power will go over the tempter's head, which power and light, were before he was. And so in the light standing still you will see your salvation, you will see the Lord's strength, you will feel the small rain, you will feel the fresh springs in the power and light, your minds being kept low; for that which is out of the power and light lifts up. But in the power and light you will see God revealing His secrets, inspiring, and His gifts coming unto you, through which your hearts will be filled with God's love; praise to Him Who lives forevermore, in which light and power His blessings are received. And so the eternal power of the Lord Jesus Christ preserve and keep you in that. And so live everyone in the power of God that you may all come to be heirs of that and know that to be your portion, and the kingdom that hath no end, and an endless life, which the seed is heir of. And so feel that over all set, which hath the promise and blessing of God.

— *George Fox*

The Journal of George Fox
E.P. Dulton

The Rarest Part

There's no music in a "rest," but there's the making of music in it. And people are always missing that part of the life melody, always talking of perseverance and courage and fortitude; but patience is the finest and worthiest part of fortitude, and the rarest, too.

— Ruskin

The New Dictionary of Thoughts
Originally Compiled by Tryon Edwards D. D.
Revised and Enlarged by C. N. Catrevas A. B.,
Jonathan Edwards A. M., & Ralph
Emerson Browns A. M.
Standard Book Co., 1961

Waiting Patiently

I waited patiently for the Lord; and he inclined unto me, and heard my cry.

He brought me up also out of an horrible pit, out of the miry clay, and set my feet upon a rock, and established my goings.

And he hath put a new song in my mouth, even praise unto our God: many shall see it, and fear, and shall trust in the Lord.

Blessed is that man that maketh the Lord his trust, and respecteth not the proud, nor such as turn aside to lies.

— Psalm 40:1-4
HOLY BIBLE

Our Longsuffering God

Then Ezra prayed, "You alone are God. You have made the skies and the heavens, the earth and the seas, and everything in them. You preserve it all; and all the angels of heaven worship you.

"You are the Lord God who chose Abram and brought him from Ur of the Chaldeans and renamed him Abraham. When he was faithful to you, you made a contract with him to forever give him and his descendants the land . . . and now you have done what you promised, for you are always true to your word.

"You saw the troubles and sorrows of our ancestors in Egypt, and you heard their cries from beside the Red Sea . . . You divided the sea for your people so they could go through on dry land! And then you destroyed their enemies in the depths of the sea . . . You led our ancestors by a pillar of cloud during the day and a pillar of fire at night so that they could find their way.

"You came down upon Mount Sinai and spoke with them from heaven and gave them good laws and true commandments . . .

"You gave them bread from heaven when they were hungry and water from the rock when they were thirsty. You commanded them to go in and conquer the land you had sworn to give them; but our ancestors were a proud and stubborn lot, and they refused to listen to your commandments.

"They refused to obey and didn't pay any attention to the miracles you did for them; instead, they rebelled and appointed a leader to take them back into slavery in Egypt! But you are a God of forgiveness, always ready to pardon, gracious and merciful, slow to become angry, and full of love and mercy; you didn't abandon them, even though they made a calf-idol and proclaimed, 'This is our God! He brought us out of Egypt!' They sinned in so many ways, but in your great mercy you didn't abandon them to die in the wilderness! The pillar of cloud led them forward day by day, and the pillar of fire showed them the way through the night. You sent your good Spirit to instruct them, and you did not stop giving them bread from heaven or water for their thirst. For forty years you sustained them in the wilderness; they lacked nothing in all that time. Their clothes didn't wear out and their feet didn't swell!

"Then you helped them conquer great kingdoms and many nations, and you placed your people in every corner of the land. . . . You subdued whole nations before them—even the kings and the people of the Canaanites were powerless! Your people captured fortified cities and fertile land; they took over houses full of good things, with cisterns and vineyards and olive yards and many, many fruit trees; so they ate and were full and enjoyed themselves in all your blessings.

"But despite all this they were disobedient and rebelled against you. They threw away your law, killed the prophets who told them to return to you, and they did many other terrible things. . . . Yet whenever your people returned to you and cried to you for help, once more you listened from heaven, and in your wonderful mercy delivered them! You were patient with them for many years. You sent your prophets to warn them about their sins, but still they wouldn't listen. . . . But in your great mercy you did not destroy them completely or abandon them forever. What a gracious and merciful God you are!"

— Nehemiah 9:6-9, 11-13, 15-22,
24-26, 28, 30-31 (TLB)
HOLY BIBLE

Be Diligent

Have patience with all things, but chiefly have patience with yourself. Do not lose courage in considering your imperfections, but instantly set about remedying them—every day begin the task anew.

— St. Francis de Sales

The Book of Unusual Quotations
Selected and Edited by Rudolf Flesch
New York: Harper and Brothers Publishers, 1957

Compassion in Slow Motion

The timing is as critical as the involvement. You don't just force your way in. Even if you've got the stuff that's needed . . . even if you hold the piece perfectly shaped to fit the other person's missing part of the puzzle . . . you can't push it into place. You must not try.

You must do the most difficult thing for compassion to do.

You must wait.

Yes, that's correct. Wait.

Even if there is rebellion? Even if there's rebellion.

Even if sin is occurring? Yes, often even then.

Even if others are suffering and disillusioned and going through the misery of misunderstanding, heartache, and sleepless nights?

Believe it or not, yes.

There are times (not always, but often) when the better part of wisdom restrains us from barging in and trying to make someone accept our help. The time isn't right, so we wait.

Like Isaiah reported to the nation whom the Lord called *"rebellious children"* (Isaiah 30:1). These people were rife with shame, reproach, unfaithful alliances, oppression, and a ruthless rejection of God's holy Word. Their unwillingness to repent added insult to injury.

But what was Jehovah's response? Hidden away in the first part of verse 18 is the incredible statement:

"Therefore the Lord longs to be gracious to you,
And therefore He waits on high to have compassion on you" (NASB).

Instead of storming into the dark alleys of Judah, screaming "Repent!" and shining bright lights to expose the filthy litter of their disobedience, the Lord tapped His foot, folded His arms . . . and waited. Not even the Lord pushed His way in. He waited until the time was right.

"O people in Zion, inhabitant in Jerusalem, you will weep no longer.
He will surely be gracious to you at the sound of your cry; when He hears it,
He will answer you" (Isaiah 30:19).

Our Lord would love to piece together the shattered fragments of your life. But He is waiting . . . graciously waiting until the time is right.

Until you are tired of the life you are living . . . until you see it for what it really is.

Until you are weary of coping . . . of taking charge of your own life . . . until you realize the mess you are making of it.

Until you recognize your need for Him.

He's waiting. . . .

— *Charles R. Swindoll*

The Finishing Touch
Charles R. Swindoll, 1994
Word, Inc., Dallas, Texas.

Relax

Nada te turbe,
Nada te espante,
Todo se pasa,
Dios no se muda,
La paciencia
Todo lo alcanza;
Quien a Dios tiene
Nada le falta:
Solo Dios basta.

Let nothing disturb thee;
Let nothing dismay thee:
All things pass;
God never changes.
Patience attains
All that it strives for.
He who has God
Finds he lacks nothing:
God alone suffices.

— *St. Teresa of Avila*

The Complete Works of St. Teresa of Jesus
Translated and Edited by E. Allison Peers
London: Sheed and Ward, 1946, Vol. 3, p. 288

Waiting on the Lord

Yet the Lord longs to be gracious to you;
  he rises to show you compassion.
For the Lord is a God of justice.
  Blessed are all who wait for him!

Do you not know?
  Have you not heard?
The Lord is the everlasting God,
  the Creator of the ends of the earth.
He will not grow tired or weary,
  and his understanding no one can fathom.
He gives stength to the weary
  and increases the power of the weak.
Even youths grow tired and weary,
  and young men stumble and fall;
but those who hope in the Lord
  will renew their strength.
They will soar on wings like eagles;
  they will run and not grow weary,
  they will walk and not be faint.

— Isaiah 30:18; 40:28-31 (NIV)
HOLY BIBLE

Waiting With Confidence

Just suppose that your boat sank in the middle of the lake one day and nobody saw you. You couldn't swim, the water was cold and you were hanging on to the sodden rigging with fingers which were getting progressively colder and weaker. You would hardly be very contented.

On the other hand, suppose that as your boat was sinking, you radioed to shore. The rescue service picked up the message, told you to hold on and dispatched a helicopter immediately. You could see it in the distance, rapidly getting nearer. Would you feel more content?

Of course you would, for you would see an end to your ordeal and you would feel confidence in your rescuers. That's how it is with the "God of peace." Instead of hanging on with growing despair and weakening fingers, you see the adequate resources and the infinite wisdom of your God at work, and you learn to be content because of what He is doing and the way He's doing it.

— *Stuart Briscoe*

Living On the Lord's Timing

Are you ever troubled with impatience? Do difficult people ever test your patience? Does what they do or fail to do get to you? Are you ever upset when people you love fail to capture your vision for them? Ever get exasperated when people do not meet your expectations of what you want them to accomplish on your time schedules? And more profoundly, knowing people's potential and what the Lord can do with the life given over to His control, do you become impatient with their slow response or imperviousness?

Perhaps our problem with impatience is that we misunderstand patience. It is not acquiescence, or perpetual placidity, or feckless lack of fiber. Patience must be rooted in an overarching confidence that there is Someone in control of this universe, our world, and our life. We need to know that God does work things together for good for those who love Him. A patient person knows the shortness of time and the length of eternity. Patience is really faith in action. No wonder it is called an aspect of the fruit of the Spirit. It is one of the matchless characteristics of Christ Himself. If we would learn patience, He alone can teach us. There are many facsimiles of the virtue, but authentic patience comes as a result of our deep personal relationship with Christ.

It would be disastrous to have anything that God did not deem best for us or to have what is best for us before God timed it.

— Lloyd John Ogilvie

Taken from *Silent Strength for My Life*
by Lloyd John Ogilvie. Copyright © 1990 by
Harvest House Publishers, Eugene, Oregon.
Used by permission.

Concerning Patience

She is a Virtue, none can truly prize
Enough her Worth and Value, but the Wise
Who have her try'd, and her great Power known;
Her sublime Virtue, as th' admired Stone,
Brings things to pass, which some don't think to see,
Strange things to pass, hid in Obscurity;
Those that possess her in their Souls, shall know
Experience by her, deep things she will show:
But those that are impatient, and do fret,
The Night o'ertakes them, and their Sun doth set;
They cannot see far off, nor night at Hand;
The Light withdraws, and Darkness fills their Land.

— Benjamin Antrobus

Buds and Blossoms of Piety
With Some Fruit of the Spirit of Love
and Directions To the Divine Wisdom
London, 1715

Running the Race

Let us lay aside every weight, and the sin which doth so easily beset us, and let us run with patience the race that is set before us, looking unto Jesus the author and finisher of our faith; who for the joy that was set before him endured the cross, despising the shame, and is set down at the right hand of the throne of God.

> — *Hebrews 12:1-2*
> HOLY BIBLE

O Master, Let Me Walk With Thee

O Master, let me walk with Thee
    in lowly paths of service free;
tell me Thy secret; help me bear
    the strain of toil, the fret of care.

Help me the slow of heart to move
    by some clear, winning word of love;
teach me the wayward feet to stay,
    and guide me in the homeward way.

Teach me Thy patience; still with Thee
    in closer, dearer company,
in work that keeps faith sweet and strong,
    in trust that triumphs over wrong;

In hope that sends a shining ray
    far down the future's broadening way,
in peace that only Thou canst give,
    with Thee, O Master, let me live.

> — *Washington Gladden*

Patience With a Smile

Be patient in little things. Learn to bear the everyday trials and annoyances of life quietly and calmly, and then, when unforseen trouble or calamity comes, your strength will not forsake you.

There is as much difference between genuine patience and sullen endurance, as between the smile of love, and the malicious gnashing of the teeth.

— *William Swan Plumer*

The New Dictionary of Thoughts
Originally Compiled by Tryon Edwards D. D.
Revised and Enlarged by C. N. Catrevas A. B.,
Jonathan Edwards A. M., & Ralph
Emerson Browns A. M.
Standard Book Co., 1961

Make a Pearl

The most extraordinary thing about the oysters is this: Irritations get into his shell. He does not like them. But when he cannot get rid of them, he uses the irritation to do the loveliest thing an oyster ever has a chance to do. If there are irritations in our lives today, there is only one prescription: make a pearl. It may have to be a pearl of patience, but, anyhow, make a pearl. And it takes faith and love to do it.

— *Harry Emerson Fosdick*

Words of Wisdom
Compiled and Edited by William Safire and Leonard Safire
New York: Simon and Schuster, 1989

We Must Be Tested

Patience does not mean indifference. We may work and trust and wait, but we ought not to be idle or careless while waiting.

Life has such hard conditions that every dear and precious gift, every rare virtue, every genial endowment, love, hope, joy, wit, sprightliness, benevolence, must sometimes be put into the crucible to distill the one elixir—patience.

— Gail Hamilton

The New Dictionary of Thoughts
Originally Compiled by Tryon Edwards D. D.
Revised and Enlarged by C. N. Catrevas A. B.,
Jonathan Edwards A. M., & Ralph
Emerson Browns A. M.
Standard Book Co., 1961

God Is Not Impatient

But, beloved, do not forget this one thing, that with the Lord one day is as a thousand years, and a thousand years as one day. The Lord is not slack concerning His promise, as some count slackness, but is longsuffering toward us, not willing that any should perish but that all should come to repentance.

But the day of the Lord will come as a thief in the night, in which the heavens will pass away with a great noise, and the elements will melt with fervent heat; both the earth and the works that are in it will be burned up. Therefore, since all these things will be dissolved, what manner of persons ought you to be in holy conduct and godliness, looking for and hastening the coming of the day of God, because of which the heavens will be dissolved, being on fire, and the elements will melt with fervent heat? Nevertheless we, according to His promise, look for new heavens and a new earth in which righteousness dwells.

Therefore, beloved, looking forward to these things, be diligent to be found by Him in peace, without spot and blameless; and consider that the longsuffering of our Lord is salvation.

— 2 Peter 3:8-15 (NKJV)
HOLY BIBLE

Patient in Prayer—Until the Answer Comes

One day Jesus told his disciples a story to illustrate their need for constant prayer and to show them that they must keep praying until the answer comes.

"There was a city judge," he said, "a very godless man who had great contempt for everyone. A widow of that city came to him frequently to appeal for justice against a man who had harmed her. The judge ignored her for a while, but eventually she got on his nerves.

"'I fear neither God nor man,' he said to himself, 'but this woman bothers me. I'm going to see that she gets justice, for she is wearing me out with her constant coming!'"

Then the Lord said, "If even an evil judge can be worn down like that, don't you think that God will surely give justice to his people who plead with him day and night? Yes! He will answer them quickly! But the question is: When I, the Messiah, return, how many will I find who have faith and are praying?"

> — *Luke 18:1-8* (TLB)
> *HOLY BIBLE*

On the Advantage of Patience

Let us, as servants and worshippers of God, show, in our spiritual obedience, the patience which we learn from heavenly teachings. For we have this virtue in common with God. From Him patience begins; from Him its glory and its dignity take their rise. The origin and greatness of patience proceed from God as its author. Man ought to love the thing which is dear to God; the good which the Divine Majesty loves, it commends. If God is our Lord and Father, let us imitate the patience of our Lord as well as our Father; because it behooves servants to be obedient, no less than it becomes sons not to be degenerate. . . .

— *Cyprian*

The Ante-Nicene Fathers
Translated by Ernest Wallis
New York, 1886

What To Wish For

The sun is just rising on the morning of another day. What can I wish that this day may bring me? Nothing shall make the world or others poorer, nothing at the expense of other men; but just those few things which in their coming do not stop with me but touch me, rather, as they pass and gather strength.

A few friends, who understand me, and yet remain my friends.

A work to do which has real value, without which the world would feel the poorer.

A return for such work small enough not to tax anyone who pays.

A mind unafraid to travel, even though the trail be not blazed.

An understanding heart.

A sight of the eternal hills, and the unresting sea, and of something beautiful which the hand of man has made.

A sense of humor, and the power to laugh.

A little leisure with nothing to do.

A few moments of quiet, silent meditation. The sense of the presence of God.

And the patience to wait for the coming of these things, with the wisdom to know them when they come, and the wit not to change this morning wish of mine

— *Walter Reid Hunt*

A Treasury of Contentment
Compiled and Edited by Ralph L. Woods
New York: Trident Press, 1969
A Division of Simon and Schuster

To the End

Grant, O God,
That we may never lose the way through our self-will,
and so end up in the far countries of the soul;
That we may never abondon the struggle,
but that we may endure to the end,
and so be saved;
That we may never drop out of the race,
but that we may ever press forward
to the goal of our high calling;
That we may never choose the cheap and passing
things, and let go the precious things
that last forever;
That we may never take the easy way,
and so leave the right way;
That we may never forget
that sweat is the price of all things,
and that without the Cross, there cannot
be the crown.

So keep up and strengthen us by Your grace that no disobedience and no weakness and no failure may stop us from entering into the blessedness which awaits those who are faithful in all the changes and the chances of life down even to the gates of death; through Jesus Christ our Lord. Amen.

— *William Barclay*

A Prayer from William Barclay,
Prayers for the Christian Year,
SCM Press © 1964

Chapter 5

KINDNESS

"Therefore as the elect of God, holy and beloved, put on tender mercies, kindness, humility, meekness, longsuffering; bearing with one another, and forgiving one another" (Colossians 3:12-13 NKJV).

Kindness is a state of being "unruffled and unflappable." In many passages in the Scriptures, it is linked with love as is *lovingkindness.* Kindness is behavior that flows from *agape,* God's love. It is, therefore, behavior that is gentle, pure and totally rooted in good and for the good of another person. While love might cause a person to make tough decisions or exert behavior that may be perceived as absolute, austere, and even harsh, "kindness" refers to loving behavior that is mellow and gentle.

Kindness, however, is in no way weak or wimpish. It does not compromise truth or back down during times of spiritual warfare. It never gives in to evil, or refrains from speaking about the goodness of God. Rather, kindness is a manner of speaking and acting. It is an attitude, a quality of behavior that stands firm without forcing others to their knees.

The Greek word for such kindness is "chrestotes" (pronounced khray-stot'-ace) and can mean:

- Mellowed with age.

- Nothing harsh or painful.

- Totally lacking the wisdom of a serpent.

Whatever Happened to Kindness?

Kindness is the steadfast love of the Lord in action toward those who fail. Throughout the Old Testament the words for "steadfast love," "mercy," and "kindness" are used interchangeably. Kindness is the persistent effort of the Lord to reach His people and enable them to return to Him.

Jesus Christ was kindness incarnate. He came to express it; lived to model it; died to offer it; and returns to impart it to us in the Holy Spirit. Paul knew this from his own experience of the kindness of God in Christ. His rigid hostility toward others and himself had been melted by an unsurpassed kindness. God never demands anything of us that He is not willing to give us. It should not be surprising that the power to be kind is available under the code name "fruit." Kindness is implanted, imputed, and ingrained into the very nature of our new heredity in Christ Jesus. It is ours to develop and express along with the other character strengths inherent in the fruit of the Spirit. Kindness can now be reflected in all our relationships. We can be as merciful and gracious to others as Christ has been to us.

Kindness is a sign of greatness.

— Lloyd John Ogilvie

Taken From: *Silent Strength for My Life*
by Lloyd John Ogilvie. Copyright © 1990
by Harvest House Publishers, Eugene, Oregon.
Used by permission

Christ Brings Kindness

Kindness, or gentleness, is a term that comes from a Greek word referring to the kindness that pervades and penetrates the whole nature. Gentleness washes away all that is harsh and austere. Indeed, gentleness is love enduring. Jesus was a gentle person. When He came into the world, there were few institutions of mercy. There were few hospitals or mental institutions, few places of refuge for the poor, few homes for orphans, few havens for the forsaken. In comparison to today, it was a cruel world. Christ changed that. Wherever true Christianity has gone His followers have performed acts of gentleness and kindness.

— *Billy Graham*

The Faithful Christian: An Anthology of Billy Graham
Compiled by William Griffin and Ruth Graham Dienert
New York: McCracken Press, 1994

It's the Word

"What is real good?"
I asked in a musing mood:
"Order," said the law court;
"Knowledge," said the school;
"Truth," said the wise man;
"Pleasure," said the fool,
"Love," said the maiden,
"Beauty," said the page,
"Freedom," said the dreamer,
"Home," said the sage,
"Fame," said the soldier,
"Equity," said the seer—
Spake my heart full sadly: "The answer is not here;"
Then, within my bosom, softly, this I heard:
"Each heart holds the secret—
Kindness is the word."

— *John Boyle O'Reilly*

The Encyclopedia of Religious Quotations
Edited and Compiled by Frank S. Mead
Fleming H. Revell, 1965

Love Is Kind

I have a number of children who talk about My love, but they are very rude to others. They take them for granted, make them feel small or even ridicule them. Love is not rude.

Don't be rude, child. One small piece of rudeness can ruin your witness in somebody else's eyes.

It is better to be kind; love is kind. I have never been rude to you. I could have said some unkind things about you—but it's not my nature to do this. I could have scorned, mocked and criticized you, but I do not do that to anyone.

Instead of being easily roused to anger, I am merciful, patient, loving, and kind. Because My love lives in you, don't be easily angered either, even when people do foolish things.

— *Colin Urquhart*

My Dear Child
Lake Myers, Florida: Creation House, 1991

Lovingkindness

Awake, my soul, to joyful lays, and sing Thy great Redeemer's praise; He justly claims a song from thee, His lovingkindness, oh, how free!

He saw me ruined by the fall, yet loved me not withstanding all; He saved me from my lost estate, His lovingkindness, oh, how great!

When trouble, like a gloomy cloud, has gathered thick and thundered loud, He near my soul has always stood, His lovingkindness, oh, how good!

Soon shall we mount and soar away to the bright realms of endless day, and sing, with rapture and surprise, His lovingkindness, in the skies.

Refrain:
Lovingkindness, lovingkindness, His lovingkindness, oh how free!

— *Samuel Medley*

A Father's Kindness

Busy in his study a minister was preparing his sermon for the coming Sunday. He reached to the shelf at his side for a book, and then remembered that he had left it downstairs. His little daughter was playing in the bedroom, and he called her. She came, running, eager and delighted at the thought that Papa needed her. He explained carefully where she could find the book, and she went gladly, returning in a moment with a book which he saw at a glance was the wrong one. But he hardly looked at the book as he took it and laid it on the table. He looked only at the eager face of his little daughter, wreathed in smiles. Gathering her close to his heart, he kissed her and said, "Thank you, darling." And when she had gone back happy and contented to her play he went quietly for the book he needed. I think I should like to listen to the sermons that man would preach.

Christian Herald
Cyclopedia of Religious Anecdotes
Compiled by James Gilchrist Lawson
Fleming H. Revell Co., 1923

And Forgive Us Our Debts,
As We Forgive Our Debtors

Jesus gives us six petitions to make. Three concern God, and three are for ourselves. All six of them are of supreme importance, yet there is one of the six on which He turns the spotlight. He does not find it necessary to emphasize that we pray that God's name be hallowed, or that God's kingdom come, or that His will be done, vital as those are.

He does not emphasize our need for bread, yet without bread we would all die. But after the Lord's Prayer is completed, our Lord feels He should turn back and lift one petition out for special comment. *"And forgive us our debts, as we forgive our debtors"* is the prayer He spotlights. He says, *"But if ye forgive not men their trespasses, neither will your Father forgive your trespasses"* (Matthew 6:15).

It isn't that God forgives on an exchange basis. Our forgiveness of others is not a condition of God's forgiveness of us. Rather, it is a condition of our ability to receive the forgiveness of God. We are told by Shakespeare, "The quality of mercy is not strain'd, it droppeth as the gentle rain from heaven." But I could cover a plant with a sheet of iron and the rain could not get to it. So, I can surround my soul with an unforgiving spirit and completely block the forgiving mercy of God.

The words "forgiving" and "forgiven" are inseparable twins. They go together. They are never separated.

On the cross our Lord prays, *"Father, forgive them; for they know not what they do"* (Luke 23:34). Often what we deplore is the innocent act of some person. But for us there is an even more important reason for not holding a grudge: "for we know not." If we understood the person, usually our judgments would not be so harsh.

With our limited understanding of each other, it is a fearful thing to set ourselves up as a judge. The Bible says, *"Vengeance is mine; I will repay, saith the Lord"* (Romans 12:19). If we are wise we will leave that business to God.

A couple had gone to an orphanage to adopt a child. One little fellow particularly appealed to them. They talked to him about all the things they would give him—clothes, toys, a good home. None of these things seemed to appeal to the boy much. So finally they asked him, "What do you want most?" He replied, "I just want somebody to love me."

That is what we all want. Deep in every human heart is a hunger for love. Loneliness is a cross for more people than we realize. Yet people are hard to love. They have so many faults, they say things they shouldn't, many have antagonistic and unattractive spirits. Yet Jesus told us to pray, "Forgive as we forgive." This is the only petition He emphasized. Maybe it is the hardest one to say.

"For if you forgive not men their trespasses"—debts—sins—! Either of those words could be used, maybe all three better express what our Lord had in mind. Debts suggest failure to discharge obligations, not merely financial. There are also such debts as the debts of friendship, citizenship, etc.

Trespasses indicate the unlawful use of another's property. We see signs, "No Trespassing," and we know that the sign means to keep off. Our friends also trespass on our time, they trespass on our name and do it harm when they talk about us wrongfully. In many ways do friends trespass on us.

Sometimes we might feel like Sir Walter Raleigh, who just a few hours before his death, wrote his wife: *To what friend to direct thee I know not, for mine have left me in the true time of trial.* Some people have been so deeply hurt that they cannot feel that Tennyson was right when he said:

> *I hold it true, whate'er befall,*
> *I feel it, when I sorrow most;*
> *'Tis better to have loved and lost,*
> *Than never to have loved at all.*

But notice carefully that Jesus said, *"Forgive us our debts."* He directs our attention first to our own debts—trespasses—sins. The faults of those about us are also in us. Maybe not exactly the same ones, but probably worse ones. He did not tell us to pray, "Forgive us if we have sinned." There is no if about it.

Let us honestly ask ourselves some questions and answer them: "What is my worst failure? That is, wherein have I not lived up to my obligations? Second, what is one way I have mistreated another person? Third, what is one sin I have committed?" Each of us has some answer for each of those questions. We all stand convicted.

But, also, do our friends have an answer for those questions? They, too, are guilty. Now, the supreme point is: If you will be willing to forgive them, then you will be able to receive God's forgiveness of you. It seems to be a good bargain for me. How about you?

— *Charles Allen*

Allen, Charles L. *God's Psychiatry*,
Fleming H. Revell Company, a division of
Baker Book House Company, © 1988.

Has God deserted Heaven,
And left it up to you,
To judge if this or that is right,
And what each one should do?

I think He's still in business,
And knows when to wield the rod,
So when you're judging others,
Just remember, you're not—God.

God's Everlasting Kindness

"Sing, O barren,
You who have not borne!
Break forth into singing, and cry aloud,
You who have not labored with child!
For more are the children of the desolate
Than the children of the married woman," says the Lord.

"Enlarge the place of your tent,
And let them stretch out the curtains of your dwellings;
Do not spare;
Lengthen your cords,
And strengthen your stakes.
For you shall expand to the right and to the left,
And your descendants will inherit the nations,
And make the desolate cities inhabited.

"Do not fear, for you will not be ashamed;
Neither be disgraced, for you will not be put to shame;
For you will forget the shame of your youth,
And will not remember the reproach of your widowhood
anymore.
For your Maker is your husband,
The Lord of hosts is His name;
And your Redeemer is the Holy One of Israel;
He is called the God of the whole earth.
For the Lord has called you
Like a woman forsaken and grieved in spirit,
Like a youthful wife when you were refused,"
Says your God.
"For a mere moment I have forsaken you,
But with great mercies I will gather you.
With a little wrath I hid My face from you for a moment;
But with everlasting kindness I will have mercy on you,"
Says the Lord, your Redeemer.

— Isaiah 54:1-8 (NKJV)
HOLY BIBLE

Pass It On

Have you had a kindness shown?
    Pass it on;
'Twas not given for thee alone,
    Pass it on;
Let it travel down the years,
Let it wipe another's tears,
'Till in Heaven the deed appears—
    Pass it on.

— Henry Burton

The Encyclopedia of Religious Quotations
Edited and Compiled by Frank S. Mead
Fleming H. Revell, 1965

Christian Community

The second service that one should perform for another in a Christian community is that of active helpfulness. This means, initially, simple assistance in trifling, external matters. There is a multitude of these things wherever people live together. Nobody is too good for the meanest service. One who worries about the loss of time that such petty, outward acts of helpfulness entail is usually taking the importance of his own career too solemnly.

— Dietrich Bonhoeffer

Taken from *Life Together* by Dietrich Bonhoeffer.
English translation copyright © 1954 by Harper & Brothers,
copyright renewed © 1982 by Helen S. Doberstein.
Reprinted by permission of HarperCollins Publishers, Inc.

A Promise of Kindness Kept

Then Jonathan told David, "I promise by the Lord God of Israel that about this time tomorrow, or the next day at the latest, I will talk to my father about you and let you know at once how he feels about you. If he is angry and wants you killed, then may the Lord kill me if I don't tell you, so you can escape and live. May the Lord be with you as he used to be with my father. And remember, you must demonstrate the love and kindness of the Lord not only to me during my own lifetime, but also to my children after the Lord has destroyed all of your enemies."

So Jonathan made a covenant with the family of David, and David swore to it. . . .

(There was a little lame grandson of King Saul's named Mephibosheth, who was the son of Prince Jonathan. He was five years old at the time Saul and Jonathan were killed at the battle of Jezreel. When the news of the outcome of the battle reached the capital, the child's nurse grabbed him and fled, but she fell and dropped him as she was running, and he became lame.)

One day David began wondering if any of Saul's family was still living, for he wanted to be kind to them, as he had promised Prince Jonathan. He heard about a man named Ziba who had been one of Saul's servants, and summoned him.

"Are you Ziba?" the king asked.

"Yes, sir, I am," he replied.

The king then asked him, "Is anyone left from Saul's family? If so, I want to fulfill a sacred vow by being kind to him."

"Yes," Ziba replied," Jonathan's lame son is still alive."

"Where is he?" the king asked.

"In Lo-debar," Ziba told him. "At the home of Machir."

So King David sent for Mephibosheth — Jonathan's son and Saul's grandson. Mephibosheth arrived in great fear and greeted the king in deep humility, bowing low before him.

But David said, "Don't be afraid! I've asked you to come so that I can be kind to you because of my vow to your father Jonathan. I will restore to you all the land of your grandfather Saul, and you shall live here at the palace!"

Mephibosheth fell to the ground before the king. "Should the king show kindness to a dead dog like me?" he exclaimed.

Then the king summoned Saul's servant Ziba. "I have given your master's grandson everything that belonged to Saul and his family," he said. "You and your sons and servants are to farm the land for him, to produce food for his family; but he will live here with me."

Ziba, who had fifteen sons and twenty servants, replied, "Sir, I will do all that you have commanded."

And from that time on, Mephibosheth ate regularly with King David, as though he were one of his own sons. Mephibosheth had a young son, Mica. All the household of Ziba became Mephibosheth's servants, but Mephibosheth (who was lame in both feet) moved to Jerusalem to live at the palace.

> *— 1 Samuel 20:12-16; 2 Samuel 4:4;*
> *9:1-13 (TLB)*
> *HOLY BIBLE*

Words of Kindness

Kind words bring no blisters on the tongue that speaks them, nor on the ear which hears them.

Kind words are never wasted. Like scattered seeds, they spring up in unexpected places.

Kindness is a conquering weapon.

Kindness should not be all on one side.

One good turn must have another as its return, or it will not be fair. He who expects kindness should show kindness.

— Charles H. Spurgeon

Spurgeon's Proverbs and Sayings With Notes Vol. I
Grand Rapids, Mich.: Baker Book House

Say It Now

If you have a friend worth loving,
  Love him. Yes, and let him know
That you love him, ere life's evening
  Tinge his brow with sunset glow.
Why should good words ne'er be said
Of a friend—till he is dead?

If you hear a song that thrills you,
  Sung by any child of song,
Praise it. Do not let the singer
  Wait deserved praises long.
Why should one who thrills your heart
Lack the joy you may impart?

If you hear a prayer that moves you
  By its humble, pleading tone,
Join it. Do not let the seeker
  Bow before his God alone.
Why should not your brother share
The strength of "two or three" in prayer?

If you see the hot tears falling
  From a brother's weeping eyes,
Share them. And by kindly sharing
  Own our kinship in the skies.
Why should anyone be glad
When a brother's heart is sad?

If a silvery laugh goes rippling
  Through the sunshine on his face,
Share it. 'Tis the wise man's saying—
  For both grief and joy a place.
There's health and goodness in the mirth
In which an honest laugh has birth.

If your work is made more easy
    By a friendly, helping hand,
Say so. Speak out brave and truly
    Ere the darkness veil the land.
Should a brother workman dear
Falter for a word of cheer?

Scatter thus your seeds of kindness
    All enriching as you go—
Leave them. Trust the Harvest Giver;
    He will make each seed to grow.
So until the happy end
Your life shall never lack a friend.

— *Unknown*

The Best Loved Poems of the American People
Selected by Hazel Felleman
Garden City, N.Y.: Doubleday & Co., Inc., 1936

God's Kindness To Us

For we also once were foolish ourselves, disobedient, deceived, enslaved to various lusts and pleasures, spending our life in malice and envy, hateful, hating one another.

But when the kindness of God our Savior and His love for mankind appeared,

He saved us, not on the basis of deeds which we have done in righteousness, but according to His mercy, by the washing of regeneration and renewing by the Holy Spirit,

whom He poured out upon us richly through Jesus Christ our Savior,

that being justified by His grace we might be made heirs according to the hope of eternal life.

– *Titus 3:3-7* (NASB)
HOLY BIBLE

The Minute We Ask

Our feeling is that it is presumptuous, and even almost impertinent, to go at once to the Lord, after having sinned against Him. It seems as if we ought to suffer the consequences of our sin first for a little while, and endure the accusings of our conscience; and we can hardly believe that the Lord can be willing at once to receive us back into loving fellowship with Himself.

A little girl once expressed this feeling to me, with a child's outspoken candor. She had asked whether the Lord Jesus always forgave us our sins as soon as we asked Him, and I had said, "Yes, of course He does." "*Just* as soon?" she repeated doubtingly. "Yes," I replied, "the very minute we ask, He forgives us." "Well," she said deliberately, "I cannot believe that. I should think He would make us feel sorry for two or three days first. And then I should think He would make us ask Him a great many times, and in a very pretty way too, not just in common talk. And I believe that is the way He does, and you need not try to make me think He forgives me right at once, no matter what the Bible says." She only said what most Christians think, and what *is* worse, what most Christians act on, making their discouragement and their remorse separate them infinitely further off from God than their sin would have done.

— *Hannah Whitall Smith*

Eerdmans' Book of Christian Classics
Compiled by Veronica Zundel
Grand Rapids, Mich.: William B. Eerdmans Pub. Co., 1985

Service and Humility

Nothing disciplines the inordinate desires of the flesh like service, and nothing transforms the desires of the flesh like serving in hiddenness. The flesh whines against service but screams against hidden service. It strains and pulls for honor and recognition. It will devise subtle, religiously acceptable means to call attention to the service rendered. If we stoutly refuse to give in to this lust of the flesh, we crucify it. Every time we crucify the flesh, we crucify our pride and arrogance. . . .

William Law made a lasting impact upon eighteenth-century England with his book *A Serious Call to a Devout and Holy Life*. In it, Law urges that every day should be viewed as a day of humility. And how does he suggest that we do this? By learning to serve others. Law understood that it is the discipline of service that brings humility into the life. If we want humility, he counsels us to ". . . condescend to all the weaknesses and infirmities of your fellow-creatures, cover their frailties, love their excellencies, encourage their virtues, relieve their wants, rejoice in their prosperities, compassionate their distress, receive their friendship, overlook their unkindness, forgive their malice, be a servant of servants, and condescend to do the lowest offices to the lowest of mankind."

— *Richard Foster*

Taken from *Celebration of Discipline:*
The Path to Spiritual Growth
by Richard J. Foster. Copyright © 1978 by
Richard J. Foster. Reprinted by permission of
HarperCollins Publishers, Inc.

Rebekah's Kindness

Now Abraham was old, advanced in age; and the Lord had blessed Abraham in every way. And Abraham said to his servant . . . "You shall go to my country and to my relatives, and take a wife for my son Isaac."

Then the servant took ten camels from the camels of his master, and set out with a variety of good things of his master's in his hand; and he arose, and went to Mesopotamia, to the city of Nahor.

And he made the camels kneel down outside the city by the well of water at evening time, the time when women go out to draw water.

And he said, "O Lord, the God of my master Abraham, please grant me success today, and show lovingkindness to my master Abraham. Behold, I am standing by the spring, and the daughters of the men of the city are coming out to draw water; now may it be that the girl to whom I say, 'Please let down your jar so that I may drink,' and who answers, 'Drink, and I will water your camels also';—may she be the one whom Thou hast appointed for Thy servant Isaac; and by this I shall know that Thou hast shown lovingkindness to my master."

And it came about before he had finished speaking, that behold, Rebekah who was born to Bethuel the son of Milcah, the wife of Abraham's brother Nahor, came out with her jar on her shoulder. And the girl was very beautiful, a virgin, and no man had had relations with her; and she went down to the spring and filled her jar, and came up.

Then the servant ran to meet her, and said, "Please let me drink a little water from your jar."

And she said, "Drink, my lord"; and she quickly lowered her jar to her hand, and gave him a drink.

Now when she had finished giving him a drink, she said, "I will draw also for your camels until they have finished drinking." So she quickly emptied her jar into the trough, and ran back to the well to draw, and she drew for all his camels.

Then it came about, when the camels had finished drinking, that the man took a gold ring weighing a half-shekel and two bracelets for her wrists weighing ten shekels in gold, and said, "Whose daughter are you? Please tell me, is there room for us to lodge in your father's house?"

And she said to him, "I am the daughter of Bethuel, the son of Milcah, whom she bore to Nahor." Again she said to him, "We have plenty of both straw and feed, and room to lodge in."

Then the man bowed low and worshiped the Lord. And he said, "Blessed be the Lord, the God of my master Abraham, who has not forsaken His lovingkindness and His truth toward my master; as for me, the Lord has guided me in the way to the house of my master's brothers."

Then the girl ran and told her mother's household about these things.

— *Genesis 24:1-2, 4, 10-20, 22-28*
(NASB)
HOLY BIBLE

Make People Smile

How easy is it for one benevolent being to diffuse pleasure around him, and how truly is a kind heart a fountain of gladness, making everything in its vicinity to freshen into smiles.

— *Washington Irving*

The New Dictionary of Thoughts
Originally Compiled by Tryon Edwards D. D.
Revised and Enlarged by C. N. Catrevas A. B., Jonathan Edwards A. M.,
& Ralph Emerson Browns A. M.
Standard Book Co., 1961

Be Forgetful

I'll forgive . . . but I'll *never* forget. We say and hear that so much that it's easy to shrug it off as "only natural." That's the problem! It is the most natural response we can expect. Not *supernatural*. It also can result in tragic consequences.

In his book, *Great Church Fights*, Leslie B. Flynn tells of two unmarried sisters who lived together, but because of an unresolved disagreement over an insignificant issue, they stopped speaking to each other (one of the inescapable results of refusing to forget). Since they were either unable or unwilling to move out of their small house, they continued to use the same rooms, eat at the same table, use the same appliances, and sleep in the same room . . . all separately . . . without one word. A chalk line divided the sleeping area into two halves, separating doorways as well as the fireplace. Each would come and go, cook and eat, sew and read without ever stepping over into her sister's territory. Through the black of the night, each could hear the deep breathing of the other, but because both were unwilling to take the first step toward forgiving and forgetting the silly offense, they co-existed for years in grinding silence.

Refusing to forgive *and forget* leads to other tragedies, like monuments of spite. How many churches split (often over nitpicking issues), then spin off into another direction, fractured, splintered, and blindly opinionated?

Whether it is a personal or a public matter, we quickly reveal whether we possess a servant's heart in how we respond to those who have offended us.

And it isn't enough simply to say, "Well, okay—you're forgiven, but don't expect me to forget it!" That means we have erected a monument of spite in our mind, and that isn't really forgiveness at all.

Servants must be big people. Big enough to go on, remembering the right and forgetting the wrong.

Perhaps Amy Carmichael put it best when she wrote in her book *If:*

If I say, "Yes, I forgive, but I cannot forget," as though the God, who twice a day washes all the sands on all the shores of all the world, could not wash such memories from my mind, then I know nothing of Calvary love.

— *Charles R. Swindoll*

The Finishing Touch, Charles Swindoll,
1994 Word, Inc., Dallas, Texas.

Soothing Words

Kind words produce their own image in men's souls; and a beautiful image it is. They soothe and quiet and comfort the hearer. They shame him out of his sour, morose, unkind feelings. We have not yet begun to use kind words in such abundance as they ought to be used.

— *Blaise Pascal*

The New Dictionary of Thoughts
Originally Compiled by Tryon Edwards D. D.
Revised and Enlarged by C. N. Catrevas A. B., Jonathan Edwards
A. M., & Ralph Emerson Browns A. M.
Standard Book Co., 1961

Kindness Leads to Friendship

We cannot tell the precise moment when friendship is formed. As in filling a vessel drop by drop, there is at last a drop which makes it run over; so in a series of kindnesses there is at last one which makes the heart run over.

— *James Boswell*

Bartlett's Familiar Quotations,16th Edition
John Bartlett
Justin Kaplan, General Editor
Boston: Little, Brown & Co., 1992

Presidential Greatness

When the late President Eisenhower was vacationing in Denver many years ago, his attention was called to an open letter in a local newspaper, which told how six-year-old Paul Haley, dying of incurable cancer, had expressed a wish to see the President of the United States. Spontaneously, in one of those gracious gestures remembered long after a man's most carefully prepared speeches are forgotten, the President decided to grant the boy's request.

So one Sunday morning in August, a big limousine pulled up outside the Haley home and out stepped the President. He walked up to the door and knocked.

Mr. Donald Haley opened the door, wearing blue jeans, an old shirt, and a day's growth of beard. Behind him was his little son, Paul. Their amazement at finding President Eisenhower on their doorstep can be imagined.

"Paul," said the President to the little boy, "I understand you want to see me. Glad to see you." Then he shook hands with the six-year-old, took him out to see the presidential limousine, shook hands again, and left.

The Haleys and their neighbors, and a lot of other people, will probably talk about this kind and thoughtful deed of a busy president for a long time to come.

— *Billy Graham*

Unto the Hills
Billy Graham, 1986
Word, Inc., Dallas, Texas. All rights reserved.

Make Me a Blessing

Out in the highways and byways of life,
Many are weary and sad;
Carry the sunshine where darkness is rife,
Making the sorrowing glad.

Tell the sweet story of Christ and His love,
Tell of His pow'r to forgive;
Others will trust Him if only you prove
True, ev'ry moment you live.

Give as 'twas given to you in your need,
Love as the Master loved you;
Be to the helpless a helper indeed,
Unto your mission be true.

Make me a blessing,
Make me a blessing,
Out of my life . . . may Jesus shine;
Make me a blessing, O Savior, I pray,
Make me a blessing to someone today.

— *Ira B. Wilson*

Melodies of Praise

Anyone Can Do It

The ministry of kindness is a ministry which may be achieved by all men, rich and poor, learned and illiterate. Brilliance of mind and capacity for deep thinking have rendered great service to humanity, but by themselves they are impotent to dry a tear or mend a broken heart.

— Anonymous

The Encyclopedia of Religious Quotations
Edited and Compiled by Frank S. Mead
Fleming H. Revell, 1965

A Becoming Quality

The quality of mercy is not strained;
It droppeth as the gentle rain from heaven
Upon the place beneath: it is twice blest—
It blesseth him that gives and him that takes:
'Tis mightiest in the mightiest; it becomes
The throned monarch better than his crown:
His sceptre shows the force of temporal power,
The attribute to awe and majesty,
Wherein doth sit the dread and fear of kings;
But mercy is above this sceptred sway—
It is enthroned in the hearts of kings,
It is an attribute to God Himself;
And earthly power doth then show likest God's,
When mercy seasons justice.

*— William Shakespeare,
"The Merchant of Venice"*

One Hundred and One Famous Poems
An Anthology Compiled by Roy J. Cook
Chicago: Contemporary Books, Inc., 1958

Mary's Greatness

She hath done what she could: she is come aforehand to anoint my body to the burying (Mark 14:8).

I imagine when Mary died, if God had sent an angel to write her epitaph, he couldn't have done better than to put over her grave what Christ said: "She hath done what she could."

I would rather have that said over my grave, if it could honestly be said, than to have all the wealth of the Rothschilds. Christ raised a monument to Mary that is more lasting than the monuments raised to Caesar or Napoleon. Their monuments crumble away, but hers endures. Her name never appeared in print while she was on earth, but today it is famous in three hundred and fifty languages.

We may never be great; we may never be known outside our circle of friends; but we may, like Mary, do what we can. May God help each one of us to do what we can! Life will soon be over; it is short at the longest. Let us rise and follow in the footsteps of Mary of Bethany.

— Dwight L. Moody

The D. L. Moody Year Book
Selected by Emma Moody Fitt
New York: Fleming H. Revell Co., 1900

His Kindness Is Better Than Life

O God, You are my God;
Early will I seek You;
My soul thirsts for You;
My flesh longs for You
In a dry and thirsty land
Where there is no water.
So I have looked for You in the sanctuary,
To see Your power and Your glory.

Because Your lovingkindness is better than life,
My lips shall praise You.
Thus I will bless You while I live;
I will lift up my hands in Your name.
My soul shall be satisifed as with marrow and fatness,
And my mouth shall praise You with joyful lips.

— Psalm 63:1-5 (NKJV)
HOLY BIBLE

Small Kindnesses Add Up

Life is made up, not of great sacrifices or duties, but of little things, in which smiles, and kindnesses, and small obligations, given habitually, are what win and preserve the heart and secure comfort.

— Sir H. Davy

The New Dictionary of Thoughts
Originally Compiled by Tryon Edwards D. D.
Revised and Enlarged by C. N. Catrevas A. B., Jonathan Edwards
A. M., & Ralph Emerson Browns A. M.
Standard Book Co., 1961

An Unpredictable Kindness

In contrast to revenge, which is the natural, automatic reaction to transgression and which, because of the irreversibility of the action process, can be expected and even calculated, the act of forgiving can never be predicted; it is the only reaction that acts in an unexpected way and thus retains, through being a reaction, something of the original character of action.

— Hannah Arendt

A Certain World—A Commonplace Book
W. H. Auden
New York: Viking Press, 1970

Forgiveness

Everyone says forgiveness is a lovely idea, until they have something to forgive, as we had during the war. And then to mention the subject at all is to be greeted with howls of anger. It is not that people think this too high and difficult a virtue: it is that they think it hateful and contemptible. "That sort of talk makes them sick," they say. And half of you already want to ask me, "I wonder how'd you feel about forgiving the Gestapo if you were a Pole or a Jew?"

So do I. I wonder very much. Just as when Christianity tells me that I must not deny my religion even to save myself from death by torture, I wonder very much what I should do when it came to the point. I am not trying to tell you . . . what I can do—I can do precious little—I am telling you what Christianity is. I did not invent it. And there, right in the middle of it, I find, "Forgive us our sins as we forgive those that sin against us." There is no slightest suggestion that we are offered forgiveness on any other terms. It is made perfectly clear that if we do not forgive we shall not be forgiven. There are no two ways about it. What are we to do?

It is going to be hard enough, anyway, but I think there are two things we can do to make it easier. When you start mathematics you do not begin with calculus; you begin with simple addition. In the same way, if we really want (but all depends on really wanting) to learn how to forgive, perhaps we had better start with something easier than the Gestapo. One might start with forgiving one's husband or wife, or parents or children, or the nearest N.C.O., for something they have done or said in the last week. That will probably keep us busy for the moment. And secondly, we might try to understand exactly what loving your neighbor as yourself means. I have to love him as I love myself. Well, how exactly do I love myself?

Now that I come to think of it, I have not exactly got a feeling of fondness or affection for myself, and I do not even always enjoy my own society. So apparently "love your neighbor" does not mean "feel fond of him." or "find him attractive." I ought to have seen that before, because, of course, you cannot feel fond of a person by trying. Do I think well of myself, think myself a nice chap? Well, I am afraid I sometimes do (and those are, no doubt, my worst moments), but that is not why I love myself. In fact, it is the other way round: my self-love makes me think myself nice, but thinking myself nice is not why I love myself. So loving my enemies does not apparently mean thinking them nice either. That is an enormous relief. For a good many people imagine that forgiving your enemies means making out that they are really not such bad fellows after all, when it is quite plain that they are. Go a step further. In my most clear-sighted moments not only do I not think myself a nice man, but I know that I am a very nasty one. I can look at some of the things I have done with loathing and horror. So apparently I am allowed to loathe and hate some of the things my enemies do. Now that I come to think of it, I remember Christian teachers telling me long ago that I must hate a bad man's actions, but not hate the bad man: or, as they would say, hate the sin but not the sinner.

For a long time I used to think this a silly, straw-splitting distinction: how could you hate what a man did and not hate the man? But years later it occurred to me that there was one man to whom I had been doing this all my life—namely myself. However much I might dislike my own cowardice or conceit or greed, I went on loving myself. There had never been the slightest difficulty about it. In fact, the very reason why I hated the things was that I loved the man. Just because I loved myself, I was sorry to find that I was the sort of man who did those things. Consequently, Christianity does not want us to reduce by one atom the hatred we feel for cruelty and treachery. We ought to hate them. Not one word of what we have said about them needs to be unsaid. But it does want us to hate them in the same way in which we hate things in ourselves: being sorry that the man should have done such things, and hoping, if it is anyway possible, that somehow, sometime, somewhere, he can be cured and made human again.

— *C. S. Lewis*

The Joyful Christian
New York: Macmillan Publishing Co., Inc.,

Forgive Our Sins As We Forgive

"Forgive our sins as we forgive,"
You taught us, Lord, to pray;
but You alone can grant
us grace to live the words
we say.

How can Your pardon reach and
bless the unforgiving heart
that broods on wrongs
and will not let old bitterness
depart?

In blazing light Your cross
reveals the truth we dimly knew:
what trivial debts are
owed to us, how great our debt
to you!

Lord, cleanse the depths within
our souls, and bid resentment cease;
then, bound to all in
bonds of love, our lives will spread
your peace.

— *Carol Owens*

United Methodist Hymnal

Volunteer Slaves

"Slave" is not a word most of us nowadays "feel comfortable"
with. It is significant that most modern Bible translations use "servant"
instead. For a slave is not his own, has no rights whatsoever, is not in
charge of what happens to him, makes no choices about what he will

do or how he is to serve, is not recognized, appreciated, thanked or even (except by his absence) noticed at all.

Once we give up our slavery to the world, which is a cruel master indeed, to become Christ's bondslave, we live out our servitude to Him by glad service to others. This volunteer slavery cannot be taken advantage of—we have chosen to surrender everything for love. It is a wholly different thing from forced labor. It is, in fact, the purest joy when it is most unobserved, most unself-conscious, most simple, most freely offered.

Lord, break the chains that hold me to myself; free me to be Your happy slave—that is, to be the happy foot-washer of anyone today who needs his feet washed, his supper cooked, his faults overlooked, his work commended, his failure forgiven, his griefs consoled, or his button sewed on. Let me not imagine that my love for You is very great if I am unwilling to do for a human being something very small.

— *Elizabeth Elliot*

The Worst Disease

I have come more and more to realize that being unwanted is the worst disease that any human being can ever experience. Nowadays we have found medicine for leprosy, and lepers can be cured. There's medicine for TB, and consumption can be cured. But for being unwanted, except there are willing hands to serve and there's a loving heart to love, I don't think this terrible disease can be cured.

— *Mother Teresa*

Encourage Him

God employs His people to encourage one another. He did not say to an angel, "Gabriel, my servant Joshua is about to lead My people into Canaan—go, encourage him." God never works needless miracles; if His purposes can be accomplished by ordinary means, He will not use a miraculous agency. Gabriel would not have been half so well-fitted for the work as Moses. A brother's sympathy is more precious than an angel's embassy. The angel, swift of wing, had better known the Master's bidding than the people's tempter. An angel had never experienced the hardness of the road, nor seen the fiery serpents, nor had he led the stiff-necked multitude in the wilderness as Moses had done. We should be glad that God usually works for man by man. It forms a bond of brotherhood, and being mutually dependent on one another, we are fused more completely into one family. Brethren, take the text as God's message to you. Labour to help others, and especially strive to encourage them. Talk cheerily to the young and anxious enquirer, lovingly try to remove stumbling-blocks out of his way. When you find a spark of grace in the heart, kneel down and blow it into a flame. Leave the young believer to discover the roughness of the road by degrees, but tell him of the strength which dwells in God, of the sureness of the promise, and of the charms of communion with Christ. Aim to comfort the sorrowful, and to animate the desponding. Speak a word in season to him who is weary, and encourage those who are fearful to go on their way with gladness. God encourages you by His promises; Christ encourages you as He points to the heaven He has won for you, and the Spirit encourages you as He works in you to will and to do of His own will and pleasure. Imitate divine wisdom, and encourage others, according to the word of this evening.

— Charles H. Spurgeon

Cheer the Lonely Heart

I remember hearing of a man in one of the hospitals who received a bouquet of flowers from the Flower Mission. He looked at the beautiful bouquet and said: "Well, if I had known that a bunch of flowers could do a fellow so much good, I would have sent some myself when I was well." If people only knew how they might cheer some lonely heart and lift up some drooping spirit, or speak some word that shall be lasting in its effects for all coming time, they would be up and about it.

— Dwight L. Moody

The D. L. Moody Year Book
Selected by Emma Moody Fitt
New York: Fleming H. Revell, 1900

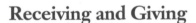

Receiving and Giving

What makes the Dead Sea dead? Because it is all the time receiving, but never giving out anything. Why is it that many Christians are cold? Because they are all the time receiving, never giving out.

— Dwight L. Moody

The D. L. Moody Year Book
Selected by Emma Moody Fitt
New York: Fleming H. Revell, 1900

My Creed

I would be true, for there are those who trust me;
    I would be pure, for there are those who care;
I would be strong, for there is much to suffer;
    I would be brave, for there is much to dare.
I would be friend of all—the foe, the friendless;
    I would be giving, and forget the gift.
I would be humble, for I know my weakness;
    I would look up—and laugh—and love—and lift.

— Howard Arnold Walter

Poems That Live Forever
Selected by Hazel Felleman
Doubleday, 1965

Sacrifice for Others

Look around you, first in your own family, then among your friends and neighbors, and see whether there be not someone whose little burden you can lighten, whose little cares you may lessen, whose little pleasures you can promote, whose little wants and wishes you can gratify. Giving up cheerfully our own occupations to attend to others, is one of the little kindnesses and self-denials. Doing little things that nobody likes to do, but which must be done by someone, is another. It may seem to many, that if they avoid little unkindnesses, they must necessarily be doing all that is right to their family and friends; but it is not enough to abstain from sharp words, sneering tones, petty contradiction, or daily little selfish cares; we must be active and earnest in kindness, not merely passive and inoffensive.

— Little Things, 1852

Joy and Strength
Mary Wilder Tileston
Worldwide Publications, 1986

A Story of Kindness and Family Loyalty: The Book of Ruth

Long ago when judges ruled in Israel, a man named Elimelech, from Bethlehem, left the country because of a famine and moved to the land of Moab. With him were his wife, Naomi, and his two sons, Mahlon and Chilion. During the time of their residence there, Elimelech died and Naomi was left with her two sons.

These young men, Mahlon and Chilion, married girls of Moab, Orpah and Ruth. But later, both men died, so that Naomi was left alone, without her husband or sons. She decided to return to Israel with her daughters-in-law, for she had heard that the Lord had blessed his people by giving them good crops again.

But after they had begun their homeward journey, she changed her mind and said to her two daughters-in-law, "Why don't you return to your parents' homes instead of coming with me? And may the Lord reward you for your faithfulness to your husbands and to me. And may he bless you with another happy marriage." Then she kissed them and they all broke down and cried.

"No," they said. "We want to go with you to your people."

But Naomi replied, "It is better for you to return to your own people. Do I have younger sons who could grow up to be your husbands? No, my daughters, return to your parents' homes, for I am too old to have a husband. And even if that were possible, and I became pregnant tonight, and bore sons, would you wait for them to grow up? No, of course not, my daughters; oh, how I grieve for you that the Lord has punished me in a way that injures you."

And again they cried together, and Orpah kissed her mother-in-law good-bye, and returned to her childhood home; but Ruth insisted on staying with Naomi.

"See," Naomi said to her, "your sister-in-law has gone back to her people and to her gods; you should do the same."

But Ruth replied, "Don't make me leave you, for I want to go wherever you go, and to live wherever you live; your people shall be my people, and your God shall be my God; I want to die where you die, and be buried there. May the Lord do terrible things to me if I allow anything but death to separate us."

And when Naomi saw that Ruth had made up her mind and could not be persuaded otherwise, she stopped urging her. So they both came to Bethlehem and the entire village was stirred by their arrival.

"Is it really Naomi?" the women asked.

But she told them, "Don't call me Naomi. Call me Mara," (Naomi means "pleasant"; Mara means "bitter") "for Almighty God has dealt me bitter blows. I went out full and the Lord has brought me home empty; why should you call me Naomi when the Lord has turned his back on me and sent such calamity!"

(Their return from Moab and arrival in Bethlehem was at the beginning of the barley harvest.)

Now Naomi had an in-law there in Bethlehem who was a very wealthy man. His name was Boaz.

One day Ruth said to Naomi, "Perhaps I can go out into the fields of some kind man to glean the free grain behind his reapers."

And Naomi said, "All right, dear daughter. Go ahead."

So she did. And as it happened, the field where she found herself belonged to Boaz, this relative of Naomi's husband.

Boaz arrived from the city while she was there. After exchanging greetings with the reapers he said to his foreman, "Hey, who's that girl over there?"

And the foreman replied, "It's that girl from the land of Moab who came back with Naomi. She asked me this morning if she could pick up the grains dropped by the reapers, and she has been at it ever since except for a few minutes' rest over there in the shade."

Boaz went over and talked to her. "Listen, my child," he said to her. "Stay right here with us to glean; don't think of going to any other fields. Stay right behind my women workers; I have warned the young men not to bother you; when you are thirsty, go and help yourself to the water."

She thanked him warmly. "How can you be so kind to me?" she asked. "You must know I am only a foreigner."

"Yes, I know," Boaz replied, "and I also know about all the love and kindness you have shown your mother-in-law since the death of your husband, and how you left your father and mother in your own land and have come here to live among strangers. May the Lord God of Israel, under whose wings you have come to take refuge, bless you for it."

"Oh, thank you, sir," she replied. "You are so good to me, and I'm not even one of your workers!"

At lunch time Boaz called to her, "Come and eat with us."

So she sat with his reapers and he gave her food, more than she could eat. And when she went back to work again, Boaz told his young men to let her glean right among the sheaves without stopping her, and to snap off some heads of barley and drop them on purpose for her to glean, and not to make any remarks. So she worked there all day, and in the evening when she had beaten out the barley she had gleaned, it came to a whole bushel! She carried it back into the city and gave it to her mother-in-law, with what was left of her lunch.

"So much!" Naomi exclaimed. "Where in the world did you glean today? Praise the Lord for whoever was so kind to you." So Ruth told her mother-in-law all about it, and mentioned that the owner of the field was Boaz.

"Praise the Lord for a man like that! God has continued his kindness to us as well as to your dead husband!" Naomi cried excitedly. "Why, that man is one of our closest relatives!"

"Well," Ruth told her, "he said to come back and stay close behind his reapers until the entire field is harvested."

"This is wonderful!" Naomi exclaimed. "Do as he has said. Stay with his girls right through the whole harvest; you will be safer there than in any other field!"

So Ruth did, and gleaned with them until the end of the barley harvest, and then the wheat harvest, too.

One day Naomi said to Ruth, "My dear, isn't it time that I try to find a husband for you, and get you happily married again? The man I'm thinking of is Boaz! He has been so kind to us, and he is a close relative. I happen to know that he will be winnowing barley tonight out on the threshing-floor. Now do what I tell you—bathe and put on some perfume and some nice clothes and go on down to the threshing-floor; but don't let him see you until he has finished his supper. Notice where he lies down to sleep; then go and lift the cover off his feet and lie down there, and he will tell you what to do concerning marriage."

And Ruth replied, "All right. I'll do whatever you say."

So she went down to the threshing-floor that night and followed her mother-in-law's instructions. After Boaz had finished a good meal, he lay down very contentedly beside a heap of grain and went to sleep. Then Ruth came quietly and lifted the covering off his feet and lay there. Suddenly, around midnight, he wakened and sat up, startled. There was a woman lying at his feet!

"Who are you?" he demanded.

"It's I, sir—Ruth," she replied. "Make me your wife according to God's law, for you are my close relative."

"Thank God for a girl like you!" he exclaimed. "For you are being even kinder to Naomi now than before. Naturally you'd prefer a younger man, even though poor. But you have put aside your personal desires [so you can give Naomi an heir by marrying me]. Now don't worry about a thing, my child; I'll handle all the details, for everyone knows what a wonderful person you are. But there is one problem. It's true that I am a close relative, but there is someone else who is more closely related to you than I am. Stay here tonight, and in the morning I'll talk to him, and if he will marry you, fine; let him do his duty; but if he won't, then I will, I swear by Jehovah; lie down until the morning."

So she lay at his feet until the morning and was up early, before daybreak, for he had said to her, "Don't let it be known that a woman was here at the threshing-floor."

"Bring your shawl," he told her. Then he tied up a bushel and a half of barley in it as a present for her mother-in-law, and laid it on her back. Then she returned to the city.

"Well, what happened, dear?" Naomi asked her when she arrived home. She told Naomi everything and gave her the barley from Boaz, and mentioned his remark that she mustn't go home without a present.

Then Naomi said to her, "Just be patient until we hear what happens, for Boaz won't rest until he has followed through on this. He'll settle it today."

So Boaz went down to the market place and found the relative he had mentioned.

"Say, come over here," he called to him. "I want to talk to you a minute."

So they sat down together. Then Boaz called for ten of the chief men of the village, and asked them to sit as witnesses.

Boaz said to his relative, "You know Naomi, who came back to us from Moab. She is selling our brother Elimelech's property. I felt that I should speak to you about it so that you can buy it if you wish, with these respected men as witnesses. If you want it, let me know right away, for if you don't take it, I will. You have the first right to purchase it and I am next."

The man replied, "All right, I'll buy it."

Then Boaz told him, "Your purchase of the land from Naomi requires your marriage to Ruth so that she can have children to carry on her husband's name, and to inherit the land."

"Then I can't do it," the man replied. "For her son would become an heir to my property, too; you buy it."

In those days it was the custom in Israel for a man transferring a right of purchase to pull off his sandal and hand it to the other party; this publicly validated the transaction. So, as the man said to Boaz, "You buy it for yourself," he drew off his sandal.

Then Boaz said to the witnesses and to the crowd standing around, "You have seen that today I have bought all the property of Elimelech, Chilion, and Mahlon, from Naomi, and that with it I have purchased Ruth the Moabitess, the widow of Mahlon, to be my wife, so that she can have a son to carry on the family name of her dead husband."

And all the people standing there, and the witnesses replied, "We are witnesses. May the Lord make this woman, who has now come into your home, as fertile as Rachel and Leah, from whom all the nation of Israel descended! May you be a great and successful man in Bethlehem, and may the descendants the Lord will give you from this young woman be as numerous and honorable as those of our ancestor Perez, the son of Tamar and Judah."

So Boaz married Ruth, and when he slept with her, the Lord gave her a son.

And the women of the city said to Naomi, "Bless the Lord who has given you this little grandson; may he be famous in Israel. May he restore your youth and take care of you in your old age; for he is the son of your daughter-in-law who loves you so much, and who has been kinder to you than seven sons!"

Naomi took care of the baby, and the neighbor women said, "Now at last Naomi has a son again!"

And they named him Obed. He was the father of Jesse and grandfather of King David.

This is the family tree of Boaz, beginning with his ancestor Perez: Perez, Hezron, Ram, Amminadab, Nashon, Salmon, Boaz, Obed, Jesse, David.

— *Ruth* (TLB)
HOLY BIBLE

Do What I Can

If I can stop one heart from breaking,
I shall not live in vain:
If I can ease one life the aching,
Or cool one pain,
Or help one fainting robin
Unto his nest again,
I shall not live in vain.

— Emily Dickinson

One Hundred and One Famous Poems
An Anthology Compiled by Roy J. Cook
Chicago: Contemporary Books, Inc., 1958

Don't Just Preach It—Do It

All of my grandparents lived out their faith on the Plains. My paternal grandparents, the Reverend John Luther Norris and his wife, Beatrice, served twelve Methodist churches in South Dakota and several more in Iowa. Prairie people have long memories, and they still tell stories about my grandfather's kindness. One man recalls that after his wife died, leaving him with several small children, he began drinking heavily. My grandfather came to his house one day to do the family's laundry, and though the man was drinking the whole time, my grandfather never preached about it; he just kept talking to him about his plans for the future, and, as he put it, "helped me straighten up my life."

— Kathleen Norris

Dakota: A Spiritual Geography
New York: Houghton Mifflin Co.

Chapter 6

GOODNESS

"*A merry heart does good, like medicine*"
(Proverbs 17:22 NKJV).

While we have talked at length throughout this volume about virtues being "moral goodness" according to biblical standards, the goodness listed as part of the fruit of the Holy Spirit in Galatians 5:22-23 is a very specific goodness. The Greek word is "agathosune" (pronounced ag-ath-o-soo'-nay). It is character that is energized to display an active goodness. This is goodness that "does good" toward others and in relationship to others.

Goodness requires both courage and restraint. It is an intentional act. And ultimately, it is our strength of character.

The truly good person does whatever is necessary to right a wrong. But goodness must be tempered with kindness. Jesus alone is our example. Jesus moved in kindness toward people, but when confronted with evil, He responded with goodness. His words and actions were always intended to move evil doers toward God. By conviction—not away from Him through harmful condemnation.

Love At Work

Goodness is love in action, love with its hand to the plow, love with the burden on its back, love following His footsteps who went about continually doing good.

— *James Hamilton*

The Encyclopedia of Religious Quotations
Edited and Compiled by Frank S. Mead
Fleming H. Revell Co., 1965

Doing Good

"Who went about doing good" — Acts 10:38

Few words, but yet an exquisite miniature of the Lord Jesus Christ. There are not many touches, but they are the strokes of a master's pencil. Of the Saviour and only of the Saviour is it true in the fullest, broadest, and most unqualified sense. "He went about doing good." From this description it is evident that He did good personally. The evangelists constantly tell us that He touched the leper with His own finger, that He anointed the eyes of the blind, and that in cases where He was asked to speak the word only at a distance, He did not usually comply, but went Himself to the sick bed, and there personally wrought the cure. A lesson to us, if we would do good, to do it ourselves. Give alms with your own hand; a kind look, or word, will enhance the value of the gift. Speak to a friend about his soul; your loving appeal will have more influence than a whole library of tracts. Our Lord's mode of doing good sets forth His incessant activity! He did not only the good which came close to hand, but He "went about" on His errands of mercy. Throughout the whole land of Judea there was scarcely a village or a hamlet which was not gladdened by the sight of Him. How this reproves the creeping, loitering manner in which many professors serve the Lord. Let us gird up the loins of our mind, and be not weary in well doing. Does not the text imply that

Jesus Christ went out of His way to do good? "He went about doing good." He was never deterred by danger or difficulty. He sought out the objects of His gracious intentions. So must we. If old plans will not answer, we must try new ones, for fresh experiments sometimes achieve more than regular methods. Christ's perseverance, and the unity of His purpose, are also hinted at, and the practical application of the subject may be summed up in the words, "He hath left us an example that we should follow in His steps."

— *Charles H. Spurgeon*

Taken from *Morning and Evening Devotions: An Updated Edition of the Classic Devotional in Today's Language* by C. H. Spurgeon. Copyright © 1987 by Thomas Nelson Publishers. Used by permission of Thomas Nelson Publishers.

The Source of Goodness

Men are ever discussing the problem of evil. If there be a God, all-good and all-powerful, why does He allow so many bad things to happen? That is a real question. But the mystery of evil in a world ruled by God is not so baffling as the mystery of goodness in a godless world. We can understand how a fatherly God must give man certain freedom in order to develop his character and how man may misuse his liberty in the excesses of evil, but if there be no God, what makes a man sacrifice for a noble cause or pray for his crucifiers?

We can explain evil as the absence or perversion of good as we explain darkness as the absence of light, but we find it as difficult to account for goodness without a good-giving God as we find it hard to account for light without a light-radiating sun. Goodness and delight are positive; evil and darkness are negative. A bad man may be understood as a good man gone wrong, but a good man is somewhat more than an evil person in reverse. Hate may be explained as love turned sour, but love is more than sweetened bitterness. A hurricane is an orderly wind gone berserk, but a rainbow is not an artificially painted cloud. Baffling indeed is the mystery of life's negative forces which turn good into evil, but the deeper problem is to explain who provides the positive forces of good.

And goodness is not only the positive but also the predominant force. The bad deeds of men are still so rare that they make the news columns. The ruthless forces of evil turn the good earth into bloody battlefields, but law and order are still the general rule. The plotters of evil are outnumbered by the planners of good. Good Samaritanism is still to be found amid the roughest drivers of our crowded highways, and the milk of human kindness has not disappeared from the doorsteps of our congested cities.

Since water does not rise higher than its source, we believe that the human manifestations of goodness are to be explained only by a Divine Creator in whom are the springs of goodness.

— *Ralph W. Sockman D.D.*

From *How To Believe* by Ralph W. Sockman, D.D. Copyright © 1953 by Ralph W. Sockman. Used by permission of Doubleday, a division of Bantam Doubleday Dell Publishing Group, Inc.

Only From the Spirit

As Christians we have no alternative but to march to the drumbeat of the Holy Spirit, following the measured steps of goodness, which pleases God.

We can do good deeds, and by practicing principles of goodness can witness to those around us that we have something "different" in our lives—perhaps something they themselves would like to possess. We may even be able to show others how to practice the principles of goodness in their own lives. But the Bible says, *"Your goodness is as a morning cloud, and as the early dew it goeth away"* (Hosea 6:4). True goodness is a "fruit of the Spirit," and our efforts to achieve it in our own strength alone can never succeed.

We should be careful that any goodness the world may see in us is the genuine fruit of the Spirit and not a counterfeit substitute, lest we unwittingly lead someone astray.

— Billy Graham

Unto the Hills
Billy Graham, 1986, Word Inc., Dallas, Texas.

Community of Light

During a riot at Washington, DC's Lorton prison complex, inmates torched several buildings; armed, menacing gangs roamed the grounds. But in the main prison yard a group of Christian inmates stood in a huge circle, arms linked, singing hymns. Their circle surrounded a group of guards and prisoners who had sought protection from the rioting inmates. These Christians were a community of light, and lives were saved.

In prison, the contrast is sharp between dark and light. Choices for Christian inmates are usually clear-cut. Yet most of us in the mainstream of Western culture live in shades of gray. It's comfortable to adopt the surrounding cultural values. Yet stand apart we must.

For as the church maintains its independence from culture, it is best able to affect culture. When the Church serves as the Church, in firm allegiance to the unseen kingdom of God, God uses it in this world: first, as a model of the values of His kingdom, and second, as His missionary to culture.

— Charles Colson

Reprinted from *Against the Night — Living in the New Dark Ages*
by Charles Colson with Ellen Santilli-Vaughn.
Copyright © 1989 by Charles Colson.
Used by permission of Servant Publications.

The Sermon on the Mount

And Jesus was going about in all Galilee, teaching in their synagogues, and proclaiming the gospel of the kingdom, and healing every kind of disease and every kind of sickness among the people.

And the news about Him went out into all Syria; and they brought to Him all who were ill, taken with various diseases and pains, demoniacs, epileptics, paralytics; and He healed them. And great multitudes followed Him from Galilee and Decapolis and Jerusalem and Judea and from beyond the Jordan. And when He saw the multitudes, He went up on the mountain; and after He sat down, His disciples came to Him. And opening His mouth He began to teach them saying,

"Blessed are the poor in spirit, for theirs is the kingdom of heaven.

"Blessed are those who mourn, for they shall be comforted.

"Blessed are the gentle, for they shall inherit the earth.

"Blessed are those who hunger and thirst for righteousness, for they shall be satisfied.

"Blessed are the merciful, for they shall receive mercy.

"Blessed are the pure in heart, for they shall see God.

"Blessed are the peacemakers, for they shall be called sons of God.

"Blessed are those who have been persecuted for the sake of righteousness, for theirs is the kingdom of heaven.

"Blessed are you when men cast insults at you, and persecute you, and say all kinds of evil against you falsely, on account of Me. Rejoice, and be glad, for your reward in heaven is great, for so they persecuted the prophets who were before you.

"You are the salt of the earth; but if the salt has become tasteless, how will it be made salty again? It is good for nothing any more, except to be thrown out and trampled under foot by men.

"You are the light of the world. A city set on a hill cannot be hidden. Nor do men light a lamp, and put it under the peck-measure, but on the lampstand; and it gives light to all who are in the house. Let your light shine before men in such a way that they may see your good works, and glorify your Father who is in heaven.

"Do not think that I came to abolish the Law or the Prophets; I did not come to abolish, but to fulfill. For truly I say to you, until heaven and earth pass away, not the smallest letter or stroke shall pass away from the Law, until all is accomplished.

"Whoever then annuls one of the least of these commandments, and so teaches others, shall be called least in the kingdom of heaven; but whoever keeps and teaches them, he shall be called great in the kingdom of heaven. For I say to you, that unless your righteousness surpasses that of the scribes and Pharisees, you shall not enter the kingdom of heaven.

"You have heard that the ancients were told, 'YOU SHALL NOT COMMIT MURDER' and 'Whoever commits murder shall be liable to the court.' But I say to you that every one who is angry with his brother shall be guilty before the court; and whoever shall say to his brother, 'Raca,' shall be guilty before the supreme court; and whoever shall say, 'You fool,' shall be guilty enough to go into the fiery hell.

"If therefore you are presenting your offering at the altar, and there remember that your brother has something against you, leave your offering there before the altar, and go your way; first be reconciled to your brother, and then come and present your offering.

"Make friends quickly with your opponent at law while you are with him on the way, in order that your opponent may not deliver you to the judge, and the judge to the officer, and you be thrown into prison. Truly I say to you, you shall not come out of there, until you have paid up the last cent.

"You have heard that it was said, 'YOU SHALL NOT COMMIT ADULTERY'; but I say to you, that every one who looks on a woman to lust for her has committed adultery with her already in his heart.

"And if your right eye makes you stumble, tear it out, and throw it from you; for it is better for you that one of the parts of your body perish, than for your whole body to be thrown into hell. And if your right hand makes you stumble, cut it off, and throw it from you; for it is better for you that one of the parts of your body perish, than for your whole body to go into hell.

"And it was said, 'WHOEVER DIVORCES HIS WIFE, LET HIM GIVE HER A CERTIFICATE OF DISMISSAL'; but I say to you that every one who divorces his wife, except for the cause of unchastity, makes her commit adultery; and whoever marries a divorced woman commits adultery.

"Again, you have heard that the ancients were told, 'YOU SHALL NOT MAKE FALSE VOWS, BUT SHALL FULFILL YOUR VOWS TO THE LORD.' But I say to you, make no oath at all, either by heaven, for it is the throne of God, or by the earth, for it is the footstool of His feet, or by Jerusalem, *for it is THE CITY OF THE GREAT KING. Nor shall you make an oath by your head, for you cannot make one hair white or black. But let your statement be, 'Yes, yes' or 'No, no'; and anything beyond these is of evil.*

"You have heard that it was said, 'AN EYE FOR AN EYE, AND A TOOTH FOR A TOOTH.' But I say to you, do not resist him who is evil; but whoever slaps you on your right cheek, turn to him the other also. And if any one wants to sue you, and take your shirt, let him have your coat also. And whoever shall force you to go one mile, go with him two. Give to him who asks of you, and do not turn away from him who wants to borrow from you.

"You have heard that it was said, 'YOU SHALL LOVE YOUR NEIGHBOR, AND HATE YOUR ENEMY.' But I say to you, love your enemies, and pray for those who persecute you in order that you may be sons of your Father who is in heaven; for He causes His sun to rise on the evil and the good, and sends rain on the righteous and the unrighteous. For if you love those who love you, what reward have you? Do not even the tax-gatherers do the same? And if you greet your brothers only, what do you do more than others? Do not even the Gentiles do the same? Therefore you are to be perfect, as your heavenly Father is perfect.

"Beware of practicing your righteousness before men to be noticed by them; otherwise you have no reward with your Father who is in heaven.

"When therefore you give alms, do not sound a trumpet before you, as the hypocrites do in the synagogues and in the streets, that they may be honored by men. Truly I say to you, they have their reward in full. But when you give alms, do not let your left hand know what your right hand is doing that your alms may be in secret; and your Father who sees in secret will repay you.

"And when you pray, you are not to be as the hypocrites; for they love to stand and pray in the synagogues and on the street corners, in order to be seen by men. Truly I say to you, they have their reward in full. But you, when you pray, GO INTO YOUR INNER ROOM, AND WHEN YOU HAVE SHUT YOUR DOOR, pray to your Father who is in secret, and your Father who sees in secret will repay you. And when you are praying, do not use meaningless repetition, as the Gentiles do, for they suppose that they will be heard for their many words. Therefore do not be like them; for your Father knows what you need, before you ask Him. Pray, then, in this way:

'Our Father who art in heaven,
            Hallowed be Thy name.
Thy kingdom come,
Thy will be done,
On earth as it is in heaven.
Give us this day our daily bread.
And forgive us our debts, as we
            also have forgiven our debtors.
And do not lead us into temptation,
            but deliver us from evil. [For
            Thine is the kingdom, and the
            power, and the glory, forever.
            Amen.]'

"For if you forgive men for their transgressions, your heavenly Father will also forgive you. But if you do not forgive men, then your Father will not forgive your transgressions.

"And whenever you fast, do not put on a gloomy face as the hypocrites do, for they neglect their appearance in order to be seen fasting by men. Truly I say to you, they have their reward in full. But you, when you fast, anoint your head, and wash your face so that you may not be seen fasting by men, but by your Father who is in secret; and your Father who sees in secret will repay you.

"Do not lay up for yourselves treasures upon earth, where moth and rust destroy, and where thieves break in and steal. But lay up for yourselves treasures in heaven, where neither moth nor rust destroys, and where thieves do not break in or steal; for where your treasure is, there will your heart be also.

"The lamp of the body is the eye; if therefore your eye is clear, your whole body will be full of light. But if your eye is bad, your whole body will be full of darkness. If therefore the light that is in you is darkness, how great is the darkness!

"No one can serve two masters; for either he will hate the one and love the other, or he will hold to one and despise the other. You cannot serve God and mammon. For this reason I say to you, do not be anxious for your life, as to what you shall eat, or what you shall drink; nor for your body, as to what you shall put on. Is not life more than food, and the body than clothing?

"Look at the birds of the air, that they do not sow, neither do they reap, nor gather into barns, and yet your heavenly Father feeds them. Are you not worth much more than they? And which of you by being anxious can add a single cubit to his life's span?

"And why are you anxious about clothing? Observe how the lilies of the field grow; they do not toil nor do they spin, yet I say to you that even Solomon in all his glory did not clothe himself like one of these. But if God so arrays the grass of the field, which is alive today and tomorrow is thrown into the furnace, will He not much more do so for you, O men of little faith? Do not be anxious then, saying, 'What shall we eat?' or 'What shall we drink?' or 'With what shall we clothe ourselves?' For all these things the Gentiles eagerly seek; for your heavenly Father knows that you need all these things. But seek first His kingdom and His righteousness; and all these things shall be added to you. Therefore do not be anxious for tomorrow; for tomorrow will care for itself. Each day has enough trouble of its own.

"Do not judge lest you be judged yourselves. For in the way you judge, you will be judged; and by your standard of measure, it shall be measured to you.

"And why do you look at the speck in your brother's eye, but do not notice the log that is in your own eye? Or how can you say to your brother, 'Let me take the speck out of your eye,' and behold, the log is in your own eye? You hypocrite, first take the log out of your own eye, and then you will see clearly enough to take the speck out of your brother's eye.

"Do not give what is holy to dogs, and do not throw your pearls before swine, lest they trample them under their feet, and turn and tear you to pieces.

"Ask, and it shall be given to you; seek, and you shall find; knock, and it shall be opened to you. For every one who asks receives, and he who seeks finds, and to him who knocks it shall be opened.

"Or what man is there among you, when his son shall ask him for a loaf, will give him a stone? Or if he shall ask for a fish, he will not give him a snake, will he? If you then, being evil, know how to give good gifts to your children, how much more shall your Father who is in heaven give what is good to those who ask Him! However you want men to treat you, so treat them, for this is the law and the prophets.

"Enter by the narrow gate; for the gate is wide, and the way is broad that leads to destruction, and many are those who enter by it. For

the gate is small, and the way is narrow that leads to life, and few are those who find it.

"Beware of false prophets, who come to you in sheep's clothing, but inwardly are ravenous wolves. You will know them by their fruits. Grapes are not gathered from thorn bushes, nor figs from thistles, are they? Even so, every good tree bears good fruit, but the rotten tree bears bad fruit. A good tree cannot produce bad fruit, nor can a rotten tree produce good fruit. Every tree that does not bear good fruit is cut down and thrown into the fire. So then, you will know them by their fruits.

"Not every one who says to Me, 'Lord, Lord,' will enter the kingdom of heaven; but he who does the will of My Father who is in heaven. Many will say to Me on that day, 'Lord, Lord, did we not prophesy in Your name, and in Your name cast out demons, and in Your name perform many miracles? And then I will declare to them, 'I never knew you; DEPART FROM ME, YOU WHO PRACTICE LAWLESSNESS.'

"Therefore every one who hears these words of Mine, and acts upon them, may be compared to a wise man, who built his house upon the rock. And the rain descended, and the floods came, and the winds blew, and burst against that house; and yet it did not fall, for it had been founded upon the rock. And every one who hears these words of Mine, and does not act upon them, will be like a foolish man, who built his house upon the sand. And the rain descended, and the floods came, and the winds blew, and burst against that house; and it fell, and great was its fall."

The result was that when Jesus had finished these words, the multitudes were amazed at His teaching; for He was teaching them as one having authority, and not as their scribes.

— Matthew 4:23-7:29 (NASB)
HOLY BIBLE

Good Works

First, then, we are about to answer the question, What are good works? Now, I daresay we shall offend many here when we tell them what good works are; for in our opinion good works are the rarest things in the world, and we believe we might walk for many a mile before we should see a good work at all. We use the word good now in its proper sense. There are many works which are good enough between man and man, but we shall use the word good in a higher sense today as regards God. We think we shall be able to show you that there are very few good works anywhere, and that there are none out of the pale of Christ's Church. We think, if we read Scripture rightly, that no work can be good unless it is commanded of God. How this cuts off a large portion of what men will do in order to win salvation! The Pharisee said he tithed mint, anise, and cummin; could he prove that God commanded him to tithe his mint, his anise, and his cummin? Perhaps not. He said he fasted so many times a week: could he prove that God told him to fast? If not, his fasting was no obedience. If I do a thing that I am not commanded to do, I do not obey in doing it. Vain, then, are all the pretenses of men, that by mortifying their bodies, by denying their flesh, by doing this, that, or the other, they shall therefore win the favour of God. No work is good unless God has commanded it. A man may build a long row of almshouses, but if he builds without reference to the commandment, he has performed no good work.

Again: nothing is a good work unless it is done with a good motive; and there is no motive which can be said to be good but the glory of God. He who performs good works with a view to save himself, does not do them from a good motive, because his motive is selfish. He who does them also to gain the esteem of his fellows and for the good of society, has a laudable motive, so far as man is concerned; but it is, after all, an inferior motive. What end had we in view? If for the benefit of our fellow-creatures, then let our fellow-creatures pay us; but that has nought to do with God.

— *C. H. Spurgeon*

The New Park Street Pulpit, Vol. II
Grand Rapids, Mich.: Zondervan Publishing House

God's Goodness

Sovereign redemptive love [of God] is one facet of the quality that Scripture calls God's goodness (Psalm 100:5; Mark 10:18), that is, the glorious kindness and generosity that touches all his creatures (Psalm 145:9, 15-16) and that ought to lead all sinners to repentance. (Romans 2:4). Other aspects of this goodness are the mercy or compassion or pity that shows kindness to persons in distress by rescuing them out of trouble (Psalms 107, 136) and the longsuffering, forbearance, and slowness to anger that continues to show kindness toward persons who have persisted in sinning (Exodus 34:6; Psalm 78:38; John 3:10-4:11; Romans 9:22; 2 Peter 3:9). The supreme expression of God's goodness is still, however, the amazing grace and inexpressible love that shows kindness by saving sinners who deserve only condemnation: saving them, moreover, at the tremendous cost of Christ's death on Calvary (Romans 3:22-24; 5:5-8; 8:32-39; Ephesians 2:1-10; 3:14-18; 5:25-27).

God's faithfulness to His purposes, promises, and people is a further aspect of His goodness and praiseworthiness. Humans lie and break their word; God does neither. In the worst of times it can still be said: "His compassions never fail. . . . Great is your faithfulness" (Lamentations 3:22-23; Psalm 36:5; cf. Psalm 89, especially vv. 1-2, 14, 24, 33, 37, 49). Though God's ways of expressing His faithfulness are sometimes unexpected and bewildering, looking indeed to the casual observer and in the short term more like unfaithfulness, the final testimony of those who walk with God through life's ups and downs is that "every promise has been fulfilled; not one has failed" (Joshua 23:14-15). God's fidelity, along with the other aspects of His gracious goodness as set forth in his Word, is always solid ground on which to rest our faith and hope.

— *J. I. Packer*

Concise Theology
Wheaton, Ill.: Tyndale House Publishers, 1993

Good for Goodness' Sake!

When we feel that God is good—good to us despite everything we have said and done, then we know that mercy takes the shape of goodness. God's goodness is that He knows our need even before we ask Him. God's goodness is that He goes before us to show the way. God's goodness was that at the time humankind deserved it least, He came in Jesus Christ to reveal Himself and to die for the sins of the whole race. He came to make men and women good from the inside.

Goodness is an inside story. We are made good not by our efforts but by the efficacy of the Atonement accomplished by Jesus Christ on the cross. Our status before God is in and through Christ. He accepts us as new creatures, made good on Calvary. We could not dare to come to God apart from the imputed goodness of our vicarious standing through the Savior. The Lord looks at us through the focused lens of Calvary. Our confidence is not in our human facsimiles of goodness, but in our relationship with Christ. We are freed from compulsive efforts to be good enough to deserve love. Instead we can live in the settled security of goodness in Christ!

The goodness of the Lord impels us to do good works. We have been conscripted to serve. Goodness does not make us "goody-goodies," but people who seek to know what is good for all and do it by Christ's power.

— Lloyd John Ogilvie
Current Chaplain, U.S. Senate

Taken from: *Silent Strength for My Life*
by Lloyd John Ogilvie
Harvest House Publishers, 1990
Copyright © 1990 by Harvest House
Publishers, Eugene, Oregon.
Used by permission.

Two Surprises

A workman plied his clumsy spade
    As the sun was going down;
The German King, with a cavalcade,
    On his way to Berlin town,

Reined up his steed at the old man's side.
    "My toiling friend," said he,
"Why not cease work at eventide
    When laborer should be free?"

"I do not slave," the old man said,
    "And I am always free!
Though I work from the time I leave my bed
    Till I can hardly see."

"How much," said the King, "is the grain in a day?"
    "Eight groschens," the man replied.
"And thou canst live on this meager pay?"
    "Like a king," he said with pride.

"Two groschens for me and my wife, good friend,
    And two for a debt I owe;
Two groschens to lend and two to spend,
    For those who can't labor, you know."

"Thy debt?" said the King; to the toiler, "Yea,
    To my mother with age oppressed,
Who cared for me, toiled for me, many a day
    And now hath need of rest."

"To whom dost lend thy daily store?"
    "To my boys—for there schooling; you see,
When I am too feeble to toil any more,
    They will care for their mother and me."

"And thy last two groschens?" the monarch said.
    "My sisters are old and lame;
I give them two groschens for raiment and bread,
    All in the Father's name."

Tears welled up in the good King's eyes.
    "Thou knowest me not," said he;
    "As thou hast given me one surprise,
    Here is another for thee."

"I am the King; give me thy hand"—
    And he heaped it high with gold.
"When more thou needest, I command
    That I at once be told."

"For I would bless with rich reward
    The man who can proudly say
That eight souls he doth keep and guard
    On eight poor groschens a day."

— R. W. McAlpine

Poems That Live Forever
Selected by Hazel Felleman
Doubleday, 1965

Degrees of Giving

A Spanish scholar of the twelfth century, Moses Maimonides, depicts seven steps in what he calls the ladder of charity and giving: The first and lowest degree is to give, but with reluctance. The second is to give cheerfully, but not in proportion to the distress of the sufferer. The third step is to give cheerfully and proportionately, but not until solicited. The fourth is to give cheerfully, proportionately and unsolicitedly, but yourself to put the gift in the poor man's hand, thus exciting in him the painful emotion of shame. The fifth is to know the object of your bounty, but to remain unknown to him. The sixth is to bestow charity in such a way that the benefactor may not know the recipient, nor the recipient his benefactor. The seventh and worthiest step is to anticipate charity by preventing poverty. This is the highest step and summit of charity's golden ladder.

— Paul S. McElroy

Quiet Thoughts
Mount Vernon, N.Y.: Peter Pauper Press

I Want To Walk as a Child of the Light

I want to walk as a child of the light.
I want to follow Jesus.
God set the stars to give light to the world.
The star of my life is Jesus.

I want to see the brightness of God.
I want to look at Jesus.
Clear Sun of Righteousness, shine on my path,
and show me the way to the Father.

I'm looking for the coming of Christ.
I want to be with Jesus.
When we have run with patience the race,
we shall know the joy of Jesus.

Chorus:
In Him there is no darkness at all.
The night and the day are both alike.
The Lamb is the light of the city of God.
Shine in my heart, Lord Jesus.

— Kathleen Thomerson

The United Methodist Hymnal

The Generous Eye

The generous eye and the generous attitude are at the basis of all sound human relationships.

The Norwegians and Swedes live together as brothers. They are different, but underneath is an unbreakable tie that binds them as one people. Why? Well, when Norway wanted her freedom, Sweden gave it, gave it out of the Christian spirit behind the ruling family in Sweden. That generosity, in giving freedom without war or bitterness, has created a basic soundness that flavors all their relationships.

Why are the relationships between Britain and India basically better than with probably any other foreign nation? A few years ago those relationships were bitter, not better. For one thing, the pressure of the Gandhian movement, the spirit of which was depressed in the statement of one of the Gandhian leaders at the time of the height of the struggle: "We can thank our lucky stars that we are fighting the British and not some other nation, for there is something within the British we can appeal to"; in other words, they were trying to see something good within the British character to which they could appeal. A new kind of warfare—looking for good in your enemies! I wrote to the commission arranging the transfer of power: "I can see in your patience and generosity what I would call nothing less than the Christian spirit in public affairs." That double generosity in the British and the Indian made it possible for India, when given her freedom, to decide to stay within the British Commonwealth.

The race relations which I consider the best in the world are between the New Zealander and the Maori. These relationships were laid by the wise statesmanship of a Christian governor and a bishop. They put through legislation that made it impossible for the Maori to alienate his land to the white man, saving him from being a landless pauper. Generosity laid a sound economic basis under their relationships, and so today these two races live side by side in mutual respect and love. A Maori was the Prime Minister of New Zealand, honored and respected. The generous eye filled with light the whole body of human relationships between two diverse races.

But the Maoris, too, were generous, even when bitter fighting was going on in the early days. The Maoris sent word: "White man hungry. Cannot fight well. So we are sending some food to the white man!" The white men couldn't forget, hence one reason for the wise legislation.

One of the most potent forces in the healing between the North and South was the spirit of Abraham Lincoln. He refused a triumphal march into Richmond after the victory. When he arrived on foot, he went to the room where Jefferson Davis had governed the Confederacy and for a long time sat at the desk with his head bowed on his arms, weeping—weeping for the fallen on both sides. That sight of the weeping President broke down more barriers and healed more wounds than all the exhortations to a resumed brotherhood.

— *E. Stanley Jones*

Growing Spiritually
Abingdon Press

The Godly Eye

"The lamp of the body is the eye; if therefore your eye is clear, your whole body will be full of light.

"But if your eye is bad, your whole body will be full of darkness. If therefore the light that is in you is darkness, how great is the darkness!"

— *Matthew 6:22-23* (NASB)
HOLY BIBLE

Stars Still Shine

Were a star quenched on high,
For ages would its light,
Still travelling downward from the sky,
Shine on our mortal sight.

So when a great man dies,
For years beyond our ken,
The light he leaves behind him lies
Upon the paths of men.

— Henry W. Longfellow

The Home Book of Quotations, Classical and Modern, 10th Edition
Selected and Arranged by Burton Stevenson
New York: Dodd, Mead & Co., 1934, 1967

Being Made Good

The spirit makes war on all that is poor, shoddy, showy; weaves the different threads of personality into good material, real hard-wearing solid stuff—and not only in the sphere of behaviour or devotion. It makes human beings into fully living men, not through their own efforts and strivings, but by the penetration of God.

— Evelyn Underhill

The Fruits of the Spirit
London: Longman House, 1949

Good Words

Jesus taught:

"Brood of vipers! How can you, being evil, speak good things? For out of the abundance of the heart the mouth speaks. A good man out of the good treasure of his heart brings forth good things, and an evil man out of the evil treasure brings forth evil things. But I say to you that for every idle word men may speak, they will give account of it in the day of judgment. For by your words you will be justified, and by your words you will be condemned."

— *Matthew 12:34-37* (NKJV)
HOLY BIBLE

Getting and Giving

To get or to give, that is the question. Each individual life should be brought to the judgment seat of the one piercing, determinative question, "Is my ruling passion to get or to give?" On the answer hangs fulfillment or frustration. For men, nations, and civilizations, the fundamental law of human life phrased a thousand times by saints and seers was stated by Jesus of Nazareth in words never surpassed when He declared: "Whosoever will save his life shall lose it; but whosoever shall lose his life for my sake . . . the same shall save it."

The most creative conception that can dawn upon a human, finding himself in the midst of mortal years with their competitive tugs in various directions, is this: "I am here to be something, not to acquire something; I am here to give, not to get." If that is once fully apprehended and accepted, all actions will fall into a master pattern.

The most pernicious aspect of our modern day, with its opulent cornucopia of riches in terms of gadgets, comforts, and amusements, is the attitude of multitudes who are continually measuring their lives by the returns and rewards made to them by people, by society, by government. It is taking the threat of another Holocaust to silence the lusty cry both from those who have much and from those who by comparison have less: "Give me! Give me!" Certainly, in the present-day demand for a paternalistic government, we have raised a generation who think much more of a bill of rights than they do of the bill of responsibilities. But once more we have come upon evil days, when unsatiable selfishness is being hurled back by the bitter harvest of self-seeking and where all may read God's righteous sentence: To survive, give!

In spite of all the glitter and hectic excitement characterizing our Western life, which is reflected in the literature, music, and art of the day, and which displays its phosphorescent rottenness in sex-saturated best sellers, there is little calm, little peace, very little genuine satisfaction in all this that is called life. Getting and spending—that is, spending on self—we have laid waste the soul. As evidence, behold our mental hospitals and psychiatrists' offices swamped by tormented personalities! Even a dominant desire to find personal peace of mind may be naught but the quest of a so-called religion which is ingrown and which itself can become one of the most selfish influences in life.

The New Testament is always warning against the peril of a facile, passive response to the good which men are bent on attaining. There is all the difference in the world between a sponge and a spring. In order to grasp what it wants, a sponge swells up to several times its size. It does that because it is a sponge. What it does is no sign of life, because it is a corpse. But the spring flows along, making the meadows green and giving to all who will partake a refreshing draught from its crystal waters. If a spring becomes stagnant, it commits suicide. The Dead Sea is dead because it takes everything in and gives nothing out. That will kill a sea and all in it. It will kill a life. To give is to find life's purest joy.

One who is counted by many as the greatest human being now alive, Albert Schweitzer, scholar, lecturer, Europe's master organist, in middle life threw everything away the successful years had brought. At last, when he had performed his first operation and had brought a black bundle of suffering humanity from the gates of death back to life, he exclaimed, "I wish my friends everywhere but knew the exquisite joy of an hour like this!" He reached that pinnacle of happiness as all must who find it, not by getting, but by giving.

Here, then, is the secret of an abundant life: to give is to live, and to live is to give. And so,

I give you the end of a golden string,
Only wind it into a ball,
It will lead you in at Heaven's gate,
Built in Jerusalem's wall.

— Frederick Brown Harris

Spires of the Spirit
New York: Abingdon-Cokesbury Press

Good Works

The Christian is in a different position from other people who are trying to be good. They hope, by being good, to please God if there is one; or—if they think there is not—at least they hope to deserve approval from good men. But the Christian thinks any good he does comes from the Christ-life inside him. He does not think God will love us because we are good, but that God will make us good because He loves us.

— C. S. Lewis

Mere Christianity
Harper Collins Ltd.

Come To Thy Senses, Clemens

Clemens has his head full of imaginary piety. He is often proposing to himself what he would do if he had a great estate. He would outdo all charitable men that are gone before him; he would retire from the world; he would have no equipage; he would allow himself only necessaries, that widows and orphans, the sick and distressed, might find relief out of his estate. He tells you that all other ways of spending an estate is folly and madness. Now, Clemens has at present a moderate estate, which he spends upon himself in the same vanities and indulgences as other people do. He might live upon one-third of his fortune and make the rest the support of the poor; but he does nothing of all this that is in his power, but pleases himself with what he would do if his power was greater. Come to thy senses, Clemens. Do not talk what thou wouldst do if thou wast an angel, but consider what thou canst do as thou art a man. Make the best use of thy present state, do now as thou thinkest thou would do with a great estate, be sparing, deny thyself, abstain from all vanities, that the poor may be better maintained, and then thou art as charitable as thou canst be in any estate. Remember the poor widow's mite.

— *William Law*

A Practical Treatise Upon Christian Perfection, 1726

No Exchanges

Wherever a man hath been made a partaker of the divine nature, in him is fulfilled the best and noblest life, and the worthiest in God's eyes, that hath been or can be. And of that eternal love which loveth Goodness as Goodness and for the sake of Goodness, a true, noble, Christ-like life is so greatly beloved that it will never be forsaken or cast off. Where a man hath tasted this life, it is impossible for him ever to part with it . . . and if he could exchange it for an angel's life, he would not.

— *Theologia Germanica*

Wesley's Rule

Do all the good you can,
By all the means you can,
In all the ways you can,
In all the places you can,
At all the times you can,
To all the people you can,
As long as ever you can.

— *John Wesley*

Bartlett's Quotations

Overcome Evil With Good

Beloved, do not avenge yourselves, but rather give place to wrath;
for it is written,

> *"'Vengeance is Mine, I will repay,'*
> *says the Lord. Therefore*
> *"If your enemy is hungry, feed him;*
> *If he is thirsty, give him a drink;*
> *For in so doing you will heap coals of fire on his*
> *head."*

Do not be overcome by evil, but overcome evil with good.

— *Romans 12:19-21 (NKJV)*
  HOLY BIBLE

Of the Divine Goodness and Philanthropy

O my great and good God, who art good in all Thy greatness, and whose chiefest greatness is to be good, how can I possibly think amiss of Thee, distrust Thee, or harbour any jealous apprehensions concerning Thee? And how unworthy should I be of this Thy goodness if I should!

But, O God, my love, 'tis my infirmity to be afraid of that excellence which I should rather love, for my love of Thee is not yet perfect enough to cast out all fear; but blessed be Thy goodness, who in the midst of my fears and doubtful surmises art pleased to remind me of Thy nature, and to say to my soul, as Thou didst once to the diffident disciples, "It is I, be not afraid."

The voice of my beloved! I will therefore turn my fears to love, and love more than I ever yet feared or loved. I will also magnify Thee, O God, my King: and I will praise Thy name forever and ever. Every day will I give thanks unto Thee and praise Thy name forever and ever. For I have tasted and seen how gracious Thou art, and I find it is a good thing to praise Thee: and that 'tis a joyful and pleasant thing to be thankful. I know, O my God, that Thy goodness is as much above my praise as Thy greatness is above my comprehension. My praises can add nothing to Thee, neither can I praise Thee according to the goodness. But, O, my God, I will praise Thee according to my strength, and I know that the same goodness of Thine, which is too great to be praised worthily, is also too great not to accept our unworthy praises.

My God, I know Thou requirest from me only the praises of a man, but I am troubled that I cannot praise Thee as an angel. O that I were now in heaven, if 'twere only that I might praise Thee as Thy angels praise Thee: this, O my God, I will do hereafter, my gratitude shall run then as high as theirs, and it shall be lasting too; it shall last as long as Thy goodness and my being lasts; and as Thy mercy, so my praise shall endure forever.

— *John Norris*

Reason and Religion
An Anthology of Devotional Literature
Compiled by Thomas S. Kepler
Grand Rapids, Mich.: Baker Book House, 1947

The Outward Flow

No man has learned to live until he can rise above the narrow confines of his individualistic concerns to the broader concerns of all humanity. Length without breadth is like a self-contained tributary having no outward flow to the ocean. Stagnant, still, and stale it lacks both life and freshness. In order to live creatively and meaningfully, our self-concern must be wedded to other concerns.

— *Martin Luther King, Jr.*

Reflections
Edited by P. J. Deagan
Amecus Street Publishers

All Goodness Comes From God

Only what is good attracts your love. The earth with its high mountains, gentle hills, level plains is good. The lovely and fertile land is good; the sturdy house with its proportions, its spaciousness and light is good. The bodies of living things are good; the mild and healthy air is good; pleasurable and health-giving food is good; health itself, a freedom from pain and exhaustion, is good. The human face with its symmetrical features, its glad countenance, its high coloring is good; the heart of a friend whose companionship is sweet and whose love is loyal is good; a righteous man is good; wealth for what it enables us to do is good; the sky with its sun, moon, and stars is good; the angels by their holy obedience are good; speech which teaches persuasively and counsels suitably is good; the poem of musical rhythm and profound meaning is good.

But enough! This is good and that is good; take away "this" and "that," and gaze if you can upon good itself: Then you will behold God, good not through the having of any other good thing, but He is the goodness of every good.

— *St. Augustine*

On the Trinity, Book 8, Chapter 3
Augustine Hippo—Selected Writings
Translation and Introduction by Mary T. Clark
New York: Paulist Press, 1984

Give What You Are

What is your unique talent? How are you communicating that special gift to the rest of the world? What are some of the ways you like to give back? Whatever you do with your life, you want to be able to have your passions shed light on others. You want to help others to understand their own journey better, and at the same time, you want to feel the continuity that long after you're dead the consequences of your acts will still be remembered.

If you are an enlightened teacher or a dedicated artist, if you are a writer, editor, publisher, a musician, or a dancer, think of the lives you can affect. If you are a designer, a decorator, mother, gourmet cook, or a collector of letters and manuscripts, think of the lives you can affect. If you are a politician, a photographer, a doctor, scientist, philosopher, or historian, think of the lives you can affect. You are doing a part, in your own style, and when you are joined by others, collectively, you can make a powerful impact.

— *Alexandra Stoddard*

From *Daring To Be Yourself*
by Alexandra Stoddard.
Copyright (1960) by Alexandra Stoddard.
Used by permission of Doubleday,
A division of Bantam Doubleday Dell Publishers, Inc.

I Sing a Song of the Saints of God

I sing a song of the saints of God, patient and brave and
       true,
who toiled and fought and lived and died for the Lord they
       loved and knew.
And one was a doctor, and one was a queen, and one was
       a shepherdess on the green;
they were all of them saints of God, and I mean, God
       helping, to be one too.

They loved their Lord so dear, so dear, and
       His love made them strong;
and they followed the right for Jesus' sake
       the whole of their good lives long.
And one was a soldier, and one was a priest, and one was
       slain by a fierce wild beast;
and there's not any reason, no, not the least, why I
       shouldn't be one too.

They lived not only in ages past; there are hundreds of
       thousands still.
The world is bright with the joyous saints who love to do
       Jesus' will.
You can meet them in school, on the street, in the store, in
       church, by sea, in the house next door;
they are saints of God, whether rich or poor, and I mean to
       be one too.

— *Lesbia Scott*

The United Methodist Hymnal

Evil and Good Kings

Manasseh

Manasseh was only twelve years old when he became king, and he reigned fifty-five years in Jerusalem. But it was an evil reign, for he encouraged his people to worship the idols of the heathen nations destroyed by the Lord when the people of Israel entered the land. He rebuilt the heathen altars his father Hezekiah had destroyed—the altars of Baal, and of the shameful images, and of the sun, moon, and stars. He even constructed heathen altars in both courts of the Temple of the Lord for worshiping the sun, moon, and stars—in the very place where the Lord had said that he would be honored forever. And Manasseh sacrificed his own children as burnt offerings in the Valley of Hinnom. He consulted spirit-mediums, too, and fortune-tellers and sorcerers, and encouraged every sort of evil, making the Lord very angry.

Think of it! He placed an idol in the very Temple of God, where God had told David and his son Solomon, "I will be honored here in this Temple and in Jerusalem—the city I have chosen to be honored forever above all the other cities of Israel. And if you will only obey my commands—all the laws and instructions given to you by Moses— I won't ever again exile Israel from this land which I gave your ancestors."

But Manasseh encouraged the people of Judah and Jerusalem to do even more evil than the nations the Lord destroyed when Israel entered the land. Warnings from the Lord were ignored by both Manasseh and his people. So God sent the Assyrian armies, and they seized him with hooks and bound him with bronze chains and carted him away to Babylon. Then at last he came to his senses and cried out humbly to God for help. And the Lord listened and answered his plea by returning him to Jerusalem and to his kingdom! At that point Manasseh finally realized that the Lord was really God!

It was after this that he rebuilt the outer wall of the City of David and the wall from west of the Spring of Gihon in the Kidron Valley, and then to the Fish Gate, and around Citadel Hill, where it was built very high. And he stationed his army generals in all of the fortified cities of Judah. He also removed the foreign gods from the hills and took his idol from the Temple, and tore down the altars he had built on the mountain, where the Temple stood, and the altars that were in Jerusalem, and dumped them outside the city. Then he rebuilt the altar of the Lord and offered sacrifices upon it—peace offerings and thanksgiving offerings—and demanded that the people of Judah worship the Lord God of Israel. However, the people still sacrificed upon the altars on the hills, but only to the Lord their God.

Amon

When Manasseh died, he was buried beneath his own palace, and his son Amon became the new king. Amon was twenty-two years old when he began to reign in Jerusalem, but he lasted for only two years. It was an evil reign like the early years of his father Manasseh; for Amon sacrificed to all the idols just as his father had. But he didn't change as his father did; instead he sinned more and more. At last his own officers assassinated him in his palace. But some public-spirited citizens killed all of those who assassinated him and declared his son Josiah to be the new king.

Josiah

Josiah was only eight years old when he became king. He reigned thirty-one years in Jerusalem. His was a good reign, as he carefully followed the good example of his ancestor King David. For when he was sixteen years old, in the eighth year of his reign, he began to search for the God of his ancestor David; and four years later he began to clean up Judah and Jerusalem, destroying the heathen altars and the shameful idols on the hills. He went out personally to watch as the altars of Baal were knocked apart, the obelisks above the altars chopped down, and the shameful idols ground into dust and scattered over the graves of those who had sacrificed to them. Then he burned the bones of the heathen priests upon their own altars, feeling that this action would clear the people of Judah and Jerusalem from the guilt of their sin of idol worship.

Then he went to the cities of Manasseh, Ephraim, and Simeon, even to distant Naphtali, and did the same thing there. He broke down the heathen altars, ground to powder the shameful idols and chopped down the obelisks. He did this everywhere throughout the whole land of Israel before returning to Jerusalem.

One day when Hilkiah the High Priest was at the Temple recording the money collected at the gates, he found an old scroll that turned out to be the laws of God as given to Moses!

"Look!" Hilkiah exclaimed to Shaphan, the king's secretary. "See what I have found in the Temple! These are the laws of God!" Hilkiah gave the scroll to Shaphan, and Shaphan took it to the king, along with his report that there was good progress being made in the reconstruction of the Temple.

"The money chests have been opened and counted, and the money has been put into the hand of the overseers and workmen," he said to the king.

Then he mentioned the scroll and how Hilkiah had discovered it. So he read it to the king. When the king heard what these laws required of God's people, he ripped his clothing in despair and summoned Hilkiah, Ahikam (son of Shaphan), Abdon (son of Micah), Shaphan the treasurer, and Asaiah, the king's personal aide.

"Go to the Temple and plead with the Lord for me!" the king told them. "Pray for all the remnant of Israel and Judah! For this scroll says that the reason the Lord's great anger has been poured out upon us is that our ancestors have not obeyed these laws that are written here."

So the men went to Huldah the prophetess. . . . When they told her of the king's trouble, she replied, "The Lord God of Israel says, Tell the man who sent you,

"'Yes, the Lord will destroy this city and its people. All the curses written in the scroll will come true. For my people have forsaken me and have worshiped heathen gods, and I am very angry with them for their deeds. Therefore, my unquenchable wrath is poured out upon this place.'

"But the Lord also says this to the king of Judah who sent you to ask me about this: Tell him, the Lord God of Israel says, 'Because you are sorry and have humbled yourself before God when you heard my words against this city and its people, and have ripped your clothing in despair and wept before me—I have heard you, says the

Lord, and I will not send the promised evil upon this city and its people until after your death.'" So they brought back to the king this word from the Lord. Then the king summoned all the elders of Judah and Jerusalem, and the priests and Levites and all the people great and small, to accompany him to the Temple. There the king read the scroll to them—the covenant of God that was found in the Temple. As the king stood before them, he made a pledge to the Lord to follow his commandments with all his heart and soul and to do what was written in the scroll. And he required everyone in Jerusalem and Benjamin to subscribe to this pact with God, and all of them did.

So Josiah removed all idols from the areas occupied by the Jews and required all of them to worship Jehovah their God. And throughout the remainder of his lifetime they continued serving Jehovah, the God of their ancestors.

> — *2 Chronicles 33:1-17, 20-25; 34:1-7, 14-33* (TLB)
> *HOLY BIBLE*

Eternal Goodness

It is a sorrow and shame to think that the Eternal Goodness is ever most graciously guiding and drawing us, and we will not yield to it. What is better and nobler than true poorness in spirit? Yet when that is held up before us, we will have none of it, but are always seeking ourselves and our own things. [We like to have our mouths always filled with good things] that we may have in ourselves a lively taste of pleasure and sweetness. When this is so, we are well pleased and think it standeth not amiss with us. [But we are yet a long way off from a perfect life. For when God will draw us up to something higher, that is, to an utter loss and forsaking of our own things, spiritual and natural, and withdraweth His comfort and sweetness from us, we faint, and are troubled, and can in no wise bring our minds to it, and we forget God and neglect holy exercises and fancy we are lost for ever.] This is a great error and a bad sign. For a true lover of God, loveth Him or the Eternal Goodness alike, in having and in not having, in sweetness and bitterness, in good or evil report, and the like, for he seeketh alone the honour of God, and not his own, either in spiritual or natural things. And therefore he standeth alike unshaken in all things, at all seasons. [Hereby let every man prove himself, how he standeth towards God, his Creator and Lord.]

— Anonymous

Theologia Germanica
Translated by Susanna Winkworth
An Anthology of Devotional Literature
Compiled by Thomas S. Kepler
Grand Rapids, Mich.: Baker Book House, 1947

Unchanging Goodness

The goodness of God breaking forth into a desire to communicate good was the cause and the beginning of the Creation. Hence, it follows that to all eternity God can have no thought or intent towards the creature but to communicate good, because He made the creature for this sole end, to receive good. The first motive towards the creature is unchangeable; it takes its rise from God's desire to communicate good, and it is an eternal impossibility that anything can ever come from God as His will and purpose towards the creature but the same love and goodness which first created it. He must always will that to which He willed at the creation of it. This is the amiable nature of God. He is the Good, the unchangeable, overflowing fountain of good that sends forth nothing but good to all eternity. He is the Love itself, the unmixed, unmeasurable Love, doing nothing but from love, giving nothing but gifts of love to everything that He has made, requiring nothing of all His creatures but the spirit and fruits of that love which brought them into being. Oh, how sweet is this contemplation of the height and depth of the riches of Divine Love! With what attraction must it draw every thoughtful man to return love for love to this overflowing fountain of boundless goodness!

— William Law

Man and God
Victor Gollancz
Boston: Houghton Mifflin Co., 1951

Prayer for Goodness

Lord, remind us that Your call is not just to the treasured time of worship or to those peaceful moments of prayer, but, because of the resurrection, it is to move with courage into the encounters and arenas of life where many have not heard the gospel's call. Help us to speak when it is not easy, to act when it is safer to just go along with wrong. Help us to know that in the day of Jesus Christ, His kingdom will come. And let us, O God, be bound by a love amazing and divine, and then go out and embrace a weary and despairing world and lift that world to You. Amen.

— Kenneth Working

Hymns for the Family of God

Your Aim

This [goodness] is derived from a Greek word referring to that quality found in the person who is ruled by and aims at what is good, that which represents the highest moral and ethical values.

Paul writes, "For the fruit of the light consists in all goodness and righteousness and truth" (Ephesians 5:9 NASB). He also says, "To this end also we pray for you always that our God may count you worthy of your calling, and fulfill every desire for goodness and the work of faith with power; in order that the name of our Lord Jesus may be glorified in you" (2 Thessalonians 1:11-12 NASB). Again, Paul says in commending the church in Rome, "And concerning you, my brethren, I myself also am convinced that you yourselves are full of goodness, filled with all knowledge, and able also to admonish one another" (Romans 15:14).

— *Billy Graham*

The Faithful Christian: An Anthology of Billy Graham
Compiled by William Griffin and Ruth Graham Dienert
New York: McCracken Press, 1994

The Goodness of God

O immeasurable goodness of our Creator! O inestimable mercy! Himself in nothing ever needing man, yet of His goodness alone He created man; creating, He adorned him with reason, that he might be able to be partaker of His happiness and His eternity, and so with Him possess forever joy and gladness.

Still further, while man in many things is contrary to Him, knowing and willfully doeth many things although they are displeasing to Him, yet He warneth him to return, to seek again the mercy of his Creator, nor for any sin, however grievous, presume to despair. For He is the fountain of lovingkindness and mercy, and all, with whatever stain of sin they are defiled, He longeth to cleanse; cleansed, to give them the joy of everlasting life.

— *St. Anselm*

Meditations
Translated by E. B. Pusey, 1856

Vision by Personal Purity

Purity is not innocence; it is much more. Purity is the outcome of sustained spiritual sympathy with God. We have to grow in purity. The life with God may be right, and the inner purity remain unsullied, and yet every now and again the bloom on the outside may be sullied. God does not shield us from this possibility, because in this way we realize the necessity of maintaining the vision by personal purity. If the spiritual bloom of our life with God is getting impaired in the tiniest degree, we must leave off everything and get it put right. Remember that vision depends on character—the pure in heart see God.

God makes us pure by His sovereign grace, but we have something to look after, this bodily life by which we come in contact with other people and with other points of view, it is these that are apt to sully. Not only must the inner sanctuary be kept right with God, but the outer courts as well are to be brought into perfect accord with the purity God gives us by His grace. The spiritual understanding is blurred immediately when the outer court is sullied. If we are going to retain personal contact with the Lord Jesus Christ, it will mean there are some things we must scorn to do or to think, some legitimate things we must scorn to touch.

A practical way of keeping personal purity unsullied in relation to other people is to say to yourself—That man, that woman, perfect in Christ Jesus! That friend, that relative, perfect in Christ Jesus!

— *Oswald Chambers*

My Utmost for His Highest
New York: Dodd Mead & Co., 1935

What Good Thing?

Now behold, one came and said to Him [Jesus], "Good Teacher, what good thing shall I do that I may have eternal life?"

So He said to him, "Why do you call Me good? No one is good but One, that is, God. But if you want to enter into life, keep the commandments."

He said to Him, "Which ones?"

Jesus said, "'You shall not murder,' 'You shall not commit adultery,' 'You shall not steal,' 'You shall not bear false witness,' 'Honor your father and your mother,' and 'You shall love your neighbor as yourself.'"

The young man said to Him, "All these things I have kept from my youth. What do I still lack?"

Jesus said to him, "If you want to be perfect, go, sell what you have and give to the poor, and you will have treasure in heaven; and come, follow Me."

But when the young man heard that saying, he went away sorrowful, for he had great possessions.

Then Jesus said to His disciples, "Assuredly, I say to you that it is hard for a rich man to enter the kingdom of heaven. And again I say to you, it is easier for a camel to go through the eye of a needle than for a rich man to enter the kingdom of God."

When His disciples heard it, they were greatly astonished, saying, "Who then can be saved?"

But Jesus looked at them and said to them, "With men this is impossible, but with God all things are possible."

— ***Matthew 19:16-26*** *(NKJV)*
HOLY BIBLE

The Father's Goodness

The Father was all in all to the Son, and the Son no more thought of His own goodness than an honest man thinks of his honesty. When the good man sees goodness, he thinks of his own evil: Jesus had no evil to think of, but neither does He think of His goodness: He delights in His Father's. "Why callest thou Me good?"

— **George MacDonald**

Unspoken Sermons
Second Series, The Way
George MacDonald, 365 Readings
Edited by C. S. Lewis
New York: Macmillan, 1947

Wise and Sensitive

A good man is good even when he is asleep; his character, which comprises several other factors in addition to mere habituation, consists in his moral readiness, the wisdom of his judgment, the sensitiveness with which he can project himself where other selves stand, and the firmness he can show in defending a vision of right.

— *Edmond Cain*

Choose Life
Bernard Mandelbaum
New York: Random House, 1968

An Alphabet of Lessons for Youth

A wise son maketh a glad father, but a foolish son is the heaviness of his mother.

B etter is a little with the fear of the Lord, than great treasure & trouble therewith.

C ome unto Christ all ye that labor and are heavy laden and he will give you rest.

D o not the abominable thing which I hate saith the Lord.

E xcept a man be born again, he cannot see the kingdom of GOD.

F oolishness is bound up in the heart of a child, but the rod of correction shall drive it far from him.

G odliness is profitable unto all things, having the promise of the life that now is, and that which is to come.

H oliness becomes GOD's house for ever.

I t is good for me to draw near unto GOD.

K eep thy heart with all diligence, for out of it are the issues of life.

L iars shall have their part in the lake which burns with fire and brimstone.

Many are the afflictions of the righteous, but the LORD delivereth them out of them all.

Now is the accepted time, now is the day of salvation.

Out of the abundance of the heart the mouth speaketh.

Pray to thy Father which is in secret; and thy Father which sees in secret shall reward thee openly.

Quit you like men, be strong, stand fast in the faith.

Remember thy Creator in the days of thy youth.

S eest thou a man wise in his own conceit, there is more hope of a fool than of him.

Trust in God at all times, ye people, pour out your hearts before him.

Upon the wicked, God shall rain an horrible tempest.

Woe to the wicked, it shall be ill with him, for the reward of his hands shall be given him.

E**X**hort one another daily while it is called to day, lest any of you be hardened thro' the deceitfulness of sin.

Young men, ye have overcome the wicked one.

Zeal hath consumed me, because thy enemies have forgotten the word of God.

— The New England Primer

The New-England Primer
Boston, 1777
(Aledo, Tex.: WallBuilder Press, 1991, Reprint)

Spelling, capitalization, and punctuation are as they appear in the Primer with the exception that "s" has been standardized throughout. This alphabet does not have "J" or "V" letters.

Salvation's Cost

The story is told of a hero of the Chinese rice-fields during an earthquake. From his hilltop farm he saw the ocean swiftly withdrawn, like some prodigious animal crouching for the leap, and knew the leap would be the tidal wave. He saw also that his neighbors working in low fields must be gathered to his hill or swept away. Without a second thought he set fire to his rice-ricks and furiously rang the temple-bell.

His neighbors thought his farm on fire and rushed to help him. Then, from that safe hill they saw the swirl of waters over fields just forsaken—and knew their salvation and its cost.

— Lafcadio Hearn

Thesaurus of Anecdotes
Edited by Edmund Fuller
New York: Crown Publishers, 1942

Don't Be Selfish

Goodness is something so simple;
always to live for others, never to seek
one's own advantage.

— Dag Hammarskjöld

Choose Life
Bernard Mandelbaum
New York: Random House, 1968

Chisel Away!

Withdraw into yourself and look. And if you do not find yourself beautiful as yet, do as does the creator of a statue that is to be made beautiful; he cuts away here, he smooths there, he makes this line lighter, this other purer, until he has shown a beautiful face upon his statue. So do you also; cut away all that is excessive, straighten all that is crooked, bring light to all that is shadowed, labour to make all glow with beauty, and do not cease chiselling your statue until there shall shine out on you the godlike splendour of virtue, until you shall see the final goodness surely established in the stainless shrine.

— Plotinus

Man and God
Victor Gollancz
Boston: Houghton Mifflin Co., 1951

A Good Samaritan

After the Chicago fire I came to New York for money, and I heard there was a rich man in Fall River who was very liberal. So I went to him. He gave me a check for a large amount, and then got into his carriage and drove with me to the houses of other rich men in the city, and they all gave me checks. When he left me at the train I grasped his hand and said:

"If you ever come to Chicago, call on me, and I will return your favor."

He said: "Mr. Moody, don't wait for me; do it to the first man who comes along."

I never forgot that remark; it had the ring of the true good Samaritan.

— Dwight L. Moody

The D. L. Moody Year Book
Selected by Emma Moody Fitt
New York: Fleming H. Revell Co., 1900

For Others

Teach us, Ruler of the universe,
      to see people by the light of the faith we profess,
that we may check in ourselves
      all ungenerous judgments, all presumptuous claims,
that, recognizing the needs and rightful claims of others,
      we may remove old hatreds and rivalries
      and hasten new understandings,
that we may bring our tributes of excellence
      to the treasury of our common humanity;
through Jesus Christ our Lord. Amen.

United Methodist Book of Worship

The Good Life

Goodness should be the highest object of human desire. When we are at our best we will never want anything evil. The good life is not some namby-pamby kind of existence, but is a life filled with joy and happiness because it shares the highest values. The good life is possible for all of us.

A story is told about Daniel Webster. During his days in the city of Washington the great statesman attended worship regularly in a little rural church outside the city. Some of his colleagues were disturbed about it. They said it lacked prestige. And they asked him why he attended a little church in the sticks when he would be welcome in the most fashionable churches in Washington.

Webster answered that when he attended church in Washington they preached to Daniel Webster, the statesman, but in the little church, they preached to Daniel Webster, the sinner.

If we are honest, we will have to admit that sin finds its place in the lives of all of us. We have failed to live up to our very best. We are not yet the best person it is possible for us to become.

We can have the good life. And the good life is not what some commercials suggest to us—the right beer or the right cigarette or driving the right automobile! The good life is that life which has the goodness of God at its very center. It is the life which recognizes that God has created us for Himself. He has given us a potential which can be fulfilled. We cannot be our best possible selves until we allow Jesus Christ to touch our lives and bring our spirits to fulfillment.

— *Herbert L. Bowdoin*

Real Riches, Real Joy
Nashville: Tidings

Signpost

Real goodness does not attach itself merely to this life—it points to another world. Political or professional reputation cannot last forever, but a conscience void of offence before God and man is an inheritance for eternity.

— *Daniel Webster*

The Encyclopedia of Religious Quotations
Edited and Compiled by Frank S. Mead
Fleming H. Revell Co., 1965

Always There

The Lord's goodness surrounds us at every moment. I walk through it almost with difficulty, as through thick grass and flowers.

— *R. W. Barbour*

A Diary of Readings
John Baillie
New York: Collier Books/Macmillan, 1955, 1986

Even When No One Is Looking

The supreme test of goodness is not in the greater but in the smaller incidents of our character and practice; not what we are when standing in the searchlight of public scrutiny, but when we reach the firelight flicker of our homes; not what we are when some clarion-call rings through the air, summoning us to fight for life and liberty, but our attitude when we are called to sentry-duty in the grey morning, when the watch-fire is burning low. It is impossible to be our best at the supreme moment if character is corroded and eaten into by daily inconsistency, unfaithfulness, and besetting sin.

— *F. B. Meyer*

Our Daily Walk

Fountain of Good Works

Verily, good works constitute a refreshing stream in this world, wherever they are found flowing. It is a pity that they are too often like Oriental torrents, "waters that fail" in the time of greatest need. When we meet the stream actually flowing, and refreshing the land, we trace it upward in order to discover the fountain whence it springs. Threading our way upward, guided by the river, we have found at length the placid lake from which the river runs. Behind all genuine good works, and above them, love will, sooner or later, certainly be found. It is never good works alone: uniformly, in fact, and necessarily in the nature of things, we find the two constituents existing as a complex whole—"love and good works," the fountain and the flowing stream.

— *Arnot*

6000 Illustrations

God's Nature

Since His goodness is so great, His will so perfect, that He does what ought to be done, not unwilling, but spontaneously, He is so much the more completely to be loved because of His very nature, and the more to be glorified because this goodness of His belongs to Him not by accident, but substantially and immutably.

— *Peter Abelard,*
   Epitome Theologiae Christianae, c. 1135

The World Treasury of Religious Quotations
Compiled and Edited by Ralph L. Woods
New York: Hawthorn Books, Inc., 1966

God Rewards the Good

Never envy the wicked! Soon they fade away like grass and disappear. Trust in the Lord instead. Be kind and good to others; then you will live safely here in the land and prosper, feeding in safety.

Be delighted with the Lord. Then he will give you all your heart's desires. Commit everything you do to the Lord. Trust him to help you do it, and he will. Your innocence will be clear to everyone. He will vindicate you with the blazing light of justice shining down as from the noonday sun.

Rest in the Lord; wait patiently for him to act. Don't be envious of evil men who prosper.

Stop your anger! Turn off your wrath. Don't fret and worry—it only leads to harm. For the wicked shall be destroyed, but those who trust the Lord shall be given every blessing. Only a little while and the wicked shall disappear. You will look for them in vain. But all who humble themselves before the Lord shall be given every blessing and shall have wonderful peace.

The Lord is laughing at those who plot against the godly, for he knows their judgment day is coming. Evil men take aim to slay the poor; they are ready to butcher those who do right. But their swords will be plunged into their own hearts, and all their weapons will be broken.

It is better to have little and be godly than to own an evil man's wealth; for the strength of evil men shall be broken, but the Lord takes care of those he has forgiven.

Day by day the Lord observes the good deeds done by godly men, and gives them eternal rewards. He cares for them when times are hard; even in famine, they will have enough. But evil men shall perish. These enemies of God will wither like grass and disappear like smoke. Evil men borrow and "cannot pay it back"! But the good man returns what he owes with some extra besides. Those blessed by the Lord shall inherit the earth, but those cursed by him shall die.

The steps of good men are directed by the Lord. He delights in each step they take. If they fall it isn't fatal, for the Lord holds them with his hand.

I have been young and now I am old. And in all my years I have never seen the Lord forsake a man who loves him; nor have I seen the children of the godly go hungry. Instead, the godly are able to be generous with their gifts and loans to others, and their children are a blessing.

So if you want an eternal home, leave your evil, low-down ways and live good lives. For the Lord loves justice and fairness; he will never abandon his people. They will be kept safe forever; but all who love wickedness shall perish.

The godly shall be firmly planted in the land and live there forever. The godly man is a good counselor because he is just and fair and knows right from wrong.

Evil men spy on the godly, waiting for an excuse to accuse them and then demanding their death. But the Lord will not let these evil men succeed, nor let the godly be condemned when they are brought before the judge.

Don't be impatient for the Lord to act! Keep traveling steadily along his pathway and in due season he will honor you with every blessing, and you will see the wicked destroyed. I myself have seen it happen: a proud and evil man, towering like a cedar of Lebanon, but when I looked again, he was gone! I searched but could not find him!

But the good man—what a different story! For the good man—the blameless, the upright, the man of peace—he has a wonderful future ahead of him. For him there is a happy ending. But evil men shall be destroyed, and their posterity shall be cut off.

The Lord saves the godly! He is their salvation and their refuge when trouble comes. Because they trust in him, he helps them and delivers them from the plots of evil men.

— *Psalm 37* (TLB)
HOLY BIBLE

Chapter 7

FAITHFULNESS

With my mouth will I make known Your faithfulness to all generations (Psalm 89:1 NKJV).

Faith and faithfulness have countless manifestations throughout the Scriptures. God is faithful to man. He is the author of faith and the giver of a measure of faith to every person. Man has faith and even great faith at times manifested in numerous ways. Man is capable of being both faithful to God and faithful to his fellowman. Furthermore, the New Testament writers use the phrase, "the faith," to refer to an entire body of doctrine as well as to all who believe it!

Faith abounds!

The word most commonly used for faith in the New Testament is "pistis" (pis'-tis). It comes from the Greek word "peitho," which means to persuade. True Christian faith means to be completely persuaded that there is no other truth apart from the Word of God on which one might build one's life.

The person of faith is the person who fully trusts God will do what He said He will do in every situation, every time. And the person of faith will continually increase as a faithful person. A faithful person is one who is committed to living a life of faith, and to manifesting that life to God and to all people at all times.

For All Time

In God's faithfulness lies eternal security.

— *Corrie Ten Boom*

Encyclopedia of Famous Quotes

Faith You Can See

What doth it profit, my brethren, though a man say he hath faith, and have not works? can faith save him? (James 2:14).

I believe in a faith that you can see; a living, working faith that prompts to action. Faith without works is like a man putting all his money into the foundation of a house; and works without faith is like building a house on sand without any foundation.

You often hear people say: "The root of the matter is in him." What would you say if I had a garden and nothing but roots in it?

— *Dwight L. Moody*

The D. L. Moody Year Book
Selected by Emma Moody Fitt
New York: Fleming H. Revell Company, 1900

Faithfulness—Love's Loyalty

The seventh fruit of the Spirit is the word for standing fast, for steadfastness. It is the quality of reliability, trustworthiness, which makes a person one on whom we can utterly rely and whose word will stand. Phillips translates this fruit "fidelity." Barclay translates it as "loyalty." Westcott wrote, "A person is said to be 'faithful' in the discharge of his duties where the trait is looked at from within outwards; and at the same time he is 'trustworthy' in virtue of that faithfulness in the judgment of those who are able to rely upon him."

Faithfulness speaks of endurance, also—a firmness of purpose, especially amid danger and calamities. It describes the faithful discharge of duties and undying devotion to persons and principles. It is the love which endures all things—difficulties, dangers, and differences.

Faithfulness is not the shrugging of the shoulders or a passive posture. Nor is it a "grin and bear it" attitude. It is a positive, active attribute. It results from a love which keeps moving forward and comes out victorious. It remains steadfast and true in the midst of evil. The faithful person does not sidestep a situation or endeavor to escape to the easy path or flee when threats come. The faithful person stays at his station.

Moffatt also translates faithfulness as "fidelity," describing it as a careful regard for the discharge of obligations, unwavering adherence to veracity and honesty. The faithful person is dependable. We can put our full faith in him. Faithfulness is love performing its prowess, never growing weary. Faithfulness is steady, true, and trustworthy. It possesses a staying power in spite of feelings and difficulties, even after the first joys seem to have disappeared.

— *John M. Drescher*

Consecration in Overalls

Faithfulness is consecration in overalls. It is the steady acceptance and performance of the common duty and immediate task without any reference to personal preferences—because it is there to be done and so is a manifestation of the will of God.

Faithfulness means continuing quietly with the job we have been given, in the situation where we have been placed; not yielding to the restless desire for change. It means tending the lamp quietly for God without wondering how much longer it has got to go on. Steady, unsensational driving, taking good care of the car. A lot of the road to heaven has to be taken at thirty miles per hour. It means keeping everything in your charge in good order for love's sake, rubbing up the silver, polishing the glass even though you know the Master will not be looking 'round the pantry next weekend. If your life is really part of the apparatus of the Spirit, that is the sort of life it must be. You have got to be the sort of cat who can be left alone with the canary: the sort of dog who follows, hungry and thirsty but tail up, to the very end of the day.

Faithfulness is the quality of the friend, refusing no test and no trouble, loyal, persevering; not at the mercy of emotional ups and downs or getting tired when things are tiresome. In the interior life of prayer faithfulness points steadily to God and His purposes, away from self and its preoccupations.

— *Evelyn Underhill*

The Fruits of the Spirit
London, 1949

Faith As Obedience

"If ye have faith and doubt not, if ye shall say unto this mountain, Be thou removed and cast into the sea, it shall be done." Good people . . . have been tempted to tempt the Lord their God upon the strength of this saying. . . Happily for such, the assurance to which they would give the name of faith generally fails them in time. Faith is that which, knowing the Lord's will, goes and does it; or, not knowing it, stands and waits. . . But to put God to the question in any other way than by saying, "What wilt thou have me to do?" is an attempt to compel God to declare Himself, or to hasten His work. . . The man is therein dissociating himself from God so far that, instead of acting by the divine will from within, he acts in God's face, as it were, to see what He will do. Man's first business is, "What does God want me to do?"— not "What will God do if I do so and so?" . . .

Do you ask, "What is faith in Him?" I answer, the leaving of your way, your objects, your self, and the taking of His and Him; the leaving of your trust in men, in money, in opinion, in character, in atonement itself, and doing as He tells you. I can find no words strong enough to serve for the weight of this obedience . . . .

Instead of asking yourself whether you believe or not, ask yourself whether you have this day done one thing because He said, "Do it," or once abstained because He said, "Do not do it." It is simply absurd to say you believe, or even want to believe, in Him, if you do not do anything He tells you. . . .

Oh the folly of any mind that would explain God before obeying Him! That would map out the character of God instead of crying, Lord, what wouldst Thou have me to do!

— *George MacDonald*

A Book of Faith
Elizabeth Goudge
New York: Coward, McCann & Geoghegan, Inc., 1976

Believe . . . See

Faith is to believe what we do not see, and the reward of this faith is to see what we believe.

— *St. Augustine*

Cyclopedia of Religious Anecdotes

Trusting in Jesus

No one can ever be made right in God's sight by doing what the law commands. For the more we know of God's laws, the clearer it becomes that we aren't obeying them; his laws serve only to make us see that we are sinners.

But now God has shown us a different way to heaven—not by "being good enough" and trying to keep his laws, but by a new way (though not new, really, for the Scriptures told about it long ago). Now God says he will accept and acquit us—declare us "not guilty"—if we trust Jesus Christ to take away our sins. And we all can be saved in this same way, by coming to Christ, no matter who we are or what we have been like. Yes, all have sinned; all fall short of God's glorious ideal; yet now God declares us "not guilty" of offending him if we trust in Jesus Christ, who in his kindness freely takes away our sins.

For God sent Christ Jesus to take the punishment for our sins and to end all God's anger against us. He used Christ's blood and our faith as the means of saving us from his wrath. In this way he was being entirely fair, even though he did not punish those who sinned in former times. For he was looking forward to the time when Christ would come and take away those sins. And now in these days also he can receive sinners in this same way because Jesus took away their sins.

But isn't this unfair for God to let criminals go free, and say that they are innocent? No, for he does it on the basis of their trust in Jesus who took away their sins.

Then what can we boast about doing to earn our salvation? Nothing at all. Why? Because our acquittal is not based on our good deeds; it is based on what Christ has done and our faith in him. So it is that we are saved by faith in Christ and not by the good things we do.

And does God save only the Jews in this way? No, the Gentiles, too, may come to him in this same manner. God treats us all the same; all, whether Jews or Gentiles, are acquitted if they have faith. Well then, if we are saved by faith, does this mean that we no longer need obey God's laws? Just the opposite! In fact, only when we trust Jesus can we truly obey him.

> *— Romans 3:20-31 (TLB)*
> *HOLY BIBLE*

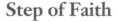

Step of Faith

Whoso draws nigh to God one step
    through doubtings dim,
God will advance a mile
    in blazing light to Him.

— Anonymous

What Do We Know?

The beginning of faith is the beginning of our groping toward understanding—without assuming in advance that we know the answer. It is a hard fact, perhaps the hardest in all religion. Yet we cannot go ahead until we are willing to accept this point: We do not know every-thing, we have not advanced to the point where all answers are available to us. . . . Faith is not in what we know, but in what we do not know and yet believe.

— *Will Oursler*

The Road to Faith, 1960

"Little" Faithfulness

Too many people are not faithful in little things. They are not to be absolutely depended upon. They do not always keep their promises. They break engagements. They fail to pay their debts promptly. They come behind time to appointments. They are neglectful and careless in little things. In general they are good people, but their life is honey-combed with small failures. One who can be positively depended upon, who is faithful in the least things as well as in the greatest, whose life and character are true through and through, gives out a light in this world which honors Christ and blesses others.

— *Rev. James R. Miller*

"Little" Faithfulness by Rev. James R. Miller.
Reprinted with the permission of Scribner,
a Division of Simon & Schuster Inc. from
A Diary of Readings by John Baillie.
Copyright © 1955 John Baillie; copyright
renewed © 1983 by Fowler Baillie.

Rewards for Faithfulness

Faithfulness, like all the other fruit of the Spirit, grows. It begins with quite small matters; indeed, if not manifested in small things, it will never have opportunity in the greater (Luke 16:10). How very great those opportunities may be only eternity will reveal.

The rewards for faithfulness include, as one of their chief and most alluring features, enlarged service (Luke 19:17).

But this is not all. The glimpses given of the final award for faithfulness are enough to inspire every fainting mind, and ravish every loving heart. *For those who are "with Him" in that bright glory are "the called, and chosen, and faithful"* (Revelation 17:14). This will be the crowning reward for faithfulness and loyalty to Christ. And after all, it is fitting that those specially marked by faithfulness should compose those armies of heaven which should follow the King of kings and Lord of lords, upon whose banner will be displayed the word *"faithful and true"* (Revelation 19:11-14).

The fruit of His Spirit, gained by walking with Him steadfastly below, will then come to its harvest. *"Be thou faithful unto death, and I will give thee a crown of life"* (Revelation 2:10).

— Donald Gee

The Fruit of the Spirit
Springfield, Mo.: Gospel Publishing House, 1928

Faithful in Little Things

God's question on the last day will not be, "How much were you noticed?" Or even, "How much did you do?" Rather, His question will be, "Were you faithful in fulfilling your calling where I placed you?" The question with God is not how obscure or prominent a place we occupy, but how faithful we are.

We must strive to be more faithful one day at a time in taking time for others, in doing deeds of kindness, in performing the small everyday run of things faithfully. We must see such as our primary responsibility. Then, says Jesus, the big things will also be taken care of. By the faithfulness with which we fulfill the common daily duties, we make the character which we will have to spend in eternity.

— *John M. Drescher*

Reprinted by permission of Herald Press from
Spirit Fruit by John M. Drescher. Copyright © 1974
by John M. Drescher. Used by permission of Herald Press.

For Childlikeness

Forgive us, Lord, that as we grow to maturity, our faith is blighted with doubts, withered with worry, tainted with sophistication. We pray that Thou wilt make us like children again in faith—not childish, but childlike in the simplicity of a faith that is willing to trust Thee even though we cannot see what tomorrow will bring.

We ask Thee to give to each of us that childlike faith, that simplicity of mind which is willing to lay aside all egotism and conceit, which recognizes vanity for what it is—an empty show, which knows that we are incapable of thinking the thoughts of God, which is willing to be humble again.

Then may we feel once more, as do our children who whisper their love to Thee, who trace with chubby little fingers the pictures of Jesus in a picture book—those pictures that portray Thee, Lord Jesus, with a hurt lamb in Thy arms or a child on Thy knee. Help us, even now, to feel again like that, that we may be as loving, as trusting, as innocent, as grateful, as affectionate.

And as we are willing to kneel again as children, then shall we discover for ourselves the glory Thou hast revealed, and find the wonder of it gripping our hearts and preparing them for Thy peace. So shall we, along with our children, enter into the Kingdom of God, and know it, and feel it, and rejoice in it. In Thy name, who didst care to come to earth as a little child, we pray. Amen.

— *Peter Marshall*

Sermons and Prayers
New York: Revell, 1950

Mind Your Place

Is your place a small place?
Tend it with care!—He set you there.
Is your place a large place?
Guard it with care!—He set you there.
Whate'er your place, it is
Not yours alone, but His
Who set you there.

— John Oxenham (1861-1941)

A Stalwart Virtue

Let us consider three of Our Lord's great lessons upon faithfulness gathered together in Matthew 25. Here are three examples of faithfulness of the difficult kind that is exercised, not towards God when we feel Him present, but to God when He seems to be absent. And these lessons show it to be a stalwart sort of virtue making great demands on us, having little connection with feeling, and not achieved without deliberate, continuous, costly effort of heart, mind and will.

First comes the story of the ten virgins: The really faithful will have to be prudent and careful as well as devoted. We have to carry on all night; it is a long job subject to temptations of weariness and inconstancy, so we make our plans accordingly. The truly faithful take the situation seriously, remembering that the ardent lamp depends on the homely oil; they do not leave it all to chance and say it will be "all right on the night." They take reasonable precautions—enough oil in the lamp, the rule of life, the necessary spiritual nourishment, the quiet devotional practice—to keep light going in the long night. And then the cry at dawn; and those who were faithful and prudent find the lamp of adoration is still alight.

Secondly comes the story of the ten talents: Faithfulnss always seeks the interests of God and uses all its ability for Him with courage and skill. That often involves risks and choices and demands which seem beyond our capacity—the faithfulness of the small creature doing a hard job in the teeth of overwhelming circumstances because this is the Master's will; forgetting all about safety first.

The third lesson is perhaps the deepest and the most searching: Faithfulness in responding to the here and now demands of men on our love and pity and service; going on and on with that loving service even though we have no sense of God; on and on with the work and the effort entailed in the feeding and clothing of the needy, the visiting of the sick—just out of loving compassion and without any glow of religious joy. That bit comes home to some of us very specially. "When saw we Thee, Lord?" We are to serve Him wherever He is; that is, wherever need appeals and love and compassion are awakened by its voice. Though we cannot realize it, the King is there—not in His beauty, but moving disguised among His people by night.

— *Evelyn Underhill*

The Fruits of the Spirit
London, 1949

Faith To Survive

And in the evening, when I lie in bed and end my prayers with the words, "I thank You, God, for all that is good and dear and beautiful," I am filled with joy. Then I think about "the good" of going into hiding, of my health and with my whole being of the "dearness" of Peter, of that which is still embryonic and impressionable and which we neither of us dare to name or touch, of that which will come sometime: love, the future, happiness and of "the beauty" which exists in the world; the world, nature, beauty and all, all that is exquisite and fine.

I don't think then of all the misery, but of the beauty that still remains. This is one of the things that Mummy and I are so entirely different about. Her counsel when one feels melancholy is: "Think of all the misery in the world and be thankful that you are not sharing in it!" My advice is: "Go outside, to the fields, enjoy nature and the sunshine, go out and try to recapture happiness in yourself and in God. Think of all the beauty that's still left in and around you and be happy!"

I don't see how Mummy's ideas can be right, because then how are you supposed to behave if you go through the misery yourself? Then you are lost. On the contrary, I've found that there is always some beauty left—in nature, sunshine, freedom, in yourself; these can all help you. Look at these things, then you find yourself again, and God, and then you regain your balance. And whoever is happy will make others happy too. He who has courage and faith will never perish in misery!

— *Anne Frank*

"Excerpts," from *Anne Frank: The Diary of a Young Girl* by Anne Frank. Copyright © 1952 by Otton H. Frank. Used by permission of Doubleday Division of Bantam Doubleday Dell Publishing Group, Inc.

On Solid Ground

In I Corinthians 16:13-14, Paul asks the Corinthians to stand on something that is deeper than the physical and social and spiritual universe, something that cannot be shaken, because all levels of the universe rest upon it, their divine ground. To stand on this ground is, in Paul's words, to stand in "the faith. . . ."

Breaking the way to this ground is the meaning of the appearance of the Christ. "Stand firm in your faith" means—don't give up that faith that alone can make you ultimately strong, because it gives you the ultimate ground on which to stand. Standing firm in one's faith does not mean adhering to a set of beliefs; it does not require us to suppress doubts about Christian or other doctrines, but points to something which lies beyond doubt in the depth in which man's being and all being is rooted. To be aware of this ground, to live in it and out of it is ultimate strength. "Be strong" and "stand in the faith" are one and the same command.

— *Paul Tillich*

Reprinted with permission of Scribner, a Division of Simon & Schuster, Inc. from *The Eternal Now* by Paul Tillich. Copyright © 1963 by Paul Tillich.

Two Prayers

Last night my little boy confessed to me
Some childish wrong;
And kneeling at my knee,
He prayed with tears—
"Dear God, make me a man
Like Daddy—wise and strong;
I know You can."

Then while he slept
I knelt beside his bed,
Confessed my sins,
And prayed with low-bowed head.
"O God, make me a child
Like my child here—
Pure, guileless,
Trusting Thee with faith sincere."

— *Andrew Gillies 1870-1942*

Masterpiece of Religious Verse
Edited by James Dalton Morrison
New York: Harper & Brothers Publishers, 1948

The Gateway of Faith

In the divine scheme of salvation the doctrine of faith is central. Every benefit flowing from the Atonement of Christ comes to the individual through the gateway of faith. We dare take nothing for granted concerning it.

For a number of years, my heart has been troubled over the doctrine of faith as it is received and taught among evangelical Christians everywhere. My fear is that the modern conception of faith is not the biblical one. Faith is not the believing of a statement we know to be true. Faith based upon reason is faith of a kind, it is true; but it is not of the character of Bible faith, for it follows the evidence infallibly and has nothing of a moral or spiritual nature in it. True faith rests upon the character of God and asks no further proof than the moral perfections of the One who cannot lie. It is enough that God said it.

Faith as the Bible knows it is confidence in God and His Son Jesus Christ; it is the response of the soul to the divine character as revealed in the Scriptures; and even this response is impossible apart from the prior inworking of the Holy Spirit. Faith is a gift of God to a penitent soul and has nothing whatsoever to do with the senses or the data they afford. Faith is a miracle; it is the ability God gives to trust His Son, and anything that does not result in action in accord with the will of God is not faith but something else short of it.

Faith and morals are two sides of the same coin. Indeed the very essence of faith is moral. Any professed faith in Christ as personal Saviour that does not bring the life under plenary obedience to Christ as Lord is inadequate and must betray its victim at the last. The man that believes will obey. God gives faith to the obedient heart only. Where real repentance is, there is obedience.

— *A. W. Tozer*

What Is Faith?

FAITH is dead to doubts—
dumb to discouragements,
blind to impossibilities,
knows nothing but success.

FAITH lifts its hand up through
the threatening clouds,
lays hold of Him who has
all power in heaven and
on earth.

FAITH makes the uplook good,
the outlook bright,
the inlook favorable,
and the future glorious.

— *V. Raymond Edman*

7700 Illustrations

God and Man

Whenever I am prone to doubt and wonder,
I check myself, and say, the mighty One
Who made the solar system cannot blunder,
And for the best all things are being done.
He who set the stars on their eternal courses,
Has fashioned this strange earth by some sure plan.
Bow low—bow low to those majestic forces,
Nor dare to doubt their wisdom, puny man.

You cannot put one little star in motion,
You cannot shape one single forest leaf,
Nor fling a mountain up, nor sink an ocean,
Presumptuous pygmy, large with unbelief!
You cannot bring one dawn of regal splendor,
Nor bid the day to shadowy twilight fall,
Nor send the pale moon forth with radiance tender;
And dare you doubt the One who has done all?

— *S. A. Nagel*

Masterpiece of Religious Verse
Edited by James Dalton Morrison
New York: Harper & Brothers Publishers, 1948

My Faith Looks Up to Thee

My faith looks up to Thee,
    Thou Lamb of Calvary, Savior divine!
Now hear me while I pray, take all my guilt away,
O let me from this day be wholly Thine!

May Thy rich grace impart
    strength to my fainting heart, my zeal inspire!
As Thou hast died for me, O may my love to Thee
    pure, warm, and changeless be, a living fire!

While life's dark maze I tread,
    and griefs around me spread, be Thou my guide;
bid darkness turn to day, wipe sorrow's tears away,
    nor let me ever stray from Thee aside.

When ends life's transient dream,
　　when death's cold, sullen stream shall o'er me roll;
blest Savior, then in love, fear and distrust remove;
　　O bear me safe above, a ransomed soul!

— *Ray Palmer*

Methodist Hymnal

Steps of Faith

An orphan girl in India was desperate to find a home. One day, she approached a visiting missionary teacher from a nearby village and asked the woman for help. The teacher had no room in her home for the girl, and no money to make a place. "But I will pray and ask God for His help," she said, "and you do the same."

That evening, the teacher returned to her home and found a letter from a friend in the U.S. It contained a small sum of money— enough to begin providing for the orphan girl. Taking this as a sign of encouragement from God, she summoned a messenger the following morning and asked him to go to the neighboring village—a day's walk from her home—and bring the girl back.

To the teacher's surprise, the messenger returned with the girl in half the expected time. "How did you travel so quickly?" the teacher asked.

The girl's answer demonstrated the strength of her faith.

"We both prayed to God for help," she reminded the teacher. "I thought I might as well start walking." She had been halfway to the teacher's house when the messenger met her on the road. She had faith that God would meet her needs—and He did.

— *Anonymous*

Key To Salvation

For by grace you have been saved through faith, and that not of yourselves; it is the gift of God, not of works, lest anyone should boast. For we are His workmanship, created in Christ Jesus for good works, which God prepared beforehand that we should walk in them.

— Ephesians 2:8-10 (NKJV)
HOLY BIBLE

Strong in Faith

Christian, take good care of thy faith; for recollect faith is the only way whereby thou canst obtain blessings. If we want blessings from God, nothing can fetch them down but faith. Prayer cannot draw down answers from God's throne except it be the earnest prayer of the man who believes. Faith is the angelic messenger between the soul and the Lord Jesus in glory. Let that angel be withdrawn, we can neither send up prayer, nor receive the answers. Faith is the telegraphic wire which links earth and heaven—on which God's messages of love fly so fast, that before we call He answers, and while we are yet speaking He hears us. But if that telegraphic wire of faith be snapped, how can we receive the promise? Am I in trouble?—I can obtain help for trouble by faith. Am I beaten about by the enemy?—my soul on her dear Refuge leans by faith. But take faith away—in vain I call to God. There is no road betwixt my soul and heaven. In the deepest wintertime faith is a road on which the horses of prayer may travel—ay, and all the better for the biting frost; but blockade the road, and how can we communicate with the Great King? Faith links me with divinity. Faith clothes me with the power of God. Faith engages on my side the omnipotence of Jehovah. Faith ensures every attribute of God in my defence. It helps me to defy the hosts of hell. It makes me march triumphant over the necks of my enemies. But without faith how can I receive anything of the Lord? Let not him that wavereth—who is like a wave of the sea—expect that he will receive anything of God! O, then, Christian, watch well thy faith; for with it thou canst win all things, however poor thou art, but without it thou canst obtain nothing. "If thou canst believe, all things are possible to him that believeth."

— *Charles H. Spurgeon*

Taken from *Morning and Evening Devotions: An Updated Edition of the Classic Devotional in Today's Language* by C. H. Spurgeon. Copyright © 1987 by Thomas Nelson Publishers. Used by permission of Thomas Nelson Publishers.

Who Needs Faith?

Masha: I think a human being has got to have some faith, or at least he's got to seek faith. Otherwise his life will be empty, empty. . . . How can you live and not know why the cranes fly, why children are born, why the stars shine in the sky! . . . You must either know why you live, or else . . . nothing matters . . . everything's just wild grass.

— *Anton Chekhov*

Three Sisters, Act II
Speaker's Resources from Contemporary Literature
Edited by Charles L. Wallis
New York: Harper & Row, 1965

Hidden Heroes

John Egglen had never preached a sermon in his life.
Never.

Wasn't that he didn't want to, just never needed to. But then one morning he did. The snow left his town of Colchester, England, buried in white. When he awoke on that January Sunday in 1850, he thought of staying home. Who would go to church in such weather?

But he reconsidered. He was, after all, a deacon. And if the deacons didn't go, who would? So he put on his boots, hat, and coat and walked the six miles to the Methodist Church.

He wasn't the only member who considered staying home. In fact, he was one of the few who came. Only thirteen people were present. Twelve members and one visitor. Even the minister was snowed in. Someone suggested they go home. Egglen would hear none of that. They'd come this far; they would have a service. Besides, they had a visitor. A thirteen-year-old-boy.

But who would preach? Egglen was the only deacon. It fell to him.

And so he did. His sermon lasted only ten minutes. It drifted and wandered and made no point in an effort to make several. But at the end, an uncharacteristic courage settled upon the man. He lifted his eyes and looked straight at the boy and challenged: "Young man, look to Jesus. Look! Look! Look!"

Did the challenge make a difference? Let the boy, now a man, answer. "I did look, and then and there the cloud on my heart lifted, the darkness rolled away, and at that moment I saw the sun."

The boy's name? Charles Haddon Spurgeon. England's prince of preachers.

— *Max Lucado*

When God Whispers Your Name
Dallas: Word Publishing, 1994

Have Faith in God

So Jesus answered and said to them, "Have faith in God. For assuredly, I say to you, whoever says to this mountain, 'Be removed and be cast into the sea,' and does not doubt in his heart, but believes that those things he says will be done, he will have whatever he says. Therefore I say to you, whatever things you ask when you pray, believe that you receive them, and you will have them.

"And whenever you stand praying, if you have anything against anyone, forgive him, that your Father in heaven may also forgive you your trespasses. But if you do not forgive, neither will your Father in heaven forgive your trespasses."

— Mark 11:22-26 (NKJV)
HOLY BIBLE

True Faith

If you are willing even in death to confess not only the articles, but in affliction and death to trust the promises; if in the lowest nakedness of poverty you can cherish yourselves with expectation of God's promises and dispensation, being as confident of food and raiment, and deliverance or support, when all is in God's hand; as you are, when it is in your own; if you can be cheerful in a storm, smile when the world frowns; be content in the midst of spiritual desertions, and anguish of spirit, expecting all should work together for the best according to the promise; if you can strengthen yourselves in God, when you are weakest, believe when ye see no hope, and entertain no jealousies or suspicions of God, though you see nothing to make you confident; then, and then only, you have faith, which in conjunction with its other parts is able to save your souls.

— Jeremy Taylor

The Great Exemplar
The Golden Grove Selected Passages
from the Sermons and Writings of Jeremy Taylor
Edited by Logan Pearsall Smith
Oxford: Clarendon Press, 1649

Breakthrough to Faith

I had certainly been seized with a wondrous eagerness to understand Paul in the epistle to the Romans, but hitherto I had been held up . . . by one word only, in chapter 1: *"The righteousness of God is revealed."* For I hated this word "righteousness of God" which . . . I had been taught to understand philosophically as what they call the formal or active righteousness, whereby God is just and punishes unjust sinners.

For my case was this: however irreproachable my life as a monk, I felt myself in the presence of God to be a sinner with a most unquiet conscience, nor could I believe Him to be appeased by the satisfaction I could offer. I did not love—nay, I hated this just God who punishes sinners . . . and so I raged with a savage and confounded conscience; yet I knocked importunately at Paul in this place, with a parched and burning desire to know what he could mean.

At last, as I meditated day and night, God showed mercy and I turned my attention to the connection of the words, namely, "The righteousness of God is revealed, as it is written: the righteous shall live by faith"—and there I began to understand that the righteousness of God is the righteousness in which a just man lives by the gift of God . . . in other words, that by which the merciful God justifies us through faith . . . . At this I felt myself straightway born afresh and to have entered through the open gates into paradise itself.

— *Martin Luther*

Autobiographical Fragment
Martin Luther
Edited by Rupp and Drewry
Eerdmans' Book of Christian Classics
Compiled by Veronica Zundel
Grand Rapids, Mich.: William B. Eerdmans Publishing Co., 1985

Augustine's Conversion

There was a small garden attached to the house where we lodged . . . I now found myself driven by the tumult in my breast to take refuge in this garden, where no one could interrupt that fierce struggle, in which I was my own contestant, until it came to its conclusion.

I probed the hidden depths of my soul and wrung its pitiful secrets from it, and when I gathered them all before the eyes of my heart, a great storm broke within me, bringing with it a great deluge of tears . . . For I felt that I was still enslaved by my sins, and in my misery I kept crying, "How long shall I go on saying, 'Tomorrow, tomorrow'? Why not now? Why not make an end of my ugly sins this moment?"

I was asking myself these questions, weeping all the while with the most bitter sorrow in my heart, when all at once I heard the sing-song voice of a child in a nearby house. Whether it was the voice of a boy or a girl I cannot say, but again and again it repeated the chorus, "Take it and read, take it and read." At this I looked up, thinking hard whether there was any kind of game in which children used to chant words like these, but I could not remember ever hearing them before. I stemmed my flood of tears and stood up, telling myself that this could only be God's command to open my book of Scripture and read the first passage on which my eyes should fall . . . .

So I hurried back to the place where Alypius was sitting, for when I stood up to move away I had put down the book containing Paul's letters. I seized it and opened it, and in silence I read the first passage on which my eyes fell: "No orgies or drunkenness, no immorality or indecency, no fighting or jealousy. Take up the weapons of the Lord Jesus Christ; and stop giving attention to your sinful nature, to satisfy its desires." I had no wish to read more and no need to do so. For in an instant, as I came to the end of the sentence, it was as though the light of faith flooded into my heart and all the darkness of doubt was dispelled.

— *St. Augustine*

Taken from *The Confessions of Saint Augustine*,
trans. by F. J. Sheed. Copyright © 1942,
renewed © 1970 by Sheed and Ward
Used by permission of Sheed and Ward Publishers

Conquering Mountains

All temptation is primarily to look within, to take our eyes off the Lord, and to take account of appearances. Faith is always meeting a mountain, a mountain of evidence that seems to contradict God's Word, a mountain of apparent contradiction in the realm of tangible fact—of failures in deed, as well as in the realm of feeling and suggestion— and either faith or the mountain has to go. They cannot both stand. But the trouble is that many a time the mountain stays and faith goes. That must not be. If we resort to our senses to discover the truth, we shall find Satan's lies are often enough true to our experience; but if we refuse to accept as binding anything that contradicts God's Word and maintain an attitude of faith in Him alone, we shall find instead that Satan's lies begin to dissolve and that our experience is coming progressively to tally with that Word.

— *Watchman Nee*

The Normal Christian Life, 1957

Faith When Darkness Comes

When the night kneels down by your bed
    In the time of your sadness,
Remember O child of the mountains
    This word of the law:
The night is the shadow of God
    Who made you for gladness,
And your sorrows are less than your strength
    Which He foresaw.

— *Preston Clark*

The Home Book of Modern Verse, Second Edition
Compiled by Burton E. Stevenson
Holt, Rinehart & Winston, 1953

Faith's Ingredients

From these premises we may see but too evidently, that though a great part of mankind pretend to be sav'd by faith, yet they know not what it is, or else wilfully mistake it, and place their hopes upon sand or the more unstable water. Believing is the least thing in a justifying faith. For faith is a conjunction of many ingredients; and faith is a covenant, and faith is a law, and faith is obedience, and faith is a work, and indeed is a sincere cleaving to and a closing with the terms of the gospel in every instance, in every particular. Alas! the niceties of a spruce understanding, and the curious nothings of useless speculation, and all the opinions of men that make the divisions of heart, and do nothing else, cannot bring us one drop of comfort in the day of tribulation; and therefore are not parts of the strength of faith. Nay, when a man begins truly to fear God, and is in the agonies of mortification, all these new nothings and curiosities will lie neglected by as baubles do by children when they are deadly sick. But that only is faith that makes us to love God, to do His will, to suffer his impositions, to trust His promises, to see through a cloud, to overcome the world, to resist the devil, to stand in the day of trial, and to be comforted in all our sorrows.

— *Jeremy Taylor*

Righteousness Evangelical
The Golden Grove Selected Passages
from the Sermons and Writings of Jeremy Taylor
Edited by Logan Pearsall Smith
Oxford: Clarendon Press, 1663

You Can Depend on Me

The steadfast nature of the Lord is like an anchor that never pulls off the bottom. It stabilizes the ship in the midst of the storm. It is because God loves us that we know He is faithful. He cannot contradict His own nature. He Himself is unmerited, unchanging, unconditional love.

The fruit of faithfulness is a result. Faith is a primary gift of the Holy Spirit. It is the imputed gift by which we respond to what God has done for us in Jesus Christ. Belief is not our accomplishment. The same God who is Source and Sustainer of all, who dwelt in Jesus Christ for the reconciliation of the world, is the same Lord who comes to each of us to give us the capacity to claim what was done for us as the basis of our hope, now and forever. This faith leads to faithfulness, a full-grown faith which dares to believe that all things are possible. It develops as a consistency in all of life. Our faithfulness is not our human follow-through, but our trust that Christ will follow through in all of life's changes and challenges. He says, "You can depend on Me!" Can we say that to Him and to others? His dependability makes us dependable.

— *Lloyd John Ogilvie*

Taken from *Silent Strength for My Life*
by Lloyd John Ogilvie. Copyright © 1990 by
Harvest House Publishers, Eugene, Oregon.
Used by permission.

Assurance

How easy for me to live with You, O Lord!
How easy for me to believe in You!
When my mind parts in bewilderment or falters,
then the most intelligent people see no further than this day's
end and do not know what must be done tomorrow.
You grant me the serene certitude
that You exist and that You will take care
that not all the paths of good be closed.
Atop the ridge of earthly fame,
I look back in wonder at the path
which I alone could never have found,
a wondrous path through despair to this point

from which I, too, could transmit to mankind
a reflection of Your rays.
And as much as I must still reflect You will give me.
But as much as I cannot take up
You will have already assigned to others.

— Aleksandr Solzhenitsyn

Hymns for the Family of God

His Compassions Never Fail

*Yet this I call to mind
    and therefore I have hope:
Because of the Lord's great love we are not consumed,
    for his compassions never fail.
They are new every morning;
    great is your faithfulness.
I say to myself, "The Lord is my portion;
    therefore I will wait for him."
The Lord is good to those whose hope is in him,
    to the one who seeks him;
it is good to wait quietly for the salvation of the Lord.*

– Lamentations 3:21-26 (NIV)
HOLY BIBLE

Where Faithfulness Leads

Don't expect wisdom to come into your life like great chunks of rock on a conveyor belt. It isn't like that. It's not splashy and bold . . . nor is it dispensed like a prescription across a counter. Wisdom comes privately from God as a by-product of right decisions, godly reactions, and the application of spiritual principles to daily circumstances. Wisdom comes . . . not from trying to do great things for God . . . but more from being faithful to the small, obscure tasks few people ever see.

— *Charles R. Swindoll*

Encyclopedia of Famous Quotes

Faith Is of the Heart

The heart has its reasons of which reason knows nothing. We feel it in a thousand things. I say that the heart naturally loves the Universal Being, and naturally loves itself; and it gives itself to one or the other, and hardens itself against one or the other, as it chooses . . . It is the heart that feels God, not the reason; this is faith.

— *Blaise Pascal*

Eerdmans' Book of Christian Classics
Compiled by Veronica Zundel
Grand Rapids, Mich.: William B. Eerdmans Publishing Company, 1985

Hold Out Your Hand

Sometimes when I was a child my mother or father would say, "Shut your eyes and hold out your hand." That was the promise of some lovely surprise. I trusted them, so I shut my eyes instantly and held out my hand. Whatever they were going to give me I was ready to take. So it should be in our trust of our heavenly Father. Faith is the willingness to receive whatever He wants to give, or the willingness not to have what He does not want to give.

> I am content to be and have what in Thy heart
> I am meant to be and have.
> *[George MacDonald, Diary of an Old Soul]*

From the greatest of all gifts, salvation in Christ, to the material blessings of any ordinary day (hot water, a pair of legs that work, a cup of coffee, a job to do and strength to do it), every good gift comes down from the Father of Lights. Every one of them is to be received gladly and, like gifts people give us, with thanks.

Sometimes we want things we were not meant to have. Because He loves us, the Father says no. Faith trusts that no. Faith is willing not to have what God is not willing to give. Furthermore, faith does not insist upon an explanation. It is enough to know His promise to give what is good—He knows so much more about that than we do.

— Elizabeth Elliot

God's Heroes

To fill a little space because God wills it; to go on cheerfully with the petty round of little duties, little avocations; to accept unmurmuringly a low position; to be misunderstood, misrepresented, maligned, without complaint, to smile for the joys of others when the heart is aching; to banish all ambition, all pride, and all restlessness, in a single regard to our Savior's work; he who does this is a greater hero than he who for one hour storms a beach, or for one day rushes onward undaunted in the flaming front of shot and shell. His works will follow him. He may be no hero to the world, but he is one of God's heroes.

— F. W. Faber

Treasure Thoughts
F. W. Faber
Edited by Rose Porter

God Can Use Our Mistakes

I believe that God can and will bring good out of evil, even out of the greatest evil. For that purpose he needs men who make the best use of everything. I believe that God will give us all the strength we need to help us resist in all time of distress. But he never gives it in advance, lest we should rely on ourselves and not on Him alone. A faith such as this should allay all our fears for the future. I believe that even our mistakes and shortcomings are turned to good account, and that it is no harder for God to deal with them than with our supposedly good deeds. I believe that God is no timeless fate, but that He waits for and answers sincere prayers and responsible actions.

— Dietrich Bonhoeffer

A Book of Faith
Elizabeth Goudge
New York: Coward, McCann & Geoghegan, Inc., 1976

More Than a Feeling

Much of my own problem with faith arose from an early misunderstanding of what faith is. First of all, I used to believe that faith had something to do with feeling. For example, when I had messed up some situation and had asked God for forgiveness, then I would peer inside myself to see if I felt forgiven. If I could locate such feelings, then I was sure that God had heard and had forgiven me. Now I know that this is an altogether false test of faith. . . .

Another misconception I once had was that faith is trying to believe something one is fairly certain is not true. But faith is not hocus-pocus, opposed to knowledge and reality. In fact, faith does not go against experience at all; rather it appeals to experience, just as science does. The difference is that it appeals to experience in a realm where our five senses are not supreme rulers. . . .

Perhaps one reason that the real meaning of faith eluded me personally for so many years was that it is so surprisingly simple, so practical. Faith in God is simply trusting Him enough to step out on that trust.

— *Catherine Marshall*

Taken from *Beyond Ourselves* by Catherine
Marshall. Copyright © 1961 by Catherine Marshall.
Used by permission of Breakthrough Prayer Ministry,
a division of The Catherine Marshall Center, Lincoln, VA.

"Catching" Faith

I doubt if I will ever unravel the mystery of intercessory prayer, for myself, for others. I know that there are powers of healing that Jesus tried to teach the disciples, and us, to tap. But the disciples could not throw out the unclean spirit from the possessed boy because their faith was not sufficient. If we had faith, we could indeed move mountains.

Great Is Thy Faithfulness

Great is Thy faithfulness, O God my Father;
there is no shadow of turning with Thee;
Thou changest not, Thy compassions, they fail not;
as Thou hast been, Thou forever wilt be.

Summer and winter and springtime and harvest,
sun, moon, and stars in their courses above
join with all nature in manifold witness
to Thy great faithfulness, mercy, and love.

Pardon for sin and a peace that endureth,
Thine own dear presence to cheer and to guide;
strength for today and bright hope for tomorrow,
blessings all mine, with ten thousand beside!

(Chorus)
Great is Thy faithfulness!
Great is Thy faithfulness!
Morning by morning new mercies I see;
all I have needed Thy hand hath provided;
great is Thy faithfulness, Lord, unto me!

— Thomas O. Chisholm

Methodist Hymnal

Faith and Salvation

Faith is the avenue to salvation. Not intellectual understanding. Not money. Not your works. Just simple faith. How much faith? The faith of a mustard seed, so small you can hardly see it. But if you will put that little faith in the person of Jesus, your life will be changed. He will come with supernatural power into your heart. It can happen to you.

— *Billy Graham*

The Quotable Billy Graham
Compiled and Edited by Cort R. Flint and the Staff of *Quote*
Anderson, S.C.: Droke House, 1966

Fidelity

The reference to faithfulness (or "faith" in the KJV) is not to faith exercised by the Christian, but rather to faithfulness or fidelity, produced by the Holy Spirit in a yielded Christian life. The same word occurs in Titus 2:10 where it is translated "fidelity" in the King James Version. This trait of character is highly commended in Scripture. Fidelity in little things is one of the surest tests of character, as our Lord indicated in the parable of the talents: "You were faithful with a few things, I will put you in charge of many things" (Matthew 25:21 NASB). Morality is not so much a matter of magnitude, but of quality. Right is right, and wrong is wrong, in small things as well as in big things.

— *Billy Graham*

The Faithful Christian: An Anthology of Billy Graham
Compiled by William Griffin and Ruth Graham Dienert
New York: McCracken Press, 1994

To Have Faith

We have the God-given ability to believe, to have faith—in God, in ourselves, and in our fellow man. Christ has told us "according to your faith, be it unto you." What a wonderful promise in those words.

We have only to put our problems before Him with a humble and faithful heart and to believe with the simple faith of a little child, and we are promised His guidance and help. If our problems are big, then our prayers should be equally big! And the minute we believe that He has answered our prayers, they have been answered, perhaps not as we wanted or expected, but answered nevertheless. And they are right answers, too.

— *Norman Vincent Peale*

I Will Lift Up Mine Eyes
Selected by Bette Bishop
Hallmark Editions

Daily Fidelity

Both faith and faithfulness are closely connected together. Faith is that indefinable power whereby we realize things unseen. It seems to me that unless we possess faith, then faithfulness is impossible. We can only be true and faithful in our relationship to things spiritual, as we have faith in the reality of these things. The best of us must confess that we are not as faithful to Him as we should be. Is the Master disappointed in your allegiance to Him? Are we more faithful to others than to Him? Are you more concerned of what people think of you than His judgment will be?

"He that is faithful in that which is least is faithful also in much" (Luke 16:10). Let us observe what our Lord says: It is not he that is faithful in that which is least will become faithful also in much, but is faithful in much. Acts of faithfulness are the golden threads which make the lustre of a fruitful life. There is unity in such a life. It is a

life consecrated through and through. Every act of faithfulness is the outburst and expression of the Life of the Spirit. They are like precious stones which the soul builds into its habitation for eternity. Our life is not made up of sudden bursts of inspiration, but of progressive efforts of daily fidelity. Even as the pasture land is made up of blades of grass, so the qualities of a faithful life, the solid strength of character, is not the outcome of one act but the result of a life of self-restraint.

— *Ivor Rosser*

The Fruit of the Spirit
Great Britain: Starling Press Limited

Always There

Almighty God is on our team. He is our faithful Sustainer. When everybody else abandons us, we can count on Him. When nobody else is willing to endure with us, He is there. He is trustworthy, reliable, and consistent. We can depend upon Him.

— *Charles Stanley*

How To Listen to God
Nashville: Thomas Nelson, 1985

Link To Promises

Unto us was the gospel preached, as well as unto them: but the word preached did not profit them, not being mixed with faith in them that heard it (Hebrews 4:2).

Faith is very important. It is the link that binds us to every promise of God—it brings us every blessing. I do not mean a dead faith, but a living faith. There is a great difference between the two. A man may tell me that ten thousand dollars are deposited in a certain bank in my name. I may believe it, but if I don't act upon it and get the money it does me no good. Unbelief bars the door and keeps back the blessing.

Some one has said there are three elements in faith—knowledge, assent, laying hold. Knowledge! A man may have a good deal of knowledge about Christ, but that does not save him. I suppose Noah's carpenters knew as much about the ark as Noah did, but they perished miserably nevertheless, because they were not in the ark. Our knowledge about Christ does not help us if we do not act upon it. But knowledge is very important. Many also assent and say—"I believe"; but that does not save them. Knowledge, assent, then laying hold: it is that last element that saves, that brings the soul and Christ together.

— Dwight L. Moody

The D. L. Moody Year Book
Selected by Emma Moody Fitt
New York: Fleming H. Revell Company, 1900

Credo

Not what, but whom do I believe!
    That in my darkest hour of need,
    Hath comfort that no mortal creed
    To mortal man may give.
Not what, but whom!
    For Christ is more than all the creeds
    And His full life of gentle deeds
    Shall all the creeds outlie.
Not what, but whom!
    Who walks beside me in the gloom?
    Who shares the burden wearisome?
    Who all the dim way doth illume?
    And bids me look beyond the tomb
    The larger life to live?
Not what I do believe, but whom!
    Not what, but whom!

— John Oxenham

Another Tassel Is Moved
Louis O. Caldwell
Grand Rapids, Mich.: Baker Book House

Sanctified Imagination

Faith. What is that? Believing things you do not understand? No. It is sanctified imagination; it is having the horizon above the world; it is believing that there are things that have no mortal forms; it is believing in a future, believing in a whole assembly of intelligence above your head; it is having a life hereafter, a greater life than this. Ah! the man who sits in his house all day knows exactly what he knows—that is the fireplace, that is the rug, that is the fender, that is the window, that is the door. That is what is called a practical person, who knows what he does know. But out of doors the whole heaven is above his head, night and day, filled with inestimable treasures.

— *Henry Ward Beecher*

A Summer in England
New York: Fords, Howard, & Hulbert, 1887

The Weaver's Hand

My life is but a weaving, between my God and me.
I do not choose the colors, He worketh steadily.
Ofttimes He weaveth sorrow, and I in foolish pride,
Forget He sees the upper, and I the underside.
Not till the loom is silent and the shuttles cease to fly,
Will God unroll the canvas and explain the reason why.
The dark threads are as needful in the skillful Weaver's hand,
As the threads of gold and silver in the pattern He has planned.

— *Unknown*

Power To Transform

Faith faces everything that makes the world uncomfortable—pain, fear, loneliness, shame, death—and acts with a compassion by which these things are transformed, even exalted.

— *Samuel H. Miller*

Look
December 19, 1961

Regardless of Circumstances

This is real faith: believing and acting obediently regardless of circumstances or contrary evidence. After all, if faith depended on visible evidence, it wouldn't be faith. "We walk by faith, not by sight," the apostle Paul wrote.

It is absurd for Christians to constantly seek new demonstrations of God's power, to expect a miraculous answer to every need, from curing ingrown toenails to finding parking spaces; this only leads to faith in miracles rather than in the Maker.

True faith depends not upon mysterious signs, celestial fireworks, or grandiose dispensation from a God who is seen as a rich, benevolent uncle; true faith, as Job understood, rests on the assurance that God is who He is. Indeed, on that we must be willing to stake our very lives.

There was a time when eleven men did just that. They staked their lives on obedience to their leader, even when doing so was contrary to all human wisdom. That act of obedience produced a faith that emboldened them to stand against the world and, in their lifetimes, change it forever.

— Charles Colson

Taken from *Loving God* by Charles W. Colson.
Copyright © 1983, 1987 by Charles W. Colson.
Used by permission of Zondervan Publishing House.

Part of the Whole

One of the most basic truths of the Bible is that faith in Christ is not just an intellectual idea, to be accepted and then stored in the back of our minds. True faith affects every aspect of our lives, for Jesus Christ is to be not only our Savior, but our Lord and Master.

— Billy Graham

Taken from "Part of the Whole" from
Courage of Conviction edited by P. L. Berman.
Copyright © by P. L. Berman. Used by permission
of Alfred A. Knopf/Random House, Inc.

Heaven Comes Down

Something greater than divine philosophy must link the heights and depths for man. It is faith. Faith lowers the heavens to earth.

— *James Edward O'Mahony*

Romanticism of Holiness
1933

Source of Faith

Fasting and long hours of prayer do not build faith.

Reading books about faith, and about men of faith and their exploits stirs in the heart a deep passion for faith, but does not build faith.

The Word alone is the source of faith.

But the Word will not build faith unless it becomes a part of us. "If ye abide in me and my words have their place in you." That is, they have their place in our conduct.

Jesus gave us the key. He said, "The words that I speak are not mine, but my Father's."

And the works that He did were not His, but His Father's.

Jesus acted on His Father's words.

Jesus never needed faith. He had it unconsciously.

Faith is built in us by the Word being built into us, by our acting upon it.

It is "the Word of faith," and so as the Father builds that into us in our daily walk, faith becomes an unconscious asset.

We come to realize that we are a part of Him as a branch is a part of the vine; that He is a part of us as the vine is a part of the branch; that we have His life, we have His ability, we have His love nature, we have His strength.

That gives us an unconscious certainty as we go into His presence.

We know that we are working together with Him to one common end.

We know that He is the strength of our life.

We know that He is our ability.

We know that we are His righteousness in Christ.

We know that He needs us to carry out His will, and so we are taking our place as a son carrying out His dream for man.

— *E. W. Kenyon*

In His Presence: The Secret of Prayer
Kenyon's Publishing Society, Inc.

Faith Means "Don't Worry"

Jesus taught:

"Don't worry about things—food, drink, and clothes. For you already have life and a body—and they are far more important than what to eat and wear. Look at the birds! They don't worry about what to eat—they don't need to sow or reap or store up food—for your heavenly Father feeds them. And you are far more valuable to him than they are. Will all your worries add a single moment to your life?

"And why worry about your clothes? Look at the field lilies! They don't worry about theirs. Yet King Solomon in all his glory was not clothed as beautifully as they. And if God cares so wonderfully for flowers that are here today and gone tomorrow, won't he more surely care for you, O men of little faith?

"So don't worry at all about having enough food and clothing. Why be like the heathen? For they take pride in all these things and are deeply concerned about them. But your heavenly Father already knows perfectly well that you need them, and he will give them to you if you give him first place in your life and live as he wants you to.

"So don't be anxious about tomorrow. God will take care of your tomorrow too. Live one day at a time."

— *Matthew 6:25-34* (TLB)
HOLY BIBLE

Have Faith in God

Faith is the foot of the soul by which it can march along the road of the commandments. Love can make the feet move more swiftly; but faith is the foot which carries the soul. Faith is the oil enabling the wheels of holy devotion and of earnest piety to move well; and without faith the wheels are taken from the chariot, and we drag heavily. With faith I can do all things; without faith I shall neither have the inclination nor the power to do anything in the service of God. If you would find the men who serve God the best, you must look for the men of the most faith. Little faith will save a man, but little faith cannot do great things for God. Poor Little-faith could not have fought "Apollyon;" it needed "Christian" to do that. Poor Little-faith could not have slain "Giant Despair;" it required "Great-heart's" arm to knock that monster down. Little-faith will go to heaven most certainly, but it often has to hide itself in a nut-shell, and it frequently loses all but its jewels. Little-faith says, "It is a rough road, beset with sharp thorns, and full of dangers; I am afraid to go;" but Great-faith remembers the promise, "Thy shoes shall be iron and brass; as thy days, so shall thy strength be:" and so she boldly ventures. Little-faith stands desponding, mingling her tears with the flood; but Great-faith sings, "When thou passest through the waters, I will be with thee; and through the rivers, they shall not overflow thee:" and she fords the stream at once. Would you be comfortable and happy? Would you enjoy religion? Would you have the religion of cheerfulness and not that of gloom? Then "have faith in God." If you love darkness, and are satisfied to dwell in gloom and misery, then be content with little faith; but if you love the sunshine; and would sing songs of rejoicing, covet earnestly this best gift, "great faith."

— *Charles H. Spurgeon*

Living Up To Faith

Young Henry (Harry) Esmond, future Colonel in the Service of Her Majesty Queen Anne, is discussing persecution with Dick Steele, one of His Majesty's Horse Guards also known as "Dick the Scholar." Steele says:

". . . For faith, everywhere multitudes die willingly enough. I have read in Monsieur Rycaut's History of the Turks, of thousands of Mahomet's followers rushing upon death in battle as upon certain Paradise; and in the great Mogul's dominions people fling themselves by hundreds under the cars of the idols annually, and the widows burn themselves on their husband's bodies, as 'tis well known. 'Tis not the dying for a faith that's so hard, Master Harry—every man of every nation has done that—'tis the living up to it that is difficult, as I know to my cost."

The History of Henry Esmond
Book I, Chapter VI
William Makepeace Thackeray

Faith of Our Fathers, Living Still

Faith of our fathers, living still
In spite of dungeon, fire and sword,
O how our hearts beat high with joy
Whene'er we hear that glorious word!

Faith of our fathers, we will strive
To win all nations unto Thee;
And through the truth that comes from God
Mankind shall then indeed be free.

Faith of our fathers, we will love
Both friend and foe in all our strife,
And preach Thee, too, as love knows how
By kindly words and virtuous life.

(Chorus)
Faith of our fathers, holy faith,
We will be true to Thee till death.

— Frederick W. Faber

Treasure Thoughts

Concerning Sufferings

Surely those People who through Faith
        In Christ, on God depend,
Need not to fear the Rage of Man,
        The Lord will them defend.
Though wicked Men rise up, and come
        God's People to annoy,
Yet they shall disappointed be,
        His Saints they shan't destroy:

Therefore ye need not for to fear,
　　When you assembled be;
Nor yet ought you to make escape,
　　And from them for to flee;
Because, except the Lord doth grant,
　　And give to Satan leave,
He has no Power to do you harm:
　　This Doctrine pray receive;
That in the Faith you firm may stand,
　　And patiently may bear
Those sufferings that may attend,
　　Casting on God your Care;
Who careful is, them to support
　　That witness to his Cause,
And never fails to give Relief
　　To those that keep his Laws.

— Benjamin Antrobus

Buds and Blossoms of Piety,
with some Fruit of the Spirit of Love
and Directions to the Divine Wisdom
London, 1715

A Time of Testing

Being a missionary is never easy. No matter how strong your faith in God, there are still times when you turn to God and say, "Why am I in this place? Am I really making a difference?"

Aside from facing down these occasional doubts, and the usual poverty and lack of education found in many countries, some missionaries also have to deal with governments and law enforcement officials who seem determined to make life as difficult and as dangerous as possible for the citizens of their city or town.

One missionary in Brazil a few years back had exactly this problem. In frustration, he watched as government policies—supposedly aimed at promoting economic growth—did nothing more than rob farmers of their land (and sometimes their lives) and cause widespread starvation. Unwilling and unable to sit idly by, this missionary wrote articles for U.S. magazines, criticizing the government's actions. He must have known that he was doing a dangerous thing, but he could not do otherwise. And he paid the price.

One day, the police came and took him away. For four days, he was physically tortured, and taunted by his captors. His only comfort was his faith; he recited the 23rd Psalm over and over again.

Then, another beam of light. One of the torturers jeeringly told him that his friends were at the church, praying for him. The missionary was elated, and encouraged. To think that his friends were risking their lives by openly praying for him! They were exhibiting their faith in the God who answers prayer.

The missionary said that during the torture, he also learned something about himself and his own faith. "All the things I had been saying I believed for the past twenty years were true," he said. ". . . I really believed!"

Intervention by the American embassy resulted in the missionary's release. Sometime after his return to the U.S., he said that he was almost grateful to his captors. Before the torture, he had been like many Christians: fairly secure in his faith, but harboring a few doubts about how strong it really was.

After being tested in such a dramatic way, he could say with confidence that his faith in God was real. And God was faithful to His own.

— *James Taylor*

An Everyday God
1981

Dead Without Works

What does it profit, my brethren, if someone says he has faith but does not have works? Can faith save him? If a brother or sister is naked and destitute of daily food, and one of you says to them, "Depart in peace, be warmed and filled," but you do not give them the things which are needed for the body, what does it profit? Thus also faith by itself, if it does not have works, is dead.

But someone will say, "You have faith, and I have works." Show me your faith without your works, and I will show you my faith by my works. You believe that there is one God. You do well. Even the demons believe— and tremble! But do you want to know, O foolish man, that faith without works is dead? Was not Abraham our father justified by works when he offered Isaac his son on the altar? Do you see that faith was working together with his works, and by works faith was made perfect? And the Scripture was fulfilled which says, "Abraham believed God, and it was accounted to him for righteousness." And he was called the friend of God. You see then that a man is justified by works, and not by faith only.

Likewise, was not Rahab the harlot also justified by works when she received the messengers and sent them out another way?

For as the body without the spirit is dead, so faith without works is dead also.

— *James 2:14-26 (NKJV)*
  Holy Bible

Faith Sayings

Faith builds a bridge from this world to the next.

Faith cannot die, nor can he die who hath faith.

Faith fears no famine.
How can she, when she can sing, "Jehovah-jireh": the Lord will provide? Sooner will the clouds rain bread than the people of God be left to die.

Faith gets most, humility keeps most, love works most.

Faith honours Christ, and Christ honours faith.

He said to the blind man, "Thy faith hath saved thee." He puts the crown on the head of faith because faith always puts the crown upon the head of her Lord.

Faith in God is never out of season.

Faith looks to precepts as well as to promises. It takes the whole Word of God, and obeys commands as well as trusts promises.

Faith makes all things possible, and love makes them easy.

Faith makes the Christian, but love proves him. Faith justifies the believer, but love justifies his faith by the works which it produces. Faith believes God to be true; love proves faith to be true.

Faith sees God, and God sees faith. Faith sees God, who is invisible, and God sees even that little faith, which would be invisible to others.

Faith unfeigned breeds hope unfailing.

Faith which never wept was never true. Repentance is the inseparable companion of a true trust in Christ. It is the tear which falls from the eye of faith at the remembrance of pardoned sin.

Faith works love, works by love, and loves to work.

Faith's barque is often tost, but never lost. An untried faith will turn out to be an untrue faith; but, however much tried, true faith will bear the strain.

Faith's eye sees in the dark. It is a God-given eye, and it is like the eye of God.

Faith's hand never knocks in vain at mercy's door.

— *Charles H. Spurgeon*

Spurgeon's Proverbs and Sayings with Notes, Vol. I
Grand Rapids, Mich.: Baker Book House

Grounded in Testimony

I believe God, that it shall be even as it was told me (Acts 27:25).

Faith is a belief in testimony. It is not a leap in the dark. God does not ask any man to believe without giving him something to believe. You might as well ask a man to see without eyes, as to bid him believe without giving him something to believe.

— *Dwight L. Moody*

The D.L. Moody Year Book
Selected by Emma Moody Fitt
New York: Fleming H. Revell Co., 1900

Faith Brings Wholeness

And as he [Jesus] entered into a certain village, there met him ten men that were lepers, which stood afar off:

And they lifted up their voices, and said, Jesus, Master, have mercy on us.

And when he saw them, he said unto them, Go shew yourselves unto the priests. And it came to pass, that, as they went, they were cleansed.

And one of them, when he saw that he was healed, turned back, and with a loud voice glorified God,

And fell down on his face at his feet, giving him thanks: and he was a Samaritan.

And Jesus answering said, Were there not ten cleansed? but where are the nine?

There are not found that returned to give glory to God, save this stranger.

And he said unto him, Arise, go thy way: thy faith hath made thee whole.

— *Luke 17:12-19 (KJV)*
HOLY BIBLE

Great Faith!

And Jesus went away from there, and withdrew into the district of Tyre and Sidon.

And behold, a Canaanite woman came out from that region, and began to cry out, saying, "Have mercy on me, O Lord, Son of David; my daughter is cruelly demon-possessed."

But He did not answer her a word. And His disciples came to Him and kept asking Him, saying, "Send her away, for she is shouting out after us."

But He answered and said, "I was sent only to the lost sheep of the house of Israel."

But she came and began to bow down before Him, saying, "Lord, help me!"

And He answered and said, "It is not good to take the children's bread and throw it to the dogs."

But she said, "Yes, Lord; but even the dogs feed on the crumbs which fall from their master's table."

Then Jesus answered and said to her, "O woman, your faith is great; be it done for you as you wish." And her daughter was healed at once.

— *Matthew 15:21-28* (NASB)
HOLY BIBLE

As a Grain of Mustard Seed

And Jesus rebuked the demon, and it came out of him; and the child was cured from that very hour.

Then the disciples came to Jesus privately and said, "Why could we not cast it out?"

So Jesus said to them, "Because of your unbelief; for assuredly, I say to you, if you have faith as a mustard seed, you will say to this mountain, 'Move from here to there,' and it will move; and nothing will be impossible for you. However, this kind does not go out except by prayer and fasting."

— *Matthew 17:18-21* (NKJV)
HOLY BIBLE

Such Great Faith

When Jesus had entered Capernaum, a centurion came to him, asking for help. "Lord," he said, "my servant lies at home paralyzed and in terrible suffering."

Jesus said to him, "I will go and heal him."

The centurion replied, "Lord, I do not deserve to have you come under my roof. But just say the word, and my servant will be healed. For I myself am a man under authority, with soldiers under me. I tell this one, 'Go,' and he goes; and that one, 'Come,' and he comes. I say to my servant, 'Do this,' and he does it."

When Jesus heard this, he was astonished and said to those following him, "I tell you the truth, I have not found anyone in Israel with such great faith. I say to you that many will come from the east and the west, and will take their places at the feast with Abraham, Isaac and Jacob in the kingdom of heaven. But the subjects of the kingdom will be thrown outside, into the darkness, where there will be weeping and gnashing of teeth."

Then Jesus said to the centurion, "Go! It will be done just as you believed it would." And his servant was healed at that very hour.

> — *Matthew 8:5-13* (NIV)
> *HOLY BIBLE*

The Right Call

God has not called me to be successful;
he has called me to be faithful.

> — *Mother Teresa*

Encyclopedia of Famous Quotes

Source of Faithfulness

In Christian service, there is an inner and an outer life, both of which are necessary to the complete idea of discipleship. Each of these has its special mission and its special danger. In the inner life, the heart must be kept right, and the motives pure, the faith, love, and zeal preserved from languishing, and fed by fresh supplies. In the outer life, there must be the expression of all these in action; the zeal finding its legitimate sphere; the love blossoming into a bright and fragrant obedience; the faith, evidenced by honest and cheerful work. It is clear, however, that, in this world of evil, there will be danger, in the inner life, of unwatchfulness and carnal security, in the outer life of unfaithfulness in the discharge of duty. Hence, our Lord uttered the parable of the ten virgins, to warn His followers against declension of the heart, that of the talents, to warn them against unbelief and disloyalty in the life. The one deals with the contemplative; the other with the energetic. The latter, with which we alone have to do, stimulates to faithfulness in action, without which there can be no true expression of religion in the life. The life that now is, is rather a stern strife than a joyous bridal. And while the forces around us are lashed into unwonted activity, and there are so many chances for the use of our entrusted talents and for profitable commerce, it were shame and sin for us either boastfully to vaunt of our talents, or faithlessly to bury them.

The faithful are those who are full of faith. No faithfulness can be genuine, constant, or permanent, which does not spring from faith in Christ as its primary source. Selfishness may prompt to a formal fidelity, or natural susceptibility give rise to a fitful one; but, for a life of fervent, constant piety, amid the world's cares and toils, no motive can be sufficient except self-consecration to Christ. Let us remember that we cannot live for Christ in the world, unless we live much with Him, apart from the world. Present grace, present help, the present realizing of the solemnity of duty and the awfulness of sin, present dependence on Christ's inwrought righteousness and the Spirit's promised help, these alone will fit us to be faithful always and everywhere, even unto death. Christian faithfulness is not so much a special duty as a something which has to do with all duties—not a tax to be periodically paid, and got rid of, at other times; but a ceaseless, all-pervading tribute to Him, who is the end of our life and being. It is not appropriate to one set of actions, and unsuitable to another, but something which, like the process of breathing, or the silent growth of the stature, may go on simultaneously with all our actions.

The theatre for the manifestation of faithfulness is the coarse, profane, common world, with its cares and crosses; its temptations, toils, and trials; its rivalries and competitions; its rough jostlings and rude contacts, its ever-recurring tests of temper and character. It matters not what a man's particular work in life be; the form is nothing, the faithfulness everything.

— *James M'Donald Inglis*

Precious Fruit
London: Seeley & Co., 1887

All That Counts

You who are trying to be justified by law have been alienated from Christ; you have fallen away from grace. But by faith we eagerly await through the Spirit the righteousness for which we hope. For in Christ Jesus neither circumcision nor uncircumcision has any value. The only thing that counts is faith expressing itself through love.

— *Galatians 5:4-6 (NIV)*
HOLY BIBLE

Solid Ground

Here in the maddening maze of times
When tossed by storm and flood
To one fixed ground my spirit clings
I know that God is good.

Another Tassel Is Moved
Louis O. Caldwell
Grand Rapids, Mich.: Baker Book House

Nothing Without Faith

Faith is the sole meaning of my life. I am not a devotee, but if I did not believe in the Creator and in all that we profess in our Christian credo, then all that I am would be meaningless and point-less. I would be nothing. All that I do I do because I have faith. . . .

People often ask me: What do you really believe? What is the basis of your faith and what are your deepest convictions? Who is God to you? . . .

Faith provides me with breathing space, with a respite. Agnostics think my faith provides me with an excuse not to accept responsibility for final outcomes, while religious people think that the presence of someone above assists me, allows me to pray and ponder. As for myself, I simply believe in Providence. I believe that I am here to execute the verdicts of Providence. This is precisely why I can accomplish signifi-cantly more than if I were just Lech Walesa, without God directing my fate. It's good to have the awareness of that great force outside us and above us directing our lives.

— Lech Walesa, 1985

Courage of Conviction
Edited by P. L. Berman

Doubts Lead to Faith

To deny the existence of God may . . . involve less unbelief than the smallest yielding to doubt of His goodness. I say yielding; for a man may be haunted with doubts, and only grow thereby in faith. Doubts are the messengers of the Living One to the honest. They are the first knock at our door of things that are not yet, but have to be, understood. . . . Doubts must precede every deeper assurance; for uncertainties are what we first see when we look into a region hitherto unknown, unexplored, unannexed.

— *George MacDonald*

A Book of Faith
Elizabeth Goudge
New York: Coward, McCann & Geoghegan, Inc., 1976

Triumphs of Faith

Now faith is the assurance of things hoped for, the conviction of things not seen.

For by it the men of old gained approval.

By faith we understand that the worlds were prepared by the word of God, so that what is seen was not made out of things which are visible.

By faith Abel offered to God a better sacrifice than Cain, through which he obtained the testimony that he was righteous, God testifying about his gifts, and through faith, though he is dead, he still speaks.

By faith Enoch was taken up so that he should not see death; AND HE WAS NOT FOUND BECAUSE GOD TOOK HIM UP; for he obtained the witness that before his being taken up he was pleasing to God.

And without faith it is impossible to please Him, for he who comes to God must believe that He is, and that He is a rewarder of those who seek Him.

By faith Noah, being warned by God about things not yet seen, in reverence prepared an ark for the salvation of his household, by which he condemned the world, and became an heir of the righteousness which is according to faith.

By faith Abraham, when he was called, obeyed by going out to a place which he was to receive for an inheritance; and he went out, not knowing where he was going.

By faith he lived as an alien in the land of promise, as in a foreign land, dwelling in tents with Isaac and Jacob, fellowheirs of the same promise; for he was looking for the city which has foundations, whose architect and builder is God.

By faith even Sarah herself received ability to conceive, even beyond the proper time of life, since she considered Him faithful who had promised; therefore, also, there was born of one man, and him as good as dead at that, as many descendants AS THE STARS OF HEAVEN IN NUMBER, AND INNUMERABLE AS THE SAND WHICH IS BY THE SEASHORE.

All these died in faith, without receiving the promises, but having seen them and having welcomed them from a distance, and having confessed that they were strangers and exiles on the earth.

For those who say such things make it clear that they are seeking a country of their own.

And indeed if they had been thinking of that country from which they went out, they would have had opportunity to return.

But as it is, they desire a better country, that is a heavenly one. Therefore God is not ashamed to be called their God; for He has prepared a city for them.

By faith Abraham, when he was tested, offered up Isaac; and he who had received the promises was offering up his only begotten son; it was he to whom it was said, "IN ISAAC YOUR DESCENDANTS SHALL BE CALLED."

He considered that God is able to raise men even from the dead; from which he also received him back as a type.

By faith Isaac blessed Jacob and Esau, even regarding things to come.

By faith Jacob, as he was dying, blessed each of the sons of Joseph, and worshiped, leaning on the top of his staff.

By faith Joseph, when he was dying, made mention of the exodus of the sons of Israel, and gave orders concerning his bones.

By faith Moses, when he was born, was hidden for three months by his parents, because they saw he was a beautiful child; and they were not afraid of the king's edict.

By faith Moses, when he had grown up, refused to be called the son of Pharaoh's daughter; choosing rather to endure ill-treatment with the people of God, than to enjoy the passing pleasures of sin; considering the reproach of Christ greater riches than the treasures of Egypt; for he was looking to the reward.

By faith he left Egypt, not fearing the wrath of the king; for he endured, as seeing Him who is unseen.

By faith he kept the Passover and the sprinkling of the blood, so that he who destroyed the first-born might not touch them.

By faith they passed through the Red Sea as though they were passing through dry land; and the Egyptians, when they attempted it, were drowned.

By faith the walls of Jericho fell down, after they had been encircled for seven days.

By faith Rahab the harlot did not perish along with those who were disobedient, after she had welcomed the spies in peace.

And what more shall I say? For time will fail me if I tell of Gideon, Barak, Samson, Jephthah, of David and Samuel and the prophets, who by faith conquered kingdoms, performed acts of righteousness, obtained promises, shut the mouths of lions, quenched the power of fire, escaped the edge of the sword, from weakness were made strong, became mighty in war, put foreign armies to flight.

Women received back their dead by resurrection; and others were tortured, not accepting their release, in order that they might obtain a better resurrection; and others experienced mockings and scourgings, yes, also chains and imprisonment.

They were stoned, they were sawn in two, they were tempted, they were put to death with the sword; they went about in sheepskins, in goatskins, being destitute, afflicted, ill-treated (men of whom the world was not worthy), wandering in deserts and mountains and caves and holes in the ground.

And all these, having gained approval through their faith, did not receive what was promised, because God had provided something better for us, so that apart from us they should not be made perfect.

Therefore, since we have so great a cloud of witnesses surrounding us, let us also lay aside every encumbrance, and the sin which so easily entangles us, and let us run with endurance the race that is set before us.

*— **Hebrews 11-12:1** (NASB)*
HOLY BIBLE

Meaningful Faith

The final test of religious faith . . . is whether it will enable men to endure insecurity without complacency or despair, whether it can so interpret the ancient verities that they will not become mere escape hatches from responsibilities but instruments of insights into what civilization means.

*— **Reinhold Niebuhr***

Saturday Evening Post
July 23, 1960

Faith To Overcome

The presence of faith is no guarantee of deliverance from times of distress and vicissitude, but there can be a certainty that nothing will be encountered that is overwhelming.

*— **William Barr Oglesby, Jr.***

Virginia Seminary Journal
May, 1983

Believing Brings Eternal Life

Jesus said:

And as Moses lifted up the serpent in the wilderness, even so must the Son of man be lifted up:

That whosoever believeth in him should not perish, but have eternal life.

For God so loved the world, that he gave his only begotten Son, that whosoever believeth in him should not perish, but have everlasting life.

For God sent not his Son into the world to condemn the world; but that the world through him might be saved.

He that believeth on him is not condemned: but he that believeth not is condemned already, because he hath not believed in the name of the only begotten Son of God.

And this is the condemnation, that light is come into the world, and men loved darkness rather than light, because their deeds were evil.

For every one that doeth evil hateth the light, neither cometh to the light, lest his deeds should be reproved.

But he that doeth truth cometh to the light, that his deeds may be made manifest, that they are wrought in God.

He that believeth on the Son hath everlasting life: and he that believeth not the Son shall not see life; but the wrath of God abideth on him.

— *John 3:14-21,36 (KJV)*
HOLY BIBLE

Chapter 8

GENTLENESS

*"**B**lessed are the meek, for they will inherit the earth"* (Matthew 5:5 NIV).

A wild horse that has been tamed to accept a saddle and harness is a picture of the Bible's concept of meekness.

Meekness' Greek word *praotes*, brings forth the meaning "not easily provoked." The horse has been "meeked" to behave in a certain way, given certain cues, under the authority of designated masters. It no longer bucks or thrashes wildly about in its pen. Rather, the horse has become so gentle that a young child can ride on its back and cause it to move in precise ways at precise times with only the slightest tug of a rein. However, at no time has the horse lost its inner power or strength to run, carry a heavy load, or rear its body against its enemies.

The person who is truly "meeked" by God, and who bears God's likeness of meekness, is a person who is easily directed by God and bears a gentleness of outward demeanor, while at the same time continues to bear great spiritual strength.

True Meekness

Meekness is essentially a true view of oneself, expressing itself in attitude and conduct with respect to others . . . The man who is truly meek is the one who is truly amazed that God and man can think of him as well as they do and treat him as well as they do.

— *Martin Lloyd Jones*

Reprinted from *Studies in the Sermon on the Mount* by Dr. Martin Lloyd-Jones. Copyright © 1959 by Dr. Martin Lloyd-Jones. Used by permission of William B. Eerdmans Publishing Company, and InterVarsity Press (IVP), U. K.

The Fruit of Meekness

The Greek word *prautes*, from which the word translated "meek" comes, has beautiful imagery. It has its background in the Greek word praus, which pictures a tame animal. The word picture is that of a highly spirited trained horse. The steed is anything but weak and mild. No, this mount holds his head proudly, nostrils flaring, poised to move with speed and power, but under the complete control of his master. Hoofs flash in the light as the horse prances, eager to conquer the land with speed and power. Nothing and no one can stop this steed, should the master give the command to go. This fully controlled yet powerful animal *"inherits the earth"* (Matthew 5:5) because he is meek.

When Jesus said, *"I am meek and lowly in heart"* (Matthew 11:29), He was not lacking humility. He was simply expressing the truth of His obedience to the Father. Meekness, however, is not simple compliance; it is rather an attitude of submission found within the spirit. This is a daring acquiescence that will trust God regardless of the circumstances and can truly believe that *"all things work together for good to them that love God, to them who are the called according to his purpose"* (Romans 8:28).

Meekness is neither a stoic indifference to circumstances nor a belief in predestination. Meekness is rather an inner attitude of faith and trust. Meekness believes that whatever the Master directs is ultimately best. This is why the words of the prophet Zechariah, *"Rejoice greatly, O daughter of Zion; shout, O daughter of Jerusalem: behold, thy King cometh unto thee: he is just, and having salvation; lowly, and riding upon an ass, and upon a colt the foal of an ass"* (Zechariah 9:9) are interpreted by Matthew, *"Tell ye the daughter of Sion, Behold, thy King cometh unto thee, meek, and sitting upon an ass, and a colt the foal of an ass"* (Matthew 21:5). Matthew interprets the words "just," "having salvation" and "lowly" with one word: meek. Jesus is meek because, as the Christ, He is opening up the events that will lead to His crucifixion. As the Lord of Calvary, He is "just," bringing in God's judgment on sin; He is "having salvation," delivering God's redemption, and "lowly," being submitted to God's will. Jesus' attitude toward His Father demonstrated His meekness. He testified:

I can of mine own self do nothing: as I hear, I judge: and my judgment is just; because I seek not mine own will, but the will of the Father which hath sent me. If I bear witness of myself, my witness is not true (John 5:30-31).

Meekness is a prerequisite for learning the things of God. The psalmist wrote, *"The meek will he guide in judgment: and the meek will he teach his way"* (Psalm 25:9). The carnal mind says, "I can understand, know and have wisdom in the things of God without spiritual guidance. I have self-sufficiency that enables me to understand deep truths." The meek spirit has an attitude that says, "I recognize my unworthiness, my inability, and the fact that without Him I can do nothing." The apostle James wrote:

Wherefore lay apart all filthiness and superfluity of naughtiness, and receive with meekness the engrafted word, which is able to save your souls (James 1:21).

Meekness is not a weakness! The one who is meek is the recipient of the power that comes from faith which is energized by God's Word.

Not only is meekness a prerequisite for receiving the power of the Word, it is imperative in transmitting that Word to others.

And the servant of the Lord must not strive; but be gentle unto all men, apt to teach, patient, in meekness instructing those that oppose themselves; if God peradventure will give them repentance to the acknowledging of the truth; and that they may recover themselves out of the snare of the devil, who are taken captive by him at his will (2 Timothy 2:24-26).

The Spirit demands that the Word of God be transmitted in an attitude of love and meekness. The Holy Spirit will no more manifest Himself or God's Word through a vessel who is imparting an attitude of condescension and insolence than He will mediate between a man whose spirit is filled with self-sufficiency and the Holy God.

— C. Paul Willis

Under Control

The word "gentleness" here (or in the KJV, meekness) comes from a Greek word meaning "mild; mildness in dealing with others." Jesus said, *"Blessed are the gentle, for they shall inherit the earth"* (Matthew 5:5 NASB). Nowhere in Scripture does this word carry with it the idea of being spiritless and timid. In biblical times, gentleness or meekness meant far more than it does in modern-day English. It carried the idea of being tamed, like a wild horse that has been brought under control. Until tamed by the Holy Spirit, Peter was a rough and ready character. Then all of his energy was used for the glory of God. Moses was called the meekest of men, but prior to God's special call to him he was an unbroken, high-spirited man who needed forty years in the desert before he was fully brought under God's control. A river under control can be used to generate power. A fire under control can heat a home. Meekness is power, strength, spirit, and wildness under control.

— *Billy Graham*

The Faithful Christian: An Anthology of Billy Graham
Compiled by William Griffin and Ruth Graham Dienert
New York: McCracken Press, 1994

He's Right

Since the Bible puts a premium on meekness, I must cultivate it. Meekness is not weakness, as many have pointed out, but in the words of a Christian brother, "Meekness is 'I accept God's dealings with me without bitterness.'" Meekness says God is always right. I must always accept what He sends me, and I must always do it with gladness of heart.

— *W. Glyn Evans*

Daily With the King
Chicago: Moody Press, 1979

Meekness and Love

Meekness is a form of love. If a man smite you in the face, your bodily nature says: "Smite him back again." If a man betrays you in the bitterest way, nature, in the bad sense of that term, says: "Give him as good as he sent." What is meekness? It is receiving personal injury, yet having such a predominant spirit of love in you that you wish the man that does it good. It is not retaliation, it is being so filled with the love and nature of Jesus Christ that you give back blessing for railing and cursing, prayers for those that despitefully use you. That is the definition. Do you know what meekness is? Any man that knows what perfect meekness is, is at liberty to rise up without any danger of disturbing this congregation.

— *Henry Ward Beecher*

A Summer in England
New York: Fords, Howard, & Hulbert, 1887

Meekness Misunderstood

In modern thinking, meekness is not a coveted quality, while there is hardly a characteristic which better distinguishes Christianity. Meekness to many means spinelessness, lack of courage or strength. It is the opposite. Most of the precious promises of the Scripture are to the meek.

We like to think, *"Blessed are the strong, the shrewd, those who stand up for their rights, those who refuse to be taken advantage of; those who always look out for slights; those who strike it rich and make a success."* We have a tendency to set high value on self-assertion. The natural standpoint is that a strong person is one who not only does what he wills, but also bends others to do his will.

Meekness is not native to the natural soil of the heart. It is not a natural disposition or psychological makeup. It grows in the garden of the Holy Spirit. Meekness is meant to characterize every Christian regardless of temperament.

Meekness has a twofold expression. Toward God, it issues in complete trust and submission to God. Meekness is to be mastered by the will of God. It results in gentleness, consideration, courtesy. It is strength under control. Meekness is the character of the one who has the power to retaliate, yet remains kind. It is from such a spirit that the expression gentle-man or gentleman arises.

Meekness is an attitude toward God which manifests itself in gentleness toward others. It is an attitude of submission and yieldedness to God which results in the harnessing of our strength in godly ways toward our fellow man. It is love which seeks first not its own, but the things of God and others. The meek accept God's will and dealings without sulking, murmuring, rebellion, or resistance.

— *C. Paul Willis*

Reprinted from *Bells and Pomegranates: The Gifts and Fruit of the Spirit* by C. Paul Willis. Copyright © 1991 by C. Paul Willis. Used by permission of Destiny Image Publishers.

For Humility on the Mountaintop of Life

Lord, forgive me that when life's circumstances lift me to the crest of the wave, I tend to forget Thee. Yet, like an errant child, I have blamed Thee with my every failure, even as I credit myself with every success.

When my fears evaporate like the morning mist, then vainly I imagine that I am sufficient unto myself, that material resources and human resources are enough.

I need Thee when the sun shines, lest I forget the storm and the dark. I need Thee when I am popular, when my friends and those who work beside me approve and compliment me. I need Thee more then, lest my head begin to swell.

O God, forgive me for my stupidity, my blindness in success, my lack of trust in Thee. Be Thou now my Saviour in success. Save me from conceit. Save me from pettiness. Save me from myself! And take this success, I pray, and use it for Thy glory. In Thy strength, I pray. Amen.

— *Peter Marshall*

Sermons and Prayers
New York: Revell, 1950

Anything But

Meekness is not weakness.

— *Sir William Gurney Benham*

Encyclopedia of Famous Quotes

Bold Humility

"Meekness" is a word which has a strong and virile meaning associated with it. The primary meaning of "meekness" is "to melt and flow in a liquid state," "to soften." True meekness possesses the softness of affection and disposition. The stony heart, the bitter spirit, the strong will, the quick temper; all must be reduced to a liquid state, all must be replaced with a life that flows. This fruit is not the product of a tasteless tree, it is the product of the sweetness of the Spirit. They who grow this fruit possess that soft and yielding disposition which we call "meekness." Possessing this fruit, it strips one of his impetuousness and softens with patience.

"Meekness" is not the natural growth of the human life, it is one of the "fruit" of the Spirit. It is described as the "meekness of wisdom" (James 3:13), that is, wisdom based on that knowledge of self which humbles, on that knowledge of God which softens, on that knowledge which melts and empties us of self-flattery. James speaks in this verse of the wise man, that he is able to present the "Word of truth" to others in the same skillful "meekness" as he himself received the "engrafted Word" (James 1:21).

Let no one think for a moment that by possessing this quality that weakness or slackness is indulged. Calmness of spirit is the best attitude to be found when trouble comes. It enables the Christian to bear, while in the process of bearing there is the self-exhaustion of evil. Meekness does not excite evil, does not forgive injuries because the offender is sorry, it goes a step further, it bridges the gulf and rescues them with a brotherly love. Deal with yourself and all others in the spirit of meekness. Keep on your life-branch the fruit of meekness. Instead of growing into the way of the world, let us grow into the way of meekness. Yet it is not enough to grow this fruit unless its energy is extended in usefulness, for we cannot be Christ's disciples without adorning His character.

It is the mark of the "little one." Meekness is the seed of child-likeness. It is the highest life expressing itself in acts of deepest humility. The highest life always claims for itself the humblest service. They lie passive in God's hand, having surrendered their will. It is a willingness to take wrong without retaliation. This meekness which is of the Spirit is power blended with gentleness, boldness with humility—the harmlessness of a dove with the strength of a lion. Was it not the meekness of Christ which attracted men to Him? Is it not the growing of this fruit in our lives which will, with its positive magnetism of meekness, that will draw men again?

True meekness is creative love in action, it is the appeal from the Highest to the highest. It leads to development of character; to a refusal to dominate others, while they themselves cannot be offended. It is one of the qualities of the new man, a virtue which has been misunderstood because it leads to positive courtesy and good manners. Its one wish is to serve others, and to forget oneself. This truth is often spoiled because of the failure of the Church to represent Him in His "meekness."

Meekness is not inactivity, but perfect poise in action, as perfect as a bird in the air. Though it describes our lowliness before God, but when assailed by cruelty and wrongdoings of men it is meekness in "action." They lie passive in God's hand and endure evil patiently. It is a fertile quality. It possesses "vitality," for it is intensively alive. Then secondly, it possesses "virility." It not only carries the suffering, it sustains the struggle. It creates "hard-bound" Christians, not "paperback" Christians. Having given up self-love and self-righteousness, they have no self-government. They have no will of their own, their will is absorbed in the Divine Will. Their heart of stone has been replaced by a heart that flows. They stoop to conquer. The exercise of such a life is the bulwark of the Church. True meekness is moral power to resist evil, having no confidence in the flesh but in the "Meek and lowly One," Who has said, "I will never leave thee, nor forsake thee" (Hebrews 13:5). The word "forsake" is best understood by reference to the Greek original which is "egkataleipo" meaning "leave behind" or, "to leave in danger"—conveying the thought of leaving comrades exposed to peril in some conflict, or, forsaking them in some crisis of danger. Christ will in no wise desert the meek in the field of conflict, or forsake them in a position of suffering. He will never let go His sustaining grasp.

— *Ivor Rosser*

The Fruit of the Spirit
Great Britain: Starling Press Limited

On Gentleness Toward Ourselves

One important direction in which to exercise gentleness is with respect to ourselves, never growing irritated with one's self or one's imperfections; for although it is but reasonable that we should be displeased and grieved at our own faults, yet ought we to guard against a bitter, angry, or peevish feeling about them. . . . What we want is a quiet, steady, firm displeasure at our own faults. A judge gives sentence more effectually speaking deliberately and calmly than if he be impetuous and passionate. . . . Believe me, beloved, as a parent's tender affectionate remonstrance has far more weight with his child than anger and sternness; so, when we judge our own heart guilty, if we treat it gently, rather in a spirit of pity than anger, encouraging it to amendment, its repentance will be much deeper and more lasting than if stirred up in vehemence and wrath. . . . If anyone does not find this gentle dealing sufficient, let him use sterner self-rebuke and admonition, provided only, that whatever indignation he may rouse against himself, he finally works it all up to a tender loving trust in God, treading in the footsteps of that great penitent who cried out to his troubled soul: "Why art thou so vexed, O my soul, and why art thou so disquieted within me? O put thy trust in God, for I will yet thank Him, which is the help of my countenance, and my God." So then, when you have fallen, lift up your heart in quietness, humbling yourself deeply before God by reason of your frailty, without marvelling that you fell; there is no cause to marvel because weakness is weak, or infirmity infirm. Heartily lament that you should have offended God, and begin anew to cultivate the lacking grace, with a very deep trust in His mercy, and with a bold, brave heart. . . .

— *St. Francis de Sales*

Introduction to the Devout Life

Sensitiveness

Time was, I shrank from what was right
From fear of what was wrong;
I would not brave the sacred fight,

Because the foe was strong.
But now I cast that finer sense
And sorer shame aside;
Such dread of sin was indolence,

Such aim at Heaven was pride.
So, when my Saviour calls, I rise
And calmly do my best;
Leaving to Him, with silent eyes

Of hope and fear, the rest.
I step, I mount where He has led;
Men count my haltings o'er—I know them;
yet, though self I dread, I love His precept more.

— Cardinal John Henry Newman

The Victorian Age, Second Edition
Edited by Bowyer and Brooks
Prentice-Hall, 1954

In Control

The meek are not those who are never at all angry, for such are insensible; but those who, feeling anger, control it, and are angry only when they ought to be. Meekness excludes revenge, irritability, morbid sensitiveness, but not self-defence, or a quiet and steady maintenance of right.

— Theophylactus

The International Dictionary of Thoughts
Edited by Bradley, Daniels & Jones
Doubleday & Co., 1969

By Definition

> It is almost a definition of a gentleman to say that
> he is one who never inflicts pain.
>
> — *Cardinal John Henry Newman*

The Idea of A University
Knowledge and Religious Duty, 1852

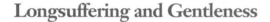

Longsuffering and Gentleness

Richard Weaver was a collier, a semi-professional pugilist in his younger days, who became a much-loved evangelist. Fighting, after drinking, seems to have been the sin to which he originally felt his flesh most perversely inclined. After his first conversion, he had a backsliding, which consisted in pounding a man who had insulted a girl. Feeling that having once fallen he might as well be hanged for a sheep as for a lamb, he got drunk and went and broke the jaw of another man who had recently challenged him to fight and taunted him with cowardice for refusing as a Christian man. I mention these incidents to show how genuine a change of heart is implied in the later conduct which he describes as follows—

'I went down the drift and found the boy crying because a fellow-workman was trying to take the wagon from him by force. I said to him, "Tom, you mustn't take that wagon." He swore at me and called me a Methodist devil. . . . "Well," I said, "let us see whether the devil and thee are stronger than the Lord and me." And the Lord and I proving stronger than the devil and he, he had to get out of the way, or the wagon would have gone over him. So I gave the wagon to the boy. Then said Tom, "I've a good mind to smack thee on the face." "Well," said I, "if that will do thee any good, thou canst do it." So he struck me on the face. I turned the other cheek to him and said, "Strike again." He struck again and again till he had struck me five times. I turned my cheek for the sixth stroke; but he turned away cursing. I shouted after him, "The Lord forgive thee, for I do, and the Lord save thee." This was on a Saturday, and when I went home from the coal-pit, my wife saw my face was swollen, and asked what was the matter with it. I said, "I've been fighting, and I've given a man a good thrashing." She burst out weeping and said, "O Richard, what made you fight?" Then I told her all about it, and she thanked the Lord that I had not struck back. But the Lord had struck, and His blows have more effect than man's. Monday came. The devil began to tempt me, saying, "The other men will laugh at thee for allowing Tom to treat thee as he did on Saturday." I cried, "Get thee behind me, Satan," and went on my way to the coal-pit. Tom was the first man I saw. I said "Good morning," but got no reply. He went down first. When I got down, I was surprised to see him sitting on the wagon-load waiting for me. When I came to him he burst into tears and said "Richard, will you forgive me for striking you?" "I have forgiven thee," said I; "ask God to forgive thee; the Lord bless thee." I gave him my hand, and we went each to his work.'

— *William James*

Freedom, Love and Truth
Compiled by William Inge
London: Longman, Green & Co., Inc., 1936

Man's Best Side

Christian meekness results, chiefly, from a deep sense of our own unworthiness, and an earnest love of our fellowman. Humility and love are among its chief ingredients. It is power-blended with humility—the harmlessness of the dove with the prowess of the lion: it is the soul, in the majesty of self-possession, elevated above the impulsive, irascible, boisterous, and revengeful. It is the soul, throwing its benign smile on the furious face of the foe, penetrating his heart, and paralyzing his arm, with the look of love. In short, meekness is that part of the grace of charity which gives us a tractable spirit, and enables us to restrain our passions.

It is first of all a state toward God. Gregory of Nyssa called humility, ' the mother of meekness.' A more modern writer has said, 'It grows out of the ashes of self-love, and on the grave of pride.' Self-will and arrogance have disappeared from the heart of the meek man. Poverty of spirit, a mournful consciousness of sin, and meekness, are not characteristics of different individuals, but parts of the same Christian character, to be exhibited by the same person. At the outset, the sinner must be stripped of fancied wealth, and reduced to spiritual beggary, that he may seek from God the alms of eternal life. He must, then, be stricken through with arrows of godly sorrow, before he can be divinely comforted, by the sweet assurance of forgiveness. God leads us, from poverty to mourning, from mourning to meekness, and then gives us the conditions of all subsequent advances to perfection.

The religion of our Lord implies, as its fundamental principle, that we are no longer our own—to do our own will, to follow the devices of our own hearts, to live for ourselves; but that we are the servants and soldiers of another, to do His will and work. This sense of belonging to, and living in obedience to, a divine will higher than our own, may be called the practical beginning of religion, in almost every heart. When we see men and women awakening to the feeling that there is a higher order above them, that there is One over them, who has not only the power but the right to command them, we can discern the beginning of religion. The natural instinct in every heart is self-assertion, not self-submission. The natural thing for us all to do is to follow our own will and desires rather than the commandments of God. The natural heart must be changed. The consciousness of a higher life than our own must be brought home to us, and made a living experience in our hearts if we are to be converted. Thus meekness toward God is the lowliness of contrition, the submission of a child-like spirit, the receptivity of a scholar in Christ's school, the humility of a devout believer. It is the true secret of yoke-wearing and burden-bearing; it makes Christ's service easy and light.

But, although meekness has thus a primary relation to God, it has its counterpart toward man. It is, when we submit ourselves most to God, and surrender our wills to His, that a gentle influence is breathed over our lives, from the calm spirit within. The result is a temper, which is not easily ruffled, and looks down with quiet serenity, on the struggling interests, which occupy the hearts of men, and crowd with passion or folly the stage of time. It is thus that men grow meek. Meekness is first of all a Christian grace, and then a human virtue. . . . This meekness is not, on its human side, cowardice, which is opposed to bravery and intrepidity, but calm energy of soul. Jesus, though meek, was the 'Lion of the tribe of Judah.' It is not social insensibility. Jesus was meek, and yet no nature was more sensitive than His. The softest zephyr rippled the deep crystal current of His heart. Apathy is as far removed from meekness as from humanity. The meek are not those who are sheltered from the shocks of life by a stupid insensibility, who have, either by nature or art, the virtue of stocks or stones, and resent nothing, for they feel nothing. Nor is meekness that constitutional easiness of disposition, that indecision of character, which acquiesces in every proposal. That is a weakness, not a virtue. As distinguished from each and all of these, meekness is a Christian grace, wrought in us by the Holy Spirit. Its main characteristics are clearly marked. It manifests a willingness to take wrong without retaliation, bears with provocation, controls all feelings of irritation. It regards wrong, pain, or insult as a medicine from God, not a poison from man. This flows from the conviction that we deserve heavier chastisements than we receive; and that all evils may be converted into blessings. The meek are bowed down in humility before God, and lie passive in His hand. Viewed in its positive aspect, meekness is the best side of a man. Under provocation, the meek man regards all his neighbours, in a candid light. His two great maxims are not to give offence and not to take offence. He enters not, with the keenness of passion, into the contentions of the violent; he keeps aloof from the contagion of party-feeling and the agitation of passion. He endeavours to allay the strifes of the contentious, to restrain the wrath of the implacable, to reconcile to one another those who are at variance.

— *James M'Donald Inglis*

Precious Fruit
London: Seeley & Co., 1887

The Face of Humility

Except in faith, nobody is humble. The mask of weakness or of Phariseeism is not the naked face of humility.

And, except in faith, nobody is proud. The vanity displayed in all its varieties by the spiritually immature is not pride.

To be, in faith, both humble and proud: that is, to live, to know that in God I am nothing, but that God is in me.

— *Dag Hammarskjöld*

From *Markings* by Dag Hammarskjöld, trans.,
Leif Sjoberg & W. H. Auden. Translation copyright
© 1964 by Alfred A. Knopf Inc. and Faber Ltd.
Reprinted by permission of Alfred A. Knopf.
New York: Alfred A. Knopf, 1964

Love's Winning Armor

Gentleness is the strongest force in the world, and the soldiers of Christ are to be priests and to fight the battle of the kingdom, robed, not in jingling shining armor or with sharp swords, nor with fierce and eager bitterness of controversy, but in the meekness which overcomes. You may take all the steam hammers that were ever forged and battle at an iceberg, and except for the comparatively little heat that is developed by the blows and melts some small portion, it will be ice still, though pulverized instead of whole. But let it move gently down to the southward, there the sunbeams smite the coldness to death, and it is dissipated in the warm ocean. Meekness is conquering.

— Alexander Maclaren

A Rosary of Christian Graces
London, 1899

The Strong Are Gentle

Insecure, weak leaders, in the world or church, usually try to rule with an iron hand. They cannot afford to have their opinions and conclusions challenged. They develop a dogmatic disposition and delight in docile disciples. Such are afraid of free discussion or trusting the group in decisions because they fear the weakness of their own viewpoints. Or they quickly label other viewpoints in order to escape dealing with contrasting concerns.

On the other hand, one who is strong is gentle and gracious. This does not mean he has no firm beliefs. It does not mean he is spineless or wishy-washy. Persons who have spiritual strength and assurance and know what they believe and why, can most easily stand differences of opinion and voices which challenge their own viewpoint. They can be gentle because they, like God, are strong in love and the desire to help.

The gentleness of God enables us to become better persons. When we sense how strong God is, we see how gentle He is to us in all our sinfulness and helplessness. When we sense this great gentleness, we rise to new spiritual stature and strength. As the psalmist expressed it in some of his last words, *"Thy gentleness hath made me great"* (2 Samuel 22:36; Psalm 18:35).

So also it is the gentle Christian who restores the erring, who helps others to God, who brings out the best in others. . . . Correction can be given in a way which discourages and drives a person to depression and despair. Correction can also be given in the spirit of gentleness which sets a person upon his feet with new courage and determination to do better. Meekness is the spirit which makes correction a stimulant and not a depressant.

— *John M. Drescher*

Reprinted by permission of Herald Press from *Spirit Fruit*
by John M. Drescher. Copyright © 1974 by John M. Drescher.
Used by permission of Herald Press.

God's Gentleness

"*Thy gentleness hath made me great*" (Psalm 18:35). The words are capable of being translated, "Thy goodness hath made me great." David gratefully ascribed all his greatness not to his own goodness, but to the goodness of God. "Thy providence," is another reading; and providence is nothing more than goodness in action. Goodness is the bud of which providence is the flower, or goodness is the seed of which providence is the harvest. Some render it, "Thy help," which is but another word for providence; providence being the firm ally of the saints, aiding them in the service of their Lord. Or again, "Thy humility hath made me great." "Thy condescension" may, perhaps, serve as a comprehensive reading, combining the ideas mentioned, including that of humility. It is God's making Himself little which is the cause of our being made great. We are so little, that if God should manifest His greatness without condescension, we should be trampled under His feet; but God, Who must stoop to view the skies, and bow to see what angels do, turns His eye yet lower, and looks to the lowly and contrite, and makes them great. There are yet other readings, as for instance, the Septuagint, which reads, "Thy discipline"—Thy fatherly correction—"hath made me great"; while the Chaldee paraphrase reads, "Thy word hath increased me." Still the idea is the same. David ascribes all his own greatness to the condescending goodness of his Father in heaven. May this sentiment be echoed in our hearts this evening while we cast our crowns at Jesus' feet and cry, "Thy gentleness hath made me great." How marvelous has been our experience of God's gentleness! How gentle have been His corrections! How gentle His forbearance! How gentle His teachings! How gentle His drawings! Meditate upon this theme, O believer. Let gratitude be awakened; let humility be deepened; let love be quickened ere thou fallest asleep tonight.

— Charles H. Spurgeon

Taken from *Morning and Evening Devotions: An Updated Edition of the Classic Devotional in Today's Language* by C. H. Spurgeon. Copyright © 1987 by Thomas Nelson Publishers. Used by permission of Thomas Nelson Publishers.

The Gentleness of Wisdom

Who among you is wise and understanding? Let him show by his good behavior his deeds in the gentleness of wisdom.

But if you have bitter jealousy and selfish ambition in your heart, do not be arrogant and so lie against the truth.

This wisdom is not that which comes down from above, but is earthly, natural, demonic.

For where jealousy and selfish ambition exist, there is disorder and every evil thing.

But the wisdom from above is first pure, then peaceable, gentle, reasonable, full of mercy and good fruits, unwavering, without hypocrisy.

And the seed whose fruit is righteousness is sown in peace by those who make peace.

— James 3:13-18 (NASB)
HOLY BIBLE

Gentleness Makes Great

Thou hast also given me the shield of thy salvation: and thy right hand hath holden me up, and thy gentleness hath made me great.

— Psalm 18:35
HOLY BIBLE

Gentle With the Opposition

And a servant of the Lord must not quarrel but be gentle to all, able to teach, patient, in humility correcting those who are in opposition, if God perhaps will grant them repentance, so that they may know the truth, and that they may come to their senses and escape the snare of the devil, having been taken captive by him to do his will.

— 2 Timothy 2:24-26 (NKJV)
HOLY BIBLE

Calvary's Death Marks

When God conquers us and takes all the flint out of our nature, and we get deep visions into the Spirit of Jesus, we then see as never before the great rarity of gentleness of spirit in this dark and unheavenly world.

The graces of the Spirit do not settle themselves down upon us by chance, and if we do not discern certain states of grace, and choose them, and in our thoughts nourish them, they never become fastened in our nature or behavior.

Every advance step in grace must be preceded by first apprehending it, and then a prayerful resolve to have it.

So few are willing to undergo the suffering out of which

thorough gentleness comes. We must die before we are turned into gentleness, and crucifixion involves suffering; it is a real breaking and crushing of self, which wrings the heart and conquers the mind.

There is a good deal of mere mental and logical sanctification nowadays, which is only a religious fiction. It consists of mentally putting one's self on the altar, and then mentally saying the altar sanctifies the gift, and then logically concluding, therefore, one is sanctified and such an one goes forth with a gay, flippant, theological prattle about the deep things of God.

But the natural heartstrings have not been snapped, and the Adamic flint has not been ground to powder, and the bosom has not throbbed with the lonely, surging sighs of Gethsemane; and not having the real death marks of Calvary, there cannot be that soft, sweet, gentle, floating, victorious, overflowing, triumphant life that flows like a spring morning from an empty tomb.

Streams in the Desert
By Mrs. Charles Cowman
Los Angeles: Cowman Publications, 1959

O Thou Great Friend to All

O Thou great Friend to all the sons of men,
Who once appeard'st in humblest guide below,
Sin to rebuke, to break the captive's chain,
To call Thy brethren forth from want and woe,

We look to Thee; Thy truth is still the light
Which guides the nations groping on their way,
Stumbling and falling in disastrous night,
Yet hoping ever for the perfect day.

Yes, Thou art still the Life;
Thou art the Way
The holiest know,
—Light, Life, and Way of heaven;
And they who dearest hope and deepest pray
Toil by the truth, life, way, that Thou hast given.

— *Theodore Parker*

Taken from "O Thou Great Friend To All"
from *Mennonite Hymnary*. Copyright by
Mennonite Publications Office, Newton, KS.

Simple in Meekness

Simplicity is an uprightness of soul that has no reference to self; it is different from sincerity, and it is a still higher virtue. We see many people who are sincere, without being simple; they only wish to pass for what they are, and they are unwilling to appear what they are not; they are always thinking of themselves, measuring their words, and recalling their thoughts, and reviewing their actions, from the fear that they have done too much or too little. These persons are sincere, but they are not simple; they are not at ease with others, and others are not at ease with them; they are not free, ingenuous, natural; we prefer people who are less correct, less perfect, and who are less artificial. . . .

Simplicity consists in a just medium, in which we are neither too much excited nor too composed. The soul is not carried away by outward things, so that it cannot make all necessary reflections; neither does it make those continual references to self, that a jealous sense of its own excellence multiplies to infinity. That freedom of the soul, which looks straight onward in its path, losing no time to reason upon its steps, to study them, or to contemplate those that it has already taken, is true simplicity. . . .

The more gentle and docile the soul is, the more it advances in this simplicity. It does not become blind to its own defects, and unconscious of its imperfections; it is more than ever sensible of them; it feels a horror of the slightest sin; it sees more clearly its own corruption; but this sensibility does not arise from dwelling upon itself, but by the light from the presence of God we see how far removed we are from infinite purity.

Thus simplicity is free in its course, since it makes no preparation; but it can only belong to the soul that is purified by a true penitence. It must be the fruit of a perfect renunciation of self, and an unreserved love of God. . . . How free, how intrepid are the motions, how glorious the progress that the soul makes, when delivered from all low, and interested, and unquiet cares!

If we desire that our friends be simple and free with us, disencumbered of self in their intimacy with us, will it not please God, who is our truest Friend, that we should surrender our souls to Him without fear or reserve, in that holy and sweet communion with Himself which He allows us? It is this simplicity which is the perfection of the true children of God. This is the end that we must have in view and to which we must be continually advancing.

— Archbishop Fenelon, 1651-1715
"True and False Simplicity"

The World's Famous Orations
William Jennings Bryan, Editor-in-chief
New York: Funk and Wagnalls Co., 1906

Gentle As a Nursing Mother

Neither at any time did we use flattering words, as you know, nor a cloak for covetousness God is witness. Nor did we seek glory from men, either from you or from others, when we might have made demands as apostles of Christ. But we were gentle among you, just as a nursing mother cherishes her own children. So, affectionately longing for you, we were well pleased to impart to you not only the gospel of God, but also our own lives, because you had become dear to us. For you remember, brethren, our labor and toil; for laboring night and day, that we might not be a burden to any of you, we preached to you the gospel of God.

— *1 Thessalonians 2:5-9 (NKJV)*
HOLY BIBLE

Acceptance

Meekness and temperance mean accepting my position, capacities, spiritual attraits, as an indication of God's will for me, and not fussing about the things other souls do or feeling despondent because I cannot do them! God hates nothing that He has made. He made it because He liked it. His creation is an act of love. And He has made me perhaps to be a temperate plant and to grow in a temperate climate. So what is required of me is to correspond with that climate and environment and to grow the fruit of His Spirit here in the ordinary English garden in which I find myself. No use trying for things that need a tropical climate or hothouse. We are all rather inclined to be a bit romantic about religion. But God is a realist. He likes home-grown stuff. He asks me for a really good apple, not for a dubious South African peach. So, not lofty thoughts of God, remarkable powers of prayer or displays of devotional fervour or difficult virtues, but gentleness, longsuffering, faithfulness, meekness, a good quality life, will prove I am growing the right way and producing as well as I can the homely fruit for which He asks.

— *Evelyn Underhill*

The Fruits of the Spirit
London, 1949

Inner Beauty

Your beauty should not come from outward adornment, such as braided hair and the wearing of gold jewelry and fine clothes. Instead, it should be that of your inner self, the unfading beauty of a gentle and quiet spirit, which is of great worth in God's sight. For this is the way the holy women of the past who put their hope in God used to make themselves beautiful.

— *1 Peter 3:3-5 (NIV)*
HOLY BIBLE

Tough or Tender?

The right kind of toughness—strength of character—ought to mark the man of today . . . but not only that. Tenderness—gentleness— is equally important. God considers it so important He places it on the list of nine qualities He feels should mark the life of His children. (Galatians 5:22-23.)

The Greek word translated "gentleness" is prautes . . . the Greeks used it when referring to people or things that demonstrated a certain soothing quality—like an ointment that took the sting out of a burn. . . . Prautes described the controlled conduct of one who had the power to act otherwise. Like a king who chose to be gracious instead of a tyrant . . . . Plato called prautes "the cement of society" as he used this word in the sense of politeness, courtesy, and kindness. . . .

Remember, our goal is balance . . . always balance. Not either-or, but both-and. Not just tough. That alone makes a man cold, distant, intolerant, unbearable. But tough and tender . . . gentle, thoughtful, teachable, considerate. Both. Like Christ.

— *Charles R. Swindoll*

Taken from *Growing Strong in the Seasons of Life* by Chuck Swindoll. Copyright © 1983 by Charles R. Swindoll, Inc. Used by permission of Zondervan Publishing House.

Slow to Anger

"The Lord is slow to anger, and great in power" (Nahum 1:3).

Jehovah "is slow to anger." When mercy cometh into the world she driveth winged steeds; the axles of her chariot-wheels are red hot with speed; but when wrath goeth forth, it toileth on with tardy footsteps, for God taketh no pleasure in the sinner's death. God's rod of mercy is ever in His hands outstretched; His sword of justice is in its scabbard, held down by that pierced hand of love which bled for the sins of men. "The Lord is slow to anger," because He is great in power. He is truly great in power who hath power over himself. When God's power doth restrain Himself, then it is power indeed: the power that binds omnipotence is omnipotence surpassed. A man who has a strong mind can bear to be insulted long, and only resents the wrong when a sense of right demands his action. The weak mind is irritated at a little: the strong mind bears it like a rock which moveth not, though a thousand breakers dash upon it, and cast their pitiful malice in spray upon its summit. God marketh His enemies, and yet He bestirs not Himself, but holdeth in His anger. If He were less divine than He is, He would long ere this have sent forth the whole of His thunders, and emptied the magazines of heaven; He would long ere this have blasted the earth with the wondrous fires of its lower regions, and man would have been utterly destroyed; but the greatness of His power brings us mercy. Dear reader, what is your state this evening? Can you by humble faith look to Jesus, and say, "My substitute, Thou art my rock, my trust"? Then, beloved, be not afraid of God's power; for now that you are forgiven and accepted, now that by faith you have fled to Christ for refuge, the power of God need no more terrify you, than the shield and sword of the warrior need terrify those whom he loves. Rather rejoice that He who is "great in power" is your Father and Friend.

— Charles H. Spurgeon

Taken from *Morning and Evening Devotions: An Updated Edition of the Classic Devotional in Today's Language* by C. H. Spurgeon. Copyright © 1987 by Thomas Nelson Publishers. Used by permission of Thomas Nelson Publishers.

He Must Increase

He must increase, but I must decrease (John 3:30).

John the Baptist reveals a basic secret of how to receive the silent strength of Christ. . . .

The Baptist was a renowned spiritual leader. He was the point person for a far-reaching revival movement. The decisive prophet stood tall in the tradition of the Old Testament prophets. He proclaimed the sovereignty of God, His requirement of absolute righteousness, and called people to repent, return to God, and be baptized. The masses flocked to the river Jordan to hear him and respond to his unmitigated message of judgment. At the height of his power, the prophet was becoming famous. He was talked about and became the center of much controversy about who he actually was. This is why the spiritual leaders of Israel came to find out who it was causing such a stir.

But John knew who he was. There was no mistake in his mind about his purpose. He was not the Christ. He knew who that was: his own cousin, Jesus of Nazareth. The Baptist had known this with divine discernment for some time. John's calling was to prepare the way for Jesus' ministry, and he knew it. There was no competition, no jockeying for recognition. He baptized with water, but he knew a greater One than he would baptize with the Holy Spirit and with fire (Luke 3:16). The result of the Father's confirmation after Jesus' baptism by John led the prophet to an amazing expression of humility: "He must increase, but I must decrease."

This is how we receive the silent strength of Christ. Our ego must be yielded to Christ. Our calling is to yield center stage to Him. He must take charge; our control must be relinquished. So often I hear people say, "I must get rid of self." This is not the secret. It's letting Christ fill the self that opens us to His strength.

— *Lloyd John Ogilvie*

Silent Strength for My Life
by Lloyd John Ogilvie. Copyright © 1990 by
Harvest House Publishers, Eugene, Oregon.
Used by permission.

The Power of Gentleness

Many people followed Jesus after He healed the man with the withered hand, and all of them who had diseases were likewise healed by Him. What a surge of enthusiasm there must have been as each healing took place.

But Jesus warned them not to speak about Him publicly. Matthew, as he thought about it, was reminded of the Isaiah passage, and he quoted it fully: "Behold, my servant, whom I have chosen; my beloved, in whom my soul is well pleased: I will put my spirit upon him, and he shall shew judgment to the Gentiles. He shall not strive, nor cry aloud, neither shall any man hear his voice in the streets. A bruised reed he will not break, and smoking flax he shall not quench, till he send forth judgment unto victory. And in his name will the Gentiles trust" (Matthew 12:18-21) .

Here we see real meekness and gentleness set before us in human flesh by the Son of God. . . . This is meekness, the quiet awareness of who He is, and of the power He has at His disposal for the accomplishment of His ends.

Now His awareness of His power enables Him to be gentle to those in need. Isaiah uses two figures of speech. The first is that of a cracked, half-broken reed. It will part in two forever under the rough treatment of men in the world.

In Jesus' hands the reed will not be further broken; in fact, it will be fully restored. When Jesus is at hand, no one is beyond hope, no matter how hopeless they may believe their lot to be.

The second is that of a flickering, almost extinguished wick. A sudden movement will quench the light entirely. But in Jesus' hands, the flame will be safe for He will be gentle and understanding.

Meekness and gentleness are not signs of weakness. They are strong and are powerful weapons in God's hands to accomplish His purposes. They require courage on the part of the one exercising them, and also great faith that God will use them as He has promised. But the fact is that sin has so bruised the human spirit that such tender treatment is required if those spirits are to be made whole again. In

these days of coldness and hatred among people, it is particularly
necessary that Christians learn gentleness.

— *John Sanderson*

Our Strength in God

When one hears the word *meekness*, immediately he thinks of a
Walter Mitty character who has little in him that is desirable. Tragically,
this is a gross misunderstanding, because meekness is not weakness, but
strength. Perhaps a word picture can be drawn to give the shape of
content.

Michael Drury recently spoke of meekness by saying, "Humility
so often seems vaguely desirable, but not really attractive. It might get
one to heaven, but it won't promote a raise in pay. It sounds somewhat
spineless, incompatible with intellect and vigorous spirit." He went on
to add that actually the reverse is true. The figures we commonly
associate with humility—Jesus, Lincoln, Gandhi, Einstein—were not
men of timid natures, but men who, while recognizing their weakness,
also remembered their destinies and acted accordingly. He concluded
by saying, "Humility is not self-disparagement; it is a tough, free,
confident characteristic."

What is often misunderstand concerning meekness is that to
which this quality relates. Meekness is our attitude toward God, not
man. It is vertical, not horizontal. This is why really meek men like
those mentioned had such great and free spirits. If meekness related to
man, then we would bend at a stronger person's will.

Meekness is understanding perfectly our worth before God and
knowing His forgiveness. Because Moses was meek before God and had
settled his personal fears and frustrations, those of others could not spill
over on him, causing him to react out of character with his calling.

Embedded in this bit of sacred history is an important psychological fact. By perfectly understanding our status with the Savior, all the fear, frustrations, and inhibitions which plagued us before Calvary are erased. Here is the miracle of the new birth. Even though our environment might have contributed to all sorts of emotional problems and complexes, yet, in the new start and making peace with our Maker, we are emotionally sound and stable.

When we realize it is God who made us and not we ourselves, that we are the sheep of His pasture, that the steps of a good man are ordered by the Lord, then what does it matter what man might say. This is when real meekness toward God gives us strength in the face of our foes. Then we will not bow to the whims and wishes of those about us. We will not react to their frustration because we know we have been ordered by Him. Therefore, criticism does not affect us and revenge is foreign to our characters.

— *Charles R. Hembree*

Hembree, Charles R. *Fruits of the Spirit*,
Baker Book House Company, © 1969.

Gentle

The word *gentle* was rarely heard before the Christian era, and the word *gentleman* was not known. This high quality of character was a direct by-product of Christian faith.

— *Billy Graham*

The Quotable Billy Graham
Compiled and Edited by Cort R. Flint and the Staff of *Quote*
Anderson, S.C.: Droke House, 1966

Christ's Example

Let this mind be in you, which was also in Christ Jesus: Who, being in the form of God, thought it not robbery to be equal with God: But made himself of no reputation, and took upon him the form of a servant, and was made in the likeness of men (Philippians 2:5-7).

It is beautiful to see the humility of Christ. This humility can be seen in the crib, in the exile in Egypt, in the hidden life, in the inability to make people understand Him, in the desertion of His apostles, in the hatred of the Jews and all the terrible sufferings and death of His passion and now in His permanent state of humility in the tabernacle, where He has reduced Himself to such a small particle of bread that the priest can hold Him with two fingers. The more we empty ourselves, the more room we give God to fill us. Let there be no pride nor vanity in the work. The work is God's work; the poor are God's poor. Work for Jesus and Jesus will work with you, pray with Jesus and Jesus will pray through you. The more you forget yourself, the more Jesus will think of you. The more you detach yourself from self, the more attached Jesus is to you.

Do not think it is a waste of time to feed the hungry, to visit and take care of the sick and the dying, to open and receive the unwanted and the homeless, for this is our love of Christ in action. We must not drift away from the humble works, because these are the works nobody will do. It is never too small. We are so small we look at things in a small way. But God, being Almighty, sees everything great. Therefore, even if you write a letter for a blind man or you just go and sit and listen, or you take the mail for him or you visit somebody or bring a flower to somebody—small things—or wash clothes for somebody or clean the house. Very humble work, that is where you and I must be. For there are many people who can do big things. But there are very few people who will do the small things.

There may be times when we appear to be wasting our precious life and burying our talents. Our lives are utterly wasted if we use only the light of reason. Our life has no meaning unless we look at Christ in His poverty.

Today when everything is questioned and changed let us go back to Nazareth. Jesus had come to redeem the world—to teach us that love of His father. How strange that He should spend thirty years just doing nothing, wasting His time! Not giving a chance to His personality or to His gifts, for we know that at the age of twelve He silenced the learned priests of the temple, who knew so much and so well. But when His parents found Him, He went down to Nazareth and was subject to them. For thirty years we hear no more of Him—so that the people were astonished when He came in public to preach, He a carpenter's son, doing just the humble work in a carpenter's shop—for thirty years!

Knowledge of God gives love and knowledge of self gives humility. Humility is nothing but truth. "What have we got that we have not received?" asks St. Paul. If I have received everything, what good have I of my own? If we are convinced of this we will never raise our head in pride. If you are humble nothing will touch you, neither praise nor disgrace, because you know what you are. If you are blamed you will not be discouraged. If they call you a saint you will not put yourself on a pedestal.

Self-knowledge puts us on our knees.

Make us worthy, Lord, to serve our fellowmen throughout the world who live and die in poverty and hunger.

Lord, grant that I may seek rather to comfort than to be comforted; to understand than to be understood; to love than to be loved; for it is by forgetting self that one finds; it is by forgiving that one is forgiven; it is by dying that one awakens to eternal life.

— *Mother Teresa*

Life in the Spirit
Harper & Row

God's Opinion

The meek man is not a human mouse afflicted with a sense of his own inferiority. Rather he may be in his moral life as bold as a lion and as strong as Samson; but he has stopped being fooled about himself. He has accepted God's estimate of his own life. He knows he is as weak and helpless as God has declared him to be, but paradoxically, he knows at the same time that he is in the sight of God of more importance than angels. In himself, nothing; in God, everything. That is his motto. He knows well that the world will never see him as God sees him and he has stopped caring. He rests perfectly content to allow God to place His own values. He will be patient to wait for the day when everything will get its own price tag and real worth will come into its own. Then the righteous shall shine forth in the Kingdom of their Father. He is willing to wait for that day.

In the meantime he will have attained a place of soul rest. As he walks on in meekness he will be happy to let God defend him. The old struggle to defend himself is over. He has found the peace which meekness brings.

Then also he will get deliverance from the burden of pretense. By this I mean not hypocrisy, but the common human desire to put the best foot forward and hide from the world our real inward poverty. For sin has played many evil tricks upon us, and one has been the infusing into us a false sense of shame. There is hardly a man or woman who dares to be just what he or she is without doctoring up the impression. The fear of being found out gnaws like rodents within their hearts. The man of culture is haunted by the fear that he will some day come upon a man more cultured than himself. The learned man fears to meet a man more learned than he. The rich man sweats under the fear that his clothes or his car or his house will sometime be made to look cheap by comparison with those of another rich man. So-called "society" runs by a motivation not higher than this, and the poorer classes on their level are little better.

Lord, make me childlike. Deliver me from the urge to compete with another for place or prestige or position. I would be simple and artless as a little child. Deliver me from pose and pretense. Forgive me for thinking of myself. Help me to forget myself and find my true peace in beholding Thee. That Thou mayest answer this prayer I humble myself before Thee. Lay upon me Thy easy yoke of self-forgetfulness that through it I may find rest. Amen.

— *A. W. Tozer*

The Pursuit of God
Harrisburg, Penn.: Christian Publications, Inc.

The Personification of Meekness

As they approached Jerusalem and came to Bethphage on the Mount of Olives, Jesus sent two disciples, saying to them, "Go to the village ahead of you, and at once you will find a donkey tied there, with her colt by her. Untie them and bring them to me. If anyone says anything to you, tell him that the Lord needs them, and he will send them right away."

This took place to fulfill what was spoken through the prophet:

"Say to the Daughter of Zion,
> *'See, your king comes to you,*
gentle and riding on a donkey,
> *on a colt, the foal of a donkey.'"*

The disciples went and did as Jesus had instructed them. They brought the donkey and the colt, placed their cloaks on them, and Jesus sat on them. A very large crowd spread their cloaks on the road, while others cut branches from the trees and spread them on the road. The crowds that went ahead of him and those that followed shouted,

> *"Hosanna to the Son of David!"*
> *"Blessed is he who comes in the name of the Lord!"*
> *"Hosanna in the highest!"*

When Jesus entered Jerusalem, the whole city was stirred and asked, "Who is this?"

The crowds answered, "This is Jesus, the prophet from Nazareth in Galilee."

Jesus entered the temple area and drove out all who were buying and selling there. He overturned the tables of the money changers and the benches of those selling doves. "It is written," he said to them, "'My house will be called a house of prayer,' but you are making it a 'den of robbers.'"

The blind and the lame came to him at the temple, and he healed them. But when the chief priests and the teachers of the law saw the wonderful things he did and the children shouting in the temple area, "Hosanna to the Son of David," they were indignant.

"Do you hear what these children are saying?" they asked him.

"Yes," replied Jesus, "have you never read,

> *'From the lips of children and infants*
> *you have ordained praise'?"*

And he left them and went out of the city to Bethany, where he spent the night.

— *Matthew 21:1-17* (NIV)
HOLY BIBLE

Gracious Savior, Gentle Shepherd

Gracious Savior, gentle Shepherd,
Little ones are dear to Thee;
Gathered with Thine arms and carried
In Thy bosom, may they be
Sweetly, fondly, safely tended,
From all want and danger free.

Tender Shepherd, never leave them
From Thy fold to go astray;
By Thy look of love directed,
May they walk the narrow way;
Thus direct them, and protect them,
Lest they fall an easy prey.
Taught to lisp the holy praises

Which on earth Thy children sing,
Both with lips and hearts unfeigned,
Glad thank-off'rings may they bring,
Then with all the saints in glory
Join to praise their Lord and King.

— Jane Eliza Leeson and John Keble

Taken from "Gracious Savior, Gentle Shephard" by
Jane Elizabeth Leeson and John Keeble from *Mennonite Hymnary*.
Copyright Mennonite Publication Office, Newton, KS.

The Lamb

Little Lamb, who made Thee?
Dost thou know who made Thee?
Gave Thee life and bid Thee feed,
By the stream and o'er the mead;
Gave Thee clothing of delight,
Softest clothing wooly bright;
Gave Thee such a tender voice,
Making all the vales rejoice!

Little Lamb, who made Thee?
Dost Thou know who made Thee?
Little Lamb, I'll tell Thee,
Little Lamb, I'll tell Thee!
He is called by Thy name,
For He calls Himself a Lamb:
He is meek and He is mild,
He became a little child:
I a child and Thou a Lamb,

We are called by His name.
Little Lamb, God bless Thee.
Little Lamb, God bless Thee.

— *William Blake, 1789*

Norton Anthology of English Literature; Third Edition
Poetry and Prose of William Blake
Doubleday, 1965

Gentle Shepherd

One of the many names of Jesus is "Good Shepherd." The Bible contains several passages that compare Jesus to the gentle, faithful shepherd, including Isaiah 40:11, Ezekiel 34:11; 16, and the beloved 23rd Psalm. After meditating on these passages for several days, author and church counselor Joyce Huggett described how she saw our gentle Savior . . . .

The picture of the Good Shepherd which rose up before me was of a Man who expresses His faithfulness through His availability: "He leads me, restores me, is with me." The Good Shepherd is One who involves Himself in the life of His flock: He gathers the lambs together, carries them, leads the ewes with gentleness. The Good Shepherd is a dedicated person: He searches for the lost, heals the sick, bandages the wounded. Communication between sheep and Shepherd seemed a two-way affair: the helpless sheep looked to the Shepherd for guidance, wisdom and direction. These resources were given constantly. The relationship which grew between a sheep and his Shepherd was one of intimacy.

The Joy of Listening to God
InterVarsity Press, 1986

His Gentle Yoke

Jesus said:

Take My yoke upon you, and learn from Me, for I am gentle and humble in heart; and YOU SHALL FIND REST FOR YOUR SOULS.

For My yoke is easy, and My load is light.

— *Matthew 11:29-30* (NASB)
HOLY BIBLE

No Use of Force

The way in which Jesus presents Himself to us is the epitome of gentleness . . . .

When our Lord Jesus was here on earth, He never forced Himself upon people. If they didn't want Him around, He left. This even happened in His own hometown, as we can read in Luke 4:16-30. . . .

As in the days when He walked in the flesh, our Lord does not force His way into your life. Since He desires a relationship of love and trust, He never attempts to coerce you, though He has the ability to do so. He seeks you, and offers Himself to you. Whether you recognize and welcome His approach is up to you.

— *Peter Lord*

Lord, Peter. *Hearing God,*
Baker Book House Company, © 1988.

Compassionate Counselor

When we unload the hurts of our spirits, the frustrations of our lives, God isn't the kind of Counselor who hurls back condemnation at us or piles guilt on top of us. Every person needs a counselor to whom the whole truth can be told, a counselor who won't retaliate angrily. If a worldly counselor can possess such compassion, certainly God can.

The kind of Counselor we as believers have is One from whom we cannot hide. He knows it all anyway, and we can tell Him anything we want to. In fact, we can tell Him how we feel about Him, even when the feelings aren't necessarily noble ones. No matter what we say, God still loves us, and as an understanding Counselor, He can take anything we give and accept us unconditionally. This understanding Counselor puts His arms around us and says, "That's okay." In fact, probably the most precious thing any counselor says to a broken, disillusioned heart is, "Everything's going to be all right."

— *Charles Stanley*

How To Listen to God
1985

A Gentle Response

Whenever He was insulted or falsely accused, Jesus was a model of restraint. Rather than respond with anger, He always had a gentle word for those who attacked Him. . . .

How utterly men failed to understand Jesus! Whatever He did was wrong in their eyes, for the light that was in them was darkness. They even dared to identify the Spirit that was in Him with Beelzebub, the prince of devils. Yet, when they accused Him of gluttony and drunkenness, what was His response? *"Father, I thank thee!"* (Matthew 11:19, 25). He was unmoved, because in Spirit He abode in the peace of God.

Or recall that last night before His passion. Everything seemed to be going wrong: a friend going out into the night to betray Him, another drawing a sword in anger, people going into hiding, or running away naked in their eagerness to escape. In the midst of it all, Jesus said to those who had come to take him, "I am He," so peacefully and so quietly that instead of Him being nervous it was they who trembled and fell backwards.

— *Watchman Nee*

Love Not the World
Tyndale House Publishers, 1968

Be Humble

There is no true and constant gentleness without humility. While we are so fond of ourselves, we are easily offended with others. Let us be persuaded that nothing is due to us, and then nothing will disturb us. Let us often think of our own infirmities, and we shall become indulgent towards those of others.

— *Fenelon*

Daily Strength for Daily Needs
Mary Tileston

Screwtape to Wormwood on Humility

Your patient has become humble; have you drawn his attention to the fact? All virtues are less formidable to us once the man is aware that he has them, but this is specially true of humility. Catch him at the moment when he is really poor in spirit and smuggle into his mind the gratifying reflection, "By jove! I'm being humble," and almost immediately pride— pride at his own humility—will appear. If he awakes to the danger and tries to smother this new form of pride, make him proud of his attempt— and so on, through as many stages as you please. But don't try this too long, for fear you awake his sense of humor and proportion, in which case he will merely laugh at you and go to bed.

But there are other profitable ways of fixing his attention on the virtue of humility. By this virtue, as by all the others, our enemy wants to turn the man's attention away from self to him, and to man's neighbors. All the abjection and self-hatred are designed, in the long run, solely for this end; unless they attain this end, they do us little harm; and they may even do us good if they keep the man concerned with himself, and above all, if self-contempt can be made the starting point for contempt of other selves, and thus for gloom, cynicism, and cruelty.

You must therefore conceal from the patient the true end of humility. Let him think of it, not as self-forgetfulness, but as a certain kind of opinion (namely, a low opinion) of his own talents and character. Some talents, I gather, he really has. Fix in his mind the idea that humility consists in trying to believe those talents to be less valuable than he believes them to be. No doubt they are in fact less valuable than he believes, but that is not the point. The great thing is to make him value an opinion for some quality other than truth, thus introducing an element of dishonesty and make-believe into the heart of what otherwise threatens to become a virtue. By this method thousands of humans have been brought to think that humility means pretty women trying to believe they are ugly and clever men trying to believe they are fools. And since what they are trying to believe may, in some cases, be manifest nonsense, they cannot succeed in believing it, and we have the chance of keeping their minds endlessly revolving on themselves in an effort to achieve the impossible.

— C. S. Lewis

The Screwtape Letters
New York: Macmillan, 1961

Rewards to the Meek

The meek shall eat and be satisfied: they shall praise the Lord that seek him: your heart shall live for ever.
— Psalm 22:26

•••

The meek will he guide in judgment: and the meek will he teach his way.
— Psalm 25:9

•••

But the meek shall inherit the earth; and shall delight themselves in the abundance of peace.
— Psalm 37:11

•••

Thou didst cause judgment to be heard from heaven; the earth feared, and was still, when God arose to judgment, to save all the meek of the earth.
— Psalm 76:8-9

*The Lord lifteth up the meek: he casteth the wicked
down to the ground.*
    — *Psalm 147:6*

• • •

*For the Lord taketh pleasure in his people: he will
beautify the meek with salvation.*
    — *Psalm 149:4*
      HOLY BIBLE

Solemn Reflection

In my first years at Mülhausen I suffered much from a home-sick longing for the church at Günsbach; I missed my father's sermons, and the services I had been familiar with all my life.

The sermons used to make a great impression on me, because I could see how much of what my father said in the pulpit was of a piece with his own life and experience. I came to see what an effort, I might say what a struggle, it meant for him to open his heart to the people every Sunday. I still remember sermons I heard from him while I was at the village school.

But what I loved best was the afternoon service, and of these I hardly ever missed a single one when I was in Günsbach. In the deep and earnest devotion of those services the plain and homely style of my father's preaching showed its real value, and the pain of thinking that the holy day was now drawing to its close gave these services a peculiar solemnity.

From the services in which I joined as a child I have taken with me into life a feeling for what is solemn, and a need for quiet and self-recollection, without which I cannot realize the meaning of my life. I cannot, therefore, support the opinion of those who would not let children take part in grownup people's services till they to some extent understand them. The important thing is not that they shall understand, but that they shall feel something of what is serious and solemn. The fact that the child sees his elders full of devotion, and has to feel something of their devotion himself, that is what gives the service its meaning for him.

— *Albert Schweitzer*

The Light Within Us
New York: Philosophical Library, 1959

Moving, Yet Still

Meekness is imperfect if it be not both active and passive, leading us to subdue our own passions and resentments, as well as to bear patiently the passions and resentments of others.

— *John Watson Foster*

International Dictionary of Thoughts
Doubleday and Company, 1969

When To Be Meek in the Church

There are certain specific matters in which Christians are very specially commanded to manifest a meek spirit in their assembly life. There is little hope of showing the world a victorious example of true meekness in big, outward issues, if we do not begin "in the family."

(a) Restoring Backsliders (Galatians 6:1)

Backsliders, if repentant, are to be restored "in a spirit of meekness," and their misdeeds forgotten, even as God forgets our forgiven sins. This warning is necessary because the pride of those who have not failed in the very way they have, would love to keep reminding them of their lapse. The reason for this—the conscious-ness of personal frailty on the part of those who sit to judge—should appeal to all men of sense. It is only the grace of God that has kept the judge from being the criminal!

Of course this does not abolish the rightful place of church discipline: it only indicates the spirit in which it must be used.

(b) Answering Opponents (1 Peter 3:15)

"Give an answer . . . with meekness." It is a splendid thing to be always ready with a convincing reply to the man who asks for it, but it must be given in a meek spirit. Our greatest spiritual blessings are no matter for self-boasting, but all of grace. We need to remember this with regard to Pentecostal blessings as much as any others.

To argue and strive in a contentious spirit, even for the most precious truths of our faith and hope, is likely to make the very spirit of our striving deny the truth of our testimony. . . .

It is also worth remembering that even if brilliant argument compels a man to an intellectual agreement, his heart may only be, for that reason, all the more antagonized against the truth we wish him to receive, unless he has felt the meekness of our spirit also. To vanquish a foe is not the same as to convert him into a friend. Our immediate purpose as Christians is conversion, not conquest.

(c) Receiving the Word (James 1:21)

Listening to the Word is a great art—perhaps as great as preaching it. If our listeners prepared themselves by prayer as much as our preachers, what a revival we should enjoy! Human hearts are like soil, and their condition determines the result of the sowing far more than the skill of the sower.

Meekness ensures a condition of receptivity likely to yield a good harvest. This does not mean a foolish credulity that soaks in every new or strange doctrine. What it does mean is a laying down of all rebellion in spirit, and a readiness to obey at any cost what may be fairly proved to be the "sincere milk of the Word." It also implies a putting away of that foolish pride which refuses to admit that anything more can be learned upon the particular subject in hand.

(d) "Meekness of Wisdom" (James 3:13)

True wisdom is always marked by humility, and the "meekness of wisdom" expresses a delightful truism. Paul recommends it to Timothy (and surely through him to all young preachers, and old ones too!): he is to "instruct (correct) those that oppose themselves" (2 Timothy 2:25), with meekness. Especially with the older men and women (1 Timothy 5:1-2). Not lording over God's people, but humbly giving a calm reason for every suggestion and reproof, that must appeal to the Spirit of Christ in every true believer.

The victories won by meekness in pastors and preachers, especially the younger, are worth far more than all the doubtful benefits of hastily standing on dignity and asserting the prerogatives of office. Probably nothing indicates a ripening of character in Christ more than an obviously meek spirit.

— Donald Gee

The Fruit of the Spirit
Springfield, Mo.: Gospel Publishing House, 1928

Choosing Gentleness

Nothing is won by force. I choose to be gentle.
If I raise my voice may it be only in praise. If I
clench my fist, may it be only in prayer. If I make
a demand, may it be only of myself.

— Max Lucado

When God Whispers Your Name
Dallas: Word Publishing, 1994

Our Gentle but Mighty Lord

Behold, the Lord God will come with might,
With His arm ruling for Him.
Behold, His reward is with Him,
And His recompense before Him.
Like a shepherd He will tend His flock,
In His arm He will gather the lambs,
And carry them in His bosom;
He will gently lead the nursing ewes.

— Isaiah 40:10-11 (NASB)
HOLY BIBLE

Benevolent Guide

We all have times in our lives when we get off course. We take detours. We decide that is the path to pursue, but sometimes the result is debilitating. How does God respond?

Scripture says that in such a situation, God's response would be something like this: "Hold it now, Charles. You're off track. Let Me show you what's going to happen if you keep pursuing this matter. Let Me reveal to you how you can return to the proper course so as to avoid unfortunate consequences in the future."

Though He may chastise us to get us back on track, nowhere in the Bible does God say that He gets angry when one of His children strays. When we disobey Him, He doesn't get angry; He is grieved in His heart. The Holy Spirit within us tracks us down, reminding us of God's love and direction.

— *Charles Stanley*

How To Listen to God, 1985

The Strength of Gentleness

There is no other way to be gentle than by the name and power the Lord gives us. Authentic gentleness is one of the most miraculous manifestations of the inner power of Christ's indwelling. It requires absolute trust in His ongoing work in others. It responds to the wonder of what people have been through, not what they have done. It addresses the emerging child, often hurt and battered, in other people.

The Lord is consistently gentle with us. He stands beside us in the midst of trouble and tragedy, nursing us through it all. This is the same kind of encouragement the people around us need.

What does it mean to be gentle in life's tensions and problems? It certainly does not mean simply having a moldable, adjustable, easy lack of concern. Moses was referred to as one of the meekest men in all of Israel, and yet he marshaled the mass exodus of a diverse company of people and brought them through the wilderness to the Promised Land.

When we are truly meek, we know who we are because we know to whom we belong. We do not have to be defensive or justify ourselves any longer. We know we are loved and are therefore free to love and free to be the unique, special, unreproducible wonders that God meant us to be. Once defensive pride is taken from us by an authentic experience of humility, we are able to treat others like God treated us.

Only a person who is afraid of himself and Christ is afraid to be gentle. Lording it over others is a sure sign we need the Lord.

— *Lloyd John Ogilvie*

Gentle Hearts of Steel

The gentleness that comes from the Holy Spirit has a broader definition than the ability to be nice. It includes the courage to do what is right and the strength to carry out God's commands . . .

Speaking Christian truth, serving as the faithful church in a new dark age, sparking the moral impulse and stimulating the moral imagination—all these sometimes seem to be losing battles, doomed efforts. It is difficult to think of fresh beginnings in times that seem so much like the end.

We may indeed be approaching midnight. But if there is any hope, it is to be found in a renewed and repentant people possessed of a moral vision informed by Scripture, respecting of tradition, and committed to the recovery of character. We must be a people of conviction, prepared to offer the world a story filled with courage, duty, commitment, and heroic effort—that will inflame the moral imagination of the West.

Will we succeed? Perhaps. Does it matter? In one sense, yes, of course. In another sense, not really. For our duty is clear no matter what the outcome.

— Charles Colson

Reprinted from *Against the Night—Living in the New Dark Ages* by Charles Colson with Ellen Santilli-Vaughn. Copyright © 1989 by Charles Colson. Used by permission of Servant Publications.

Answer With Gentleness

Always be prepared to give an answer to everyone who asks you to give the reason for the hope that you have. But do this with gentleness and respect, keeping a clear conscience, so that those who speak maliciously against your good behavior in Christ may be ashamed of their slander. It is better, if it is God's will, to suffer for doing good than for doing evil.

— 1 Peter 3:15b-17 (NIV)
HOLY BIBLE

No Room for Rudeness

On one occasion a nurse in one of the London hospitals complained to the Chaplain-General to the forces that she had been rudely treated by some patients. "Thank God for that," was the reply. "What do you mean?" asked the astonished nurse. The Bishop explained, "If you are carrying a pitcher and somebody knocks up against you, you can only spill out of the pitcher what is inside. And when people misjudge and persecute us, we can only spill what is inside. In the case of a godless man, he will probably swear. But if you are filled with the Holy Ghost, you will manifest the gentleness of Christ, and make men astonished."

The Sunday School Chronicle

A Christian Tongue

I need Thee, O Lord, for a curb on my tongue; when I am tempted to making carping criticisms and cruel judgments, keep me from speaking barbed words that hurt, and in which I find a perverted satisfaction.

Keep me from unkind words and from unkind silences.

Restrain my judgments.

Make my criticisms kind, generous, and constructive.

Make me sweet inside, that I may be gentle with other people, gentle in the things I say, kind in what I do.

Create in me that warmth of mercy that shall enable others to find Thy strength for their weakness, Thy peace for their strife, Thy joy for their sorrow, Thy love for their hatred, Thy compassion for their weakness. In Thine own strong name, I pray. Amen.

— Peter Marshall

Sermons and Prayers
New York: Revell, 1950

Prayer for Gentleness

O Almighty God, give to Thy servant a meek and gentle spirit, that I may be slow to anger, and easy to mercy and forgiveness. . . . Give me a wise and constant heart, that I may never be moved to an intemperate anger for any injury that is done or offered. Lord, let me ever be courteous and easy to be entreated; let me never fall into a peevish or contentious spirit, but follow peace with all men; offering forgiveness, inviting them by courtesies, ready to confess my own errors, apt to make amends, and desirous to be reconciled. Let no sickness or cross accident, no employment or weariness, make me angry or ungentle and discontented, or unthankful and uneasy to them that minister to me; but in all things make me like unto the holy Jesus. Amen.

— Bishop Jeremy Taylor (1613-1667)

Freedom, Love and Truth
Compiled by William Inge
London: Longman, Green & Co., Inc., 1936

Under God's Control

You should make a special point of asking God every morning to give you, before all else, that true spirit of meekness which He would have His children possess. You must also make a firm resolution to practise yourself in this virtue, especially in your interaction with those persons to whom you chiefly owe it. You must make it your main object to conquer yourself in this matter. Call it to mind a hundred times during the day, commending your efforts to God. It seems to me that no (gift) more than this is needed in order to subject your soul entirely to His will, and then you will become more gentle day by day, trusting wholly in His goodness. You will be very happy, my dearest child, if you can do this, for God will dwell in your heart, and where He reigns all is peace. But if you should fail, and commit some of your old faults, do not be disheartened, but rise up and go on again, as though you had not fallen.

— *St. Francis de Sales*

Daily Strength for Daily Needs
Mary Tileston

A Meek and Quiet Spirit

Through meekness, a man hath always fair weather within. Through meekness, he gives no manner of offense, or disturbance anywhere abroad. And in particular, I may say these (following) several things of the meek and quiet spirit.

First: There is no ungrounded passion; no boisterous motion; no exorbitance, nothing of fury. No perplexity of mind, nor over-thoughtfulness. Men that are thus disquieted know not what to do, can give no answer, nor can resolve on anything. No confusion of thought; for that is darkness within, and brings men into such disorder that they know not what is before them. No eagerness of desire; no impetuosity. . . .

Secondly: Through this meekness of spirit, there is good carriage and behavior toward others. The meek are never injurious or censorious, but are ready to take in good part, and make the best construction that the case will bear. . . . The meek man is a good neighbor, a good friend; a credit to religion, one who governs himself according to reason, makes no injury by any misconstruction and, in case of any wrong done, sits down with easy satisfaction. . . .

— *Benjamin Whichcote*

The Excellence of a Meek and Quiet Spirit
An Anthology of Devotional Literature
Compiled by Thomas S. Kepler
Grand Rapids, Mich.: Baker Book House, 1947

Tenderhearted

The hurrying, bustling and pressurized life we live tends to make even some of the finest of Christians annoyed at the interruptions of the "little people." The Lord Jesus' gentle Spirit serves as an illustration when contrasted with the disciples' cruel attitude toward the children who had been brought by their parents to be blessed by Him. The Scripture tells us that the disciples rebuked those who brought them, but Jesus said, *Suffer the little children to come unto me, and forbid them not* (Mark 10:13-14).

This gentle characteristic of the Holy Spirit never asks such questions as, "How often must I forgive my brother when he sins against me?" or, "Should I forgive a brother who does not ask for forgiveness?" or, "Isn't there a limit to how much a person can stand?" The Holy Spirit is able to give gentleness in the face of all kinds of pressures.

Jesus, who possessed the Holy Spirit "without measure," pictured Himself as a shepherd gently caring for easily injured sheep, and He, through His followers, tenderly cares today.

— *Tim LaHaye*

Spirit-Controlled Temperament
Wheaton: Tyndale House Publishers

Singularly Focused

Why has Jesus been so effective in changing hearts and lives? Not because He is following a business plan, but because He loves the Father, personifies the Father's love for us, and is devoted to doing the Father's will. In Jesus, obedience and love have come together to create a gentle, irresistible spirit. We absorb that spirit as we devote ourselves to loving and obeying Him. When our eyes and our thoughts are on Him alone, instead of on how many good works we can do and how many people we can reach, we draw others to Him as surely as we ourselves have been drawn . . . .

Today we have substituted doctrinal belief for personal belief, and that is why so many people are devoted to causes and so few are devoted to Jesus Christ. People do not really want to be devoted to Jesus, but only to the cause He started. Jesus Christ is deeply offensive to the educated minds of today, to those who only want Him to be their Friend, and who are unwilling to accept Him in any other way. Our Lord's primary obedience was to the will of His Father, not to the needs of people—the saving of people was the natural outcome of His obedience to the Father. If I am devoted solely to the cause of humanity, I will soon be exhausted and come to the point where my love will waver and stumble. But if I love Jesus Christ personally and passionately, I can serve humanity, even though people may treat me like a "doormat." The secret of a disciple's life is devotion to Jesus Christ, and the characteristic of that life is its seeming insignificance and its meekness. Yet it is like a grain of wheat that "falls into the ground and dies"—it will spring up and change the entire landscape (John 12:24).

— *Oswald Chambers*

A Light in the Dark

Solitude molds self-righteous people into gentle, caring, forgiving persons who are so deeply convinced of their own great sinfulness and so fully aware of God's even greater mercy that their life itself becomes a ministry. In such a ministry there is hardly any difference left between doing and being. When we are filled with God's merciful presence, we can do nothing other than minister because our whole being witnesses to the light that has come into the darkness.

— *Henri J. M. Nouwen*

Encyclopedia of Famous Quotes

The Way To Humility

A servant of God cannot know the extent of his patience and humility so long as all goes well with him. But when a time comes that those who should ream him well do the opposite, then he shows the true extent of his patience and humility, and no more.

Blessed is the servant who does not esteem himself as better when he is praised and promoted by men than when they look on him as vile, stupid, and contemptible; for, whatever a man is in the sight of God, that he is, and no more.

Blessed is the servant who accepts rebuke with courtesy, obeys respectfully, confesses humbly, and makes amends gladly. Blessed is the servant who is not in a hurry to excuse himself, but humbly accepts shame and reproach for a fault even when he is not to blame.

Where there is charity and wisdom,
> there is neither fear nor ignorance.

Where there is patience and humility,
> there is neither anger nor vexation.

Where there is poverty with joy,
> there is neither greed nor avarice.

Of Gentleness and Anger

Humility makes our lives acceptable to God, meekness makes us acceptable to men. . . . Depend upon it, it is better to learn how to live without being angry than to imagine one can moderate and control anger lawfully; and if through weakness and frailty one is overtaken by it, it is far better to put it away forcibly than to parley with it; for give anger ever so little way, and it will become your master, like the serpent, who easily works in its body wherever it can once introduce its head. You will ask how to put away anger. My child, when you feel its first movement, collect yourself gently and seriously, not hastily or with impetuosity. Sometimes in a law court the officials who enforce quiet make more noise than those they affect to hush; and so, if you are impetuous in restraining your temper, you will throw your heart into worse confusion than before, and, amid the excitement, it will lose all self-control. . . . Moreover, when there is nothing to stir your wrath, lay up a store of meekness and kindliness, speaking and acting in things great and small as gently as possible. . . .

So we must not only speak gently to our neighbour, but we must be filled, heart and soul, with gentleness; and we must not merely seek the sweetness of aromatic honey in courtesy and suavity with strangers, but also the sweetness of milk among those of our own household and our neighbours; a sweetness terribly lacking to some who are as angels abroad and devils at home. . . .

— *St. Francis de Sales*

Introduction to the Devout Life

Instruments of Sympathy

We are certainly not Christ; we are not called on to redeem the world by our own deeds and sufferings, and we need not try to assume such an impossible burden. We are not lords, but instruments in the hand of the Lord of history; and we can share in other people's sufferings only in a very limited degree. We are not Christ, but if we want to be Christians, we must have some share in Christ's large-heartedness by acting with responsibility and in freedom when the hour of danger comes, and by showing a real sympathy that springs, not from fear, but from the liberating and redeeming love of Christ for all who suffer. Mere waiting and looking on is not Christian behaviour. The Christian is called to sympathy and action, not in the first place by his own sufferings, but by the sufferings of his brethren, for whose sake Christ suffered.

— *Dietrich Bonhoeffer*

Letters and Papers from Prison

Inherit the Earth

"Meek" people, Jesus added, "shall inherit the earth." One would have expected the opposite. One would think that "meek" people get nowhere because everybody ignores them or else rides roughshod over them and tramples them underfoot. It is the tough, the overbearing, who succeed in the struggle for existence; weaklings go to the wall. Even the children of Israel had to fight for their inheritance, although the Lord their God gave them the promised land. But the condition on which we enter our spiritual inheritance in Christ is not might but meekness, for . . . everything is ours if we are Christ's.

— *John Stott*

Reprinted from *Christian Counter-Culture*
by John R. W. Stott. Used by permission of
InterVarsity Press, P. O. Box 1400,
Downers Grove, IL 60515.

Worthy

Walk worthy of the vocation wherewith ye are called, with all lowliness and meekness, with longsuffering, forbearing one another in love (Ephesians 4:1-2).

> Meekness, humility, and love,
> Did through thy conduct shine;
> Oh may my whole deportment prove
> A copy, Lord, of Thine.

Lincoln's Devotional
Greatneck, N.Y.: Channel Press, Inc., 1957

Chapter 9

SELF-CONTROL

*"**K**eep yourself pure"* (1 Timothy 5:22 *NIV*).

Self-control implies the restraining of oneself. But from what? What is it that we are to keep ourselves from doing or saying?

Society's answer is inevitably that we each must maintain self-control for the common good. It says we must restrain ourselves from doing what society says is wrong or not good. The list of "wrong behaviors" is often in flux.

The Bible goes far beyond that reason. The Bible states that we are to restrain ourselves from "sin" as God defines it and that, in so doing, we benefit not only ourselves, but others as well. We are to keep ourselves from engaging in whatever entices us to break God's laws and breach our relationship with God . . . whether by thought, word, or deed.

- We are to keep control of our thoughts, taking every thought captive (See 2 Corinthians 10:5).
- We are to guard our tongues. (See James 3:1-9.) We are told explicitly not to lie, bear false witness, or gossip.
- We are to avoid sinning in our relationships with others—refusing to kill, covet, engage in adultery or fornication, steal, cheat, or engage in quarrels and fights. (See James 4:1-2.)

The Greek word for self-control is "egkrateia" (pronounced eng-khra'-ti-a). It is made up of two roots: "en" meaning infused with or by, and "kratos", which means vigor, dominion, power, strength. To have "egkrateia" is to have great might and force— in other words, a very strong will, but one firmly held in rein.

We are to manifest self-control so that we can be like Him, so that we may intimately experience more and more of His presence and power in our lives.

Self-control is a high form of worship before God. It is "living out" His commandments by doing what He compels us to do, so that God can bless us fully and trust us explicitly.

Focusing the Wind

Self-control, the last fruit of the Spirit, is the one that makes all the rest operative. To the Greek, "self-control" meant to have "power over oneself." Paul grasped this quality from the four cardinal virtues of the Stoics and claimed it as one of the imputed vibrancies of the Holy Spirit. The Greek word, *egkrateia*, rooted in *kratos*, "strength," means to have strength to control the self. We know this is not possible until we surrender to Christ's management.

This sublime fruit of the Spirit is not negative. It does not delineate what we are against or will not do. Rather, it consists of a very positive capacity to know who we are and what we will do because the Spirit is in control of our abilities and aptitudes, as well as appetites. We can have power over ourselves only when we have submitted to the Spirit's control and power in us. Christ's control is the basis of self-control.

The fruit of Christ's indwelling is more than just not flying off the handle or always being Mr. Perfect or Miss Smooth. Instead, it's being centered so that all our energies, when multiplied by the Spirit, can be used creatively rather than be squandered. A person who has the fruit of self-control becomes like a wind channel in which the power of the wind is channeled. It's silent strength that's focused to do what the Master commands.

— Lloyd John Ogilvie

Growth in Self-Control

We come now to the last of the nine fruits of the Spirit, self-control. The nine Beatitudes could be pronounced on those who bear these nine fruits, and there could well be special emphasis on the last: "Blessed are the self-controlled."

It is interesting that Paul puts self-control last. Most systems, ancient and modern, would put it first. Confucianism through self-control would strive to produce "the superior man"; Hinduism through breath- and thought-control would try to produce "the realized man"; Stoicism through will-control desires to produce "the detached man"; modern cults through mind-control strive to produce "the happy man." The Christian Way produces through Christ-control the self-controlled man. But note that self-control is not so much a means as an end. You do not gain Christ through self-control; you gain self-control through Christ.

"The love of Christ constraineth us"—or, literally, "narrows us to His way," controls us. If you begin with self-control, then you are the center, you are controlling yourself. And will be anxious lest yourself slip out from beneath your control.

But if you begin, as Paul does here, with love, then the spring of action is love for a Person, someone outside yourself. You are released from yourself and from self-preoccupation. The "expulsive power of a new affection" breaks the tyranny of self-love and releases your powers. This means that you are a relaxed and, therefore a released person. When you begin with love, you end in self-control. But it is not a nervous, anxious, tied-up self-control; it is a control that is natural and unstrained, therefore beautiful.

Interestingly enough, this is the only place where the word *self-control* is used in the New Testament. And here it is used last as a by-product of love for Christ. "Love Christ and do as you like," for you'll like what He likes.

O Christ, let me move over and let Thee take the wheel, and then I'll get through this business of living without mishap. Amen.

— *E. Stanley Jones*

Growing Spiritually
Nashville, Tenn.: Abingdon Press

The Supremacy of God's Will

But what is self-denial? Wherein are we to deny ourselves? And whence does the necessity of this arise? I answer, the will of God is the supreme, unalterable rule for every intelligent creature; equally binding every angel in heaven, and every man upon earth. Nor can it be otherwise: this is the natural, necessary result of the relation between creatures and their Creator. But if the will of God be our own rule of action in everything, great and small, it follows, by undeniable consequence, that we are not to do our own will in anything. Here, therefore, we see at once the nature, with the ground and reason, of self-denial. We see the nature of self-denial: it is the denying or refusing to follow our own will, from a conviction that the will of God is the only rule of action to us. And we see the reason thereof, because we are creatures; because "it is He that hath made us, and not we ourselves."

— John Wesley

John Wesley's Theology: A Collection from His Works
Edited by Robert W. Burtner and Robert E. Chiles
Nashville, Tenn.: Abingdon Press

Conquered by Quiet

I remember that once a man came to our house red with wrath. He was boiling over with rage. He had, or supposed he had, a grievance to complain of. My father listened to him with great attention and perfect quietness until he had got it all out, and then he said to him, in a soft and low tone, "Well, I suppose you only want what is just and right?" The man said, "Yes," but went on to state the case over again.

Very gently Father said to him, "If you have been misinformed, I presume you would be perfectly willing to know what the truth is?" He said he would. Then Father very quietly and gently made a statement of the other side; and when he was through the man got up and said, "Forgive me, Doctor. Forgive me." Father had beaten him by his quiet, gentle way. I saw it, and it gave me an insight into the power of self-control. It was a striking illustration of the passage, "He that ruleth his spirit is better than he that taketh a city."

— *Henry Ward Beecher*

Cyclopedia of Religious Anecdotes
Fleming H. Revell Co., 1923

An End to Troubles

Cry for grace from God to be able to see God's hand in every trial, and then for grace . . . to submit at once to it. Not only to submit, but to acquiesce, and to rejoice in it . . . I think there is generally an end to troubles when we get to that.

— *Charles H. Spurgeon*

Power in Praise
Merlin Carothers
Plainfield, N.J.: Logos International, 1971

Trait of the Mature

Since an overseer is entrusted with God's work, he must be blameless— not overbearing, not quick-tempered, not given to drunkenness, not violent, not pursuing dishonest gain. Rather he must be hospitable, one who loves what is good, who is self-controlled, upright, holy and disciplined. He must hold firmly to the trustworthy message as it has been taught, so that he can encourage others by sound doctrine and refute those who oppose it.

Teach the older men to be temperate, worthy of respect, self-controlled, and sound in faith, in love and in endurance.

Likewise, teach the older women to be reverent in the way they live, not to be slanderers or addicted to much wine, but to teach what is good. Then they can train the younger women to love their husbands and children, to be self-controlled and pure, to be busy at home, to be kind, and to be subject to their husbands, so that no one will malign the word of God.

Similarly, encourage the young men to be self-controlled. In every-thing set them an example by doing what is good. In your teaching show integrity, seriousness and soundness of speech that cannot be condemned, so that those who oppose you may be ashamed because they have nothing bad to say about us.

— *Titus 1:7-9; 2:2-8* (NIV)
HOLY BIBLE

Take My Life and Let It Be

Take my life, and let it be
Consecrated Lord to Thee.
Take my moments and my days,
Let them flow in ceaseless praise.
Take my hands, and let them move
At the impulse of Thy love.
Take my feet and let them be
Swift and beautiful for Thee.

Take my voice, and let me sing
Always, only, for my King.
Take my lips, and let them be
Filled with messages from Thee.
Take my silver and my gold;
Not a mite would I withhold.
Take my intellect, and use
Every power as Thou shalt choose.

Take my will, and make it Thine;
It shall be no longer mine.
Take my heart, it is Thine own;
It shall be Thy royal throne.
Take my love, my Lord, I pour
At Thy feet its treasure store.
Take myself, and I will be
Ever, only, all for Thee.

— Frances R. Havergal

Methodist Hymnal

Doing What God Says

A person who has learned the meaning of self-control, and who practices it, is a person who has taken one of the steps necessary to become more like Jesus Christ. Self-control in a Christian means that instead of insisting on having our own way, we choose God's way; we turn to Him for our marching orders and we obey His loving commands. We agree to allow God's Holy Spirit to live in us and work God's will through us. Then, when the Spirit has free reign, He is able to bring us closer to God's ideal of perfection, and holiness. . . .

Obedience is the path to holiness, because it is the path to union with God's holy will. . . . Obedience itself is not holiness, but as the will opens itself to accept and to do the will of God, God communicates Himself and His holiness. . . .

Begin by doing at once whatever appears right to do. Give up at once whatever conscience tells you is not according to the will of God. Not only pray for light and strength, but act. Do what God says. *"Whoever does God's will is My brother and sister and mother,"* said

Jesus in Mark 3:35. Every son of God has been begotten of the will of God; in doing that will, he has his life. To do the Father's will is the meat, the strength, the mark of every son of God.

— Andrew Murray

The Believer's Secret of Holiness
Bethany House Publishers, 1984

Indispensable

If a person mounts a high-spirited horse, it is important that he should be able to control him; otherwise he may be dashed in pieces. If an engineer undertakes to conduct a locomotive, it is necessary that he should be able to guide or check the panting engine at his pleasure; else his own life and the lives of others may be sacrificed. But it is still more indispensable that an individual who is entrusted with the care of himself should be able to govern himself.

— S. G. Goodrich

6000 Illustrations

Mastery

Self-control ("temperance" in the *KJV*) comes from a Greek word meaning strong, having mastery, able to control one's thoughts and actions. John Wesley's mother once wrote him while he was a student at Oxford that "anything which increases the authority of the body over the mind is an evil thing." This definition has helped me understand "self-control."

— Billy Graham

The Faithful Christian: An Anthology of Billy Graham
Compiled by William Griffin and Ruth Graham Dienert
New York: McCracken Press, 1994

Hold Your Horses

The Greek word, here translated 'temperance,' is one of wide meaning. It denotes the mastery over ourselves in body and spirit. The idea is that of holding in horses, with a firm hand. The wicked and thoughtless too often toss the reins on the neck of passion, and allow the steed to plunge on in its mad course. The Christian, on the other hand, will, by the grace of God, keep a watchful eye and a firm hand upon his appetites, passions, and desires, making them servants, not masters. Perhaps the best English translation of the Greek word is 'self-control.'

Temperance is self-control, or the government of our passions— 'A prudent self-control is wisdom's root.' The Holy Spirit alone can change our hearts, and make us new creatures in Christ Jesus; but grace does not destroy passion nor eradicate appetite. After the vital change has taken place, the internal warfare begins between the old man and the new. The Bible nowhere tells us that, at conversion, a process is begun, which will, of necessity, complete its curve round its orbit, without any pains or struggle on our part. There is a dead heathen underlying every living Christian. There are possibilities of resurrection for the old man, whom we thought crucified long ago. We took him to the cross, and nailed him there, and thought him dead; when, all at once, in some evil thought or passion, he manifested vitality once more, and we learned, in our bitter experience, that the flesh is not yet subdued. Wilfulness and waywardness, anger and malice, pride and passion, dishonesty and untruthfulness, intemperance and impurity, often disfigure the lives of God's professed people, and lead to those sad declensions or falls with which the Church is only too familiar.

Our passions are either misdirected, or, though directed aright, liable to run to excess. If, therefore, we would govern our passions, we must first ascertain the proper objects of their pursuit, and then restrain their exercise in that sphere, within the bounds of reason and conscience. It should be our aim to seek after a firm mind, which the infatuation of passion shall not seduce, nor its violence shake; which shall, in the midst of contending emotions, remain master of itself, able calmly to listen to the voice of conscience, and ready to obey its dictates without hesitation.

How, then, are we to govern our passions? Let us begin by forming just views of the relative importance of those objects which draw forth our desires. Let us anticipate, by reflection, that knowledge which experience often purchases at too dear a price. Let the thought of the vanity of the world, the shortness of life, the certainty of death, judgment, and eternity, allay the heat of passion. Let us remember that the favor of God, a contented mind, and a peaceful life, form the chief elements of human happiness. Early should we learn the lesson of self-denial. That does not consist in perpetual austerity and universal renunciation of the innocent pleasures of the world. The Gospel demands no such sacrifice; but it requires us to abstain from pleasure, if need be, for the sake of duty and conscience, or for the attainment of some higher good. If we have not learned this lesson, desire, not conscience, will become the ruling principle of life. Begin early to curb passion, and you will be able to stand in the evil day, when the critical moment comes. If you have not learned the lesson before the hour when temptation influences the mind, passion will then rise in its might, to shake the soul. Therefore, oppose the beginnings of evil; avoid everything calculated to excite the wicked passions in your nature. Do not make light of any desire which seems to be gaining such progress within you as to threaten entire dominion. Gently it may steal into the heart; but as it advances, it will pierce its victim through with many sorrows. Of our passions it may be said that their beginning is treacherous; their growth imperceptible; their end death. Above all, to our own endeavours for regulating our passions, let us unite earnest prayer to God. Here, if anywhere, divine assistance is indispensably requisite. Such is the present blindness and imperfection of human nature, that even to discover all the disorders of our heart is difficult, to rectify them impossible. While we do our part with resolution and vigilance, let us earnestly and persistently pray God that He would forgive our weakness, strengthen our power of resistance, and enable us, by His grace, to 'keep the body under, and bring it into subjection.' A strong will, allied with right religious motives, is a source of blessing to the individual, and its influence becomes magnetic.

— *James MacDonald Inglis*

Precious Fruit
London: Seeley & Co., 1887

Holding One's Tongue

There is the service of guarding the reputation of others . . . . How necessary this is if we are to be saved from backbiting and gossip. The apostle Paul taught us to *"speak evil of no one" (Titus 3:2)*. We may clothe our backbiting in all the religious respectability we want, but it will remain a deadly poison. There is a discipline in holding one's tongue that works wonders within us.

Nor should we be a party to be the slanderous talk of others. In one church I served, we had a rule on the pastoral team that the members came to appreciate. We refused to allow any person in the congregation to speak disparagingly of one pastor to another pastor. Gently, but firmly, we would ask them to go directly to the offending pastor. Eventually, people understood that we simply would not allow them to talk to us about pastor "so-and-so." This rule, held to by the entire team, had beneficial results.

Bernard [of Clairvaux] warns us that the spiteful tongue "strikes a deadly blow at charity in all who hear him speak and, so far as it can, destroys root and branch, not only in the immediate hearers but also in all others to whom the slander, flying from lip to lip, is afterwards repeated." Guarding the reputation of others is a deep and lasting service.

— *Richard Foster*

Taken from *Celebration of Discipline:*
The Path To Spiritual Growth by Richard J. Foster.
Copyright © 1978 by Richard J. Foster.
Reprinted by permission of HarperCollins Publishers, Inc.

What Do You Think?

We have no control over how we feel, how we act—our attitudes, and actions—except as they are determined by our thoughts. All these elements are irrevocably tied together.

But since we do have control over what we think, it is possible to control our attitudes and actions. . . .

All thoughts can be divided into two basic categories: true and false. The thoughts that come from God are true. He is the God of all truth and has sent the Holy Spirit to dwell in us and to guide us into all truth.

If I can receive God's thoughts, I can think the truth. Therefore I will have the right attitudes and actions.

How do you get the air out of a glass? By filling it with water. How do you get rid of wrong and untrue thoughts? By filling your mind with true and right thoughts from God. The control of our thought life, then, comes by thinking God's thoughts with Him.

— Peter Lord

Lord, Peter. *Hearing God,*
Baker Book House Company, © 1988.

Take Care

If we allow some area of our life to spin out of control, God will continue to bring it up until we deal with it. . . .

Many of us appear to be all right in general, but there are still some areas in which we are careless and lazy; it is not a matter of sin, but the remnants of our carnal life that tend to make us careless. Carelessness is an insult to the Holy Spirit. We should have no carelessness about us either in the way we worship God, or even in the way we eat and drink.

Not only must our relationship to God be right, but the outward expression of that relationship must also be right. Ultimately,

God will allow nothing to escape; every detail of our lives is under His scrutiny. God will bring us back in countless ways to the same point over and over again. And He never tires of bringing us back to that one point until we learn the lesson, because His purpose is to produce the finished product. . . .

Beware of becoming careless over the small details of life and saying, "Oh, that will have to do for now." Whatever it may be, God will point it out with persistence until we become entirely His.

— *Oswald Chambers*

My Utmost for His Highest
An Updated Edition in Today's Language, 1992

Fighting Against Our Lusts

What, then, has He [Christ] hereby taught us? To fight against our lusts. For ye are about to put away your sins in holy baptism; but lusts will still remain, wherewith ye must fight after that ye are regenerate. For a conflict with your own selves still remains. Let no enemy from without be feared: conquer thine own self, and the whole world is conquered. What can any tempter from without, whether the devil or the devil's minister, do against thee? Whosoever sets the hope of gain before thee to seduce thee, let him only find no covetousness in thee; and what can he who would tempt thee by gain effect? Whereas, if covetousness be found in thee, thou takest fire at the sight of gain, and art taken by the bait of this corrupt food; but if he find no covetousness in thee the trap remains spread in vain.

Or should the tempter set before thee some woman of surpassing beauty; if chastity be within, iniquity from without is overcome. Therefore, that he may not take thee with the bait of a strange woman's beauty, fight with thine own lust within; thou hast no sensible perception of thine enemy, but of thine own concupiscence thou hast. Thou dost not see the devil, but the object that engageth thee thou dost see. Get the mastery, then, over that of which thou art sensible within. Fight valiantly, for He who hath regenerated thee is thy Judge; He hath arranged the lists, He is making ready the crown.

And truly it is a great temptation, dearly beloved, it is a great temptation in this life, when that in us is the subject of temptation whereby we obtain pardon if, in any of our temptations, we have fallen. It is a frightful temptation when that is taken from us whereby we may be healed from the wounds of other temptations. I know that ye have not yet understood me. Give me your attention that ye may understand. Suppose avarice tempts a man and he is conquered in a single temptation (for sometimes even a good wrestler and fighter may get roughly handled): avarice, then, has got the better of a man, good wrestler tho he be, and he has done some avaricious act. Or there has been a passing lust; it has not brought the man to fornication nor reached unto adultery—for when this does take place the man must at all events be kept back from the criminal act. But he "hath seen a woman to lust after her": he has let his thoughts dwell on her with more pleasure than was right; he has admitted the attack; excellent combatant tho he be, he has been wounded, but he has not consented to it; he has beaten back the motion of his lust, has chastised it with the bitterness of grief; he has beaten it back, and has prevailed. Still, in the very fact that he had slipped has he ground for saying, "Forgive us our debts." And so of all other temptations, it is a hard matter that in them all there should not be occasion for saying, "Forgive us our debts."

What, then, is that frightful temptation which I have mentioned, that grievous, that tremendous temptation, which must be avoided with all our strength, with all our resolution; what is it? When we go about to avenge ourselves. Anger is kindled and the man burns to be avenged. Oh, frightful temptation! Thou art losing that whereby thou hadst to attain pardon for other faults. If thou hadst committed any sin as to other senses and other lusts, hence mightst thou have had thy cure in that thou mightst say, "Forgive us our debts, as we also forgive our debtors." But whoso instigateth thee to take vengeance will lose for thee the power thou hadst to say, "As we also forgive our debtors." When that power is lost all sins will be retained; nothing at all is remitted.

Our Lord and Master and Savior, knowing this dangerous temptation in this life . . . took none of them for Himself to treat of and to commend to us with greater earnestness than this one.

— St. Augustine

The World's Famous Orations
William Jennings Bryan, Editor-in-chief
New York: Funk and Wagnalls Co., 1906

Refusing To Eat from the King's Table

Three years after King Jehoiakim began to rule in Judah, Babylon's King Nebuchadnezzar attacked Jerusalem with his armies, and the Lord gave him victory over Jehoiakim. When he returned to Babylon, he took along some of the sacred cups from the Temple of God and placed them in the treasury of his god in the land of Shinar.

Then he ordered Ashpenaz, who was in charge of his palace personnel, to select some of the Jewish youths brought back as captives—young men of the royal family and nobility of Judah—and to teach them the Chaldean language and literature. "Pick strong, healthy, good-looking lads," he said; "those who have read widely in many fields, are well informed, alert and sensible, and have enough poise to look good around the palace."

The king assigned them the best of food and wine from his own kitchen during their three-year training period, planning to make them his counselors when they graduated.

Daniel, Hananiah, Mishael, and Azariah were four of the young men chosen, all from the tribe of Judah. However, their superintendent gave them Babylonian names, as follows:

Daniel was called Belteshazzar;
Hananiah was called Shadrach;
Mishael was called Meshach;
Azariah was called Abednego.

But Daniel made up his mind not to eat the food and wine given to them by the king. He asked the superintendent for permission to eat other things instead. Now as it happened, God had given the superintendent a special appreciation for Daniel and sympathy for his predicament. But he was alarmed by Daniel's suggestion.

"I'm afraid you will become pale and thin compared with the other youths your age," he said, "and then the king will behead me for neglecting my responsibilities."

Daniel talked it over with the steward who was appointed by the superintendent to look after Daniel, Hananiah, Mishael, and Azariah, and suggested a ten-day diet of only vegetables and water; then, at the end of this trial period the steward could see how they looked in comparison with the other fellows who ate the king's rich food and decide whether or not to let them continue their diet.

The steward finally agreed to the test. Well, at the end of the ten days, Daniel and his three friends looked healthier and better nourished than the youths who had been eating the food supplied by the king! So after that the steward fed them only vegetables and water, without the rich foods and wines!

God gave these four youths great ability to learn, and they soon mastered all the literature and science of the time; and God gave to Daniel special ability in understanding the meanings of dreams and visions.

When the three-year training period was completed, the super-intendent brought all the young men to the king for oral exams, as he had been ordered to do. King Nebuchadnezzar had long talks with each of them, and none of them impressed him as much as Daniel, Hananiah, Mishael, and Azariah. So they were put on his regular staff of advisors. And in all matters requiring information and balanced judgment, the king found these young men's advice ten times better than that of all the skilled magicians and wise astrologers in his realm.

— **Daniel 1:1–20** (TLB)
   HOLY BIBLE

Putting Passions in Their Place

Not all appetites are bad. Some are needed for our survival. But as Charles G. Finney indicates in this selection, we should examine each one and determine if it is in our best interests at that moment. If not, we need to deny it or tone it down. Above all—with the Holy Spirit's help—we need to be in control of our passions . . . .

"Some have supposed that when persons are entirely sanctified, all the passions, desires and appetites of the sensibility will invariably impel the will in the same direction the reason does. However, such persons do not know what they say, for all these propensities seek their objects for their own sake and are blind to everything else. They always and necessarily urge the will to seek their respective objects for the sake of gratification. This is temptation and creates a warfare. The appetite for food, for example, seeks food for its own sake, and so does the desire for knowledge. It is nonsense, then, to say that they will not solicit the will to gratify them under improper circumstances. But when the mind is entirely sanctified, instead of the various propensities creating such a fiery and turbulent warfare when excited, the will will have them under control, so that all their actions will be bland and tranquilized.

The most that will or can be done is to harmonize them, and it is by no means desirable that they should be annihilated. Suppose, for example, the desire for knowledge were annihilated. What a calamity that would be! Or, the desire for food! The truth is, all the constitutional desires should remain. They were all given for useful purposes, and all call for their appropriate objects—for food, for knowledge, etc., and are thus constantly feeling after those things which are essential to our very existence, and that of our race. Besides, to regulate them is a good exercise for the will, and it is difficult to see how a mind could be virtuous at all if all the susceptibilities of its sensibility were destroyed; and if any of them were removed, it would doubtless be a great evil—otherwise God was not benevolent in our creation and did not make us in the best way."

— *Charles Finney*

Taken from "Putting Passions in Their Place" from
Principles of Holiness compiled and edited by Louis G. Parkhurst, Jr.
Copyright © 1984 by Louis G. Parkhurst, Jr.
Used by permission of Bethany House Publishers.

Worthwhile Work

Thank God every morning when you get up that you have something to do that day which must be done, whether you like it or not. Being forced to work, and forced to do your best will breed in you temperance and self-control, diligence and strength of will, cheerfulness and content, and a hundred virtues which the idle will never know.

— *Charles Kingsley*

A Treasury of Contentment
Compiled and edited by Ralph L. Woods
New York: Trident Press, 1969
A Division of Simon and Schuster

Basic Virtue of a Saint

How useful is the nature of the horse! For how swiftly soever the horse runneth, he yet letteth himself be ruled and guided, and leapeth hither and thither, and forward and backward, according to the will of his rider: and so, likewise, ought the servant of God to do, to wit, he should let himself be ruled, guided, turned aside, and bent, according to the will of his superior, or of any other man, for love of Christ. If thou wouldst be perfect, strive diligently to be full of grace and virtue, and fight valiantly against vice, enduring patiently every adversity for the love of thy Lord, that was mocked and afflicted and reviled and scourged and crucified and slain for love of thee, and not for His own sin, nor for His glory, nor for His profit, but only for thy salvation. And to do all this that I have told thee, above all things it is necessary that thou overcome thyself; for little shall it profit a man to lead and draw souls to God, if first he overcome to himself, and lead and draw himself to God.

— *St. Francis of Assisi*

The Little Flowers of St. Francis
Everyman's Library
Translated by Thomas Okey
E. P. Dutton & Co.

Temperance

Take heed to yourselves, lest at any time your hearts be overcharged with surfeiting, and drunkenness, and cares of this life, and so that day come upon you unawares (Luke 21:34).

> The world employs its various snares,
> Of hopes and pleasures, pains and cares,
>   And chain'd to earth I lie:
> When shall my fetter'd powers be free,
> And leave these seats of vanity,
>   And upward learn to fly?

Lincoln's Devotional
Introduction by Carl Sandburg
Greatneck, N.Y.: Channel Press, Inc., 1957

The Choice

I choose self-control . . . .

I am a spiritual being. After this body is dead, my spirit will soar. I refuse to let what will rot, rule the eternal. I choose self-control. I will be drunk only by joy. I will be impassioned only by my faith. I will be influenced only by God. I will be taught only by Christ. I choose self-control .

— *Max Lucado*

When God Whispers Your Name
Dallas: Word Publishing, 1994

Empty Calories?

It takes a lot of willpower, or self-control, to avoid fattening foods and stay on a diet. That same type of self-control is required in our spiritual lives if we are to take in only what is nourishing and uplifting . . .

The trouble with believers today is not that we do not take in good spiritual food; most of us do that. The problem is all of the junk that we take in (with our eyes and ears) along with the "good food." If physically I ate ninety percent bad food, and only ten percent good food, I would not have a healthy body. Likewise, in a given day, if I were to take in fifteen minutes of good, solid spiritual food and three hours of spiritual junk food, I would not wind up healthy on the spiritual level.

If you are overweight and you decide to lose weight and keep it off in order to maintain a healthy body, it means a permanent change in your physical eating habits. If you decide to become really healthy spiritually, in like manner you are looking at a permanent change in your "eating habits" concerning what you feed your mind and spirit. Your spiritual diet can prevent the power of God from flowing through you.

— Dr. James McKeever

Supernatural Power
Omega Publications, 1990

Must-Have Power

The capacity for self-control, the ability to master one's sinful impulses and deal with them constructively, is itself a crucial moral power.

— Will Herberg

Choose Life
Bernard Mandelbaum
New York: Random House, 1968

True Royalty

The command of one's self is the greatest empire a man can aspire unto, and consequently, to be subject to our own passions is the most grievous slavery. He who best governs himself is best fitted to govern others.

He who reigns within himself and rules his passions, desires and fears is more than a king.

— John Milton

The New Dictionary of Thoughts
Originally Compiled by Tryon Edwards D. D.
Revised and enlarged by C. N. Catrevas A. B.,
Jonathon Edwards A. M., & Ralph Emerson Browns A. M.
Standard Book Co., 1961

Rule Your Own Kingdom

Jesus Christ makes self-governing men. Every Christian who grows this fruit on their life-branch is a crowned king. Wherever you are ruler, be ruler within your own kingdom. You must either govern yourself or go to pieces. It is no use to tell a dethroned monarch to reign over his kingdom when his soldiers are in full revolt. Authority without power is weakness. The men Christ makes are strong men, and stronger men. There is a quality offered to every one of us in "the Fruit of the Spirit" which will turn our weakness into strength. From this inner principle arises sober-mindedness and self-restraint, which produce a well-balanced character. The end product of temperance is Christ-likeness.

Power to resist and to overcome temptation is a sign of growth in self-mastery. If we desire to grow this fruit in our lives we do well to consider and understand the forces that are hostile to growth. We must grow wisely, so that our lives may not be wanting in control, in balance, or dignity. Whenever the principle of the flesh is dominant in our lives there is a self-germinant power in it, and a self-reproduction. External influences are ever at work seeking to control the inner life. Growth is the one secret that robs the works of the flesh of its power. When the fuller life of the Holy Spirit is within us, the boundlessness of our possibilities in spiritual attainment are immeasurable. However full may be our union, it may always be made fuller; however close we may be in Christ, it is always possible to come closer. As we climb new heights and advance further in the Christian character, the more are we conscious of the infinite depths that remain to be traversed. One great element of blessedness arises, namely, that we need not fear of ever coming to the end of the growth in self-mastery that is possible to us.

— *Ivor Rosser*

The Fruit of the Spirit
Great Britain: Starling Press Limited

I Surrender All

All to Jesus I surrender,
All to Him I freely give;
I will ever love and trust Him,
In His presence daily live.

All to Jesus I surrender,
Humbly at His feet I bow,
Worldly pleasures all forsaken,
Take me, Jesus, take me now.

All to Jesus I surrender,
Make me, Savior, wholly Thine;
May Thy Holy Spirit fill me,
May I know Thy pow'r divine.

All to Jesus I surrender,
Lord, I give myself to Thee;
Fill me with Thy love and power,
Let Thy blessing fall on me.

(Chorus)
I surrender all,
I surrender all.
All to Thee, my blessed Savior, I surrender all.

— *Judson W. Van DeVenter*

Hymns of Faith

Controlling the Tongue

If anyone can control his tongue, it proves that he has perfect control over himself in every other way. We can make a large horse turn around and go wherever we want by means of a small bit in his mouth. And a tiny rudder makes a huge ship turn wherever the pilot wants it to go, even though the winds are strong.

So also the tongue is a small thing, but what enormous damage it can do. A great forest can be set on fire by one tiny spark. And the tongue is a flame of fire. It is full of wickedness and poisons every part of the body. And the tongue is set on fire by hell itself and can turn our whole lives into a blazing flame of destruction and disaster.

Men have trained, or can train, every kind of animal or bird that lives and every kind of reptile and fish, but no human being can tame the tongue. It is always ready to pour out its deadly poison. Sometimes it praises our heavenly Father, and sometimes it breaks out into curses against men who are made like God. And so blessing and cursing come pouring out of the same mouth. Dear brothers, surely this is not right! Does a spring of water bubble out first with fresh water and then with bitter water? Can you pick olives from a fig tree, or figs from a grape vine? No, and you can't draw fresh water from a salty pool.

— *James 3:1-12* (TLB)
HOLY BIBLE

Daily Dogged Discipline

I'm a great believer in what I have sometimes called "the daily dogged discipline" of the Christian life. The greatest enemies of discipline are laziness and emotionalism. Lazy people can't be bothered to acquire disciplined habits, and emotional or temperamental people prefer to live by their feelings. The "I'll see what I feel like" attitude is certain to end in disaster. We do not read God's Word and pray only on days when we feel like it, but every day (better twice a day), whether we feel like it or not. We do not join the Lord's people for worship on those Sundays when we feel like it, but every Sunday, whether we feel like it or not, because it is the Lord's Day. Do we only come to work when we feel like it? Then why should we give our heavenly Lord a service inferior to what we give our earthly employer? "We serve the Lord Christ" (Colossians 3:24). Then let's give Him better service, greater faithfulness, and more discipline than to any human master.

— *John Stott*

Reprinted from *Baptism and Fullness: The Work of the Holy Spirit Today* by John R. W. Stott. Second edition © 1975 by InterVarsity Press, P. O. Box 1400, Downers Grove, IL 60515.

It Takes Time

Willpower, (Nick Lansing) saw, was not a thing one could suddenly decree oneself to possess. It must be built up imperceptibly and laboriously out of a succession of small efforts to meet definite objects, out of the facing of daily difficulties instead of cleverly eluding them or shifting their burden on others. The making of the substance called character was a process about as slow and arduous as the building of the Pyramids.

— *Edith Wharton*

The Glimpses of the Moon

The Secret of Self-Control

Here was a man who had spent two hundred hours in trying to help an alcoholic get control of himself. Then the alcoholic decided to get on his knees, surrender to Christ, and let Christ control him. He got up from his knees a free man. He never touched alcohol again. He found self-control through Christ-control.

I tried the Christian life as self-control. Every day I would start out with the thought and purpose that I would keep myself from sin that day. And every night I came back a failure. For how could an uncontrolled will control an uncontrolled self? A diseased will could not heal a diseased soul. Then Christ moved into the affections. I began to love Him. Then the lesser loves dropped away.

Professor Royce, in his philosophy of "Loyalty," says: "There is only one way to be an ethical individual, and that is to choose your cause and then to serve it." This central loyalty to a cause puts other loyalties in their places as subordinate. Then life as a whole is coordinated, since the lesser loyalties are subordinated. To the Christian the "cause" is Christ and His Kingdom: we seek these first, and then all other things, including self-control, are added.

But not automatically. We have to cooperate. We have to throw our wills on the side of being disciplined. There are many who throw their wills on the other side—indiscipline, sometimes called freedom. A junior-high-school girl had on her belt this declaration of wants: "We want more holidays, less homework, more TV, and later hours for bedtime." Her crowd wanted to be free to do as they liked, not to be free to do as they ought. The result is inward and outward chaos. People who try to be free through indiscipline are "free in the sense that a ship is free when it has lost both compass and rudder." "The undisciplined person may sit at a piano," says Trueblood, "but he is not free to strike the notes he would like to strike. He is not free because he has not paid the necessary price for that particular freedom." Freedom is the by-product of a disciplined person. Then you are not merely "free from"; you are "free to."

Heavenly Father, help me to be the kind of person who is "free to"—free to do the very highest I am capable of doing. Amen.

— *E. Stanley Jones*

Growing Spiritually
Nashville, Tenn.: Abingdon Press

Free Will

What did God put a will into you for, but that you ought to be able to say *not* "I like" or "I was tempted, and I could not help it," but that you might, before each action, be able to say "I will"; and that passions, and the strings of lust and sense, of appetite and flesh, and emotions and affections, and vagrant fancies and wandering thoughts, and virtues that were running to seed, and weaknesses that might be cultivated into strength, might all know the master touch of a governing will, and might obey as becomes them. . . .

And what did God give you a conscience for, but that the will, which commands all the rest, might take its orders from it? There are parts of your nature which are intended to be slaves, and there are parts which are intended to be masters.

— Alexander Maclaren

A Rosary of Christian Graces
London, 1899

Silent Before His Accusers

Now Jesus stood before the governor, and the governor questioned Him, saying, "Are You the King of the Jews?" And Jesus said to him, "It is as you say."

And while He was being accused by the chief priests and elders, He made no answer.

Then Pilate said to Him, "Do You not hear how many things they testify against You?"

And He did not answer him with regard to even a single charge, so that the governor was quite amazed.

— Matthew 27:11-14 (NASB)
HOLY BIBLE

Deferring To Others

We must be continually sacrificing our own wills, as opportunity serves, to the will of others; bearing, without notice, sights and sounds that annoy us; setting about this or that task, when we had far rather be doing something very different; persevering in it, often, when we are thoroughly tired of it; keeping company for duty's sake, when it would be a great joy to us to be by ourselves.

— John Keble

Daily Strength for Daily Needs
Mary Tileston

Athletic Training

Paul seems to have been impressed by the stamina, the skill, and the temperance of athletes. Their self-control involves an aim, a list of training rules, and constant, sustained effort.

Aim—The athlete runs so he can win a prize. Now some laggards also run, but they don't care about winning a prize. Hence, their self-control is minimal. Whatever temperance they might have had is nullified by the multitude of desires which pull them in every direction. So they never "obtain."

The champion athlete aims for a prize that soon withers—a mere wreath. The Christian has an incorruptible prize: all the greater reason for self-control.

A list of training rules—The champion athlete has an eye for all the rules in his training sheet. We can control ourselves in the case of things we really don't want. Temperance becomes a problem when our desires are actively set on some things. It becomes a question of aim. If we really want the prize, we will desire other things less.

Constant, sustained effort—"I am running . . . I am fighting . . . I am buffeting. . . ." The verbs are present tense. When an athlete trained for the Isthmian games which were held near Corinth, he devoted his full time to practice. There were, of course, other things to do—lawful things, good things—but not good enough. So the athlete excluded from his life anything which would harm his body.

When this is applied to the Christian, it will be seen that he is in "full-time service." The fruit of the Spirit which is self-control is not some luxury to be enjoyed by an elite among Christians; it is a reality in the life of everyone who has been claimed by Christ. Hence, to be a Christian is to be self-controlled all the time.

We should not misunderstand Paul here. He is not urging a monastic life: self-control is not a withdrawal from the affairs of men. Temperance is the decision to have a well-defined goal, an intelligent manner of life which will make that goal possible, and a continual pressing toward the goal until it is reached.

— John Sanderson

Taken from *The Fruit of the Spirit* by
Prof. John Sanderson, Zondervan Publishing Co.
Copyright © 1972 by John Sanderson. Used by
permission of Prof. John W. Sanderson, Jr.

Firm Control

There must be firm control of the sex impulses. This God-given instinct has been dragged through the gutter by modern thinking, and we have made a cheap toy out of the most sacred gifts God has ever given to man. Our procreative powers need to be dedicated to Christ.

— Billy Graham

The Quotable Billy Graham
Compiled and Edited by Cort R. Flint and the Staff of Quote
Anderson, S.C.: Droke House, 1966

Choosing the Good

How great a virtue is temperance, how much of moment through the whole life of man! Yet God commits the managing so great a trust, without particular law or prescription, wholly to the demeanor of every grown man . . . God uses not to captivate under a perpetual childhood of prescription, but trusts him with the gift of reason to be his own chooser.

Good and evil we know in the field of this world grew up together almost inseparably; and the knowledge of good is so involved and interwoven with the knowledge of evil, and in so many cunning resemblances hardly to be discerned, that those confused seeds which were imposed upon psyche as an incessant labor to cull out, and sort asunder, were not more intermixed. It was from out of the rind of one apple tasted that the knowledge of good and evil, as two twins cleaving together, leaped forth into the world. And perhaps this is that doom which Adam fell into of knowing good and evil—that is to say, of knowing good by evil. As, therefore, the state of man now is, what wisdom can there be to choose, what continence to forbear without the knowledge of evil? He that can apprehend and consider vice with all her baits and seeming pleasures, and yet abstain, and yet distinguish, and yet prefer that which is truly better, he is the true wayfaring Christian.

— John Milton, 1608-1674

The World's Famous Orations
William Jennings Bryan, Editor-in-chief
New York: Funk and Wagnalls Co., 1906

Non-Sense

Temperance is not the absence of passion but is the transfiguring of passion into wholeness. Without it . . . you will have the senses usurping sovereignty and excluding the spirit; you will have them deciding good and evil and excluding God.

— Gerald Vann

The Heart of Man, 1945

Discipline To Resist Temptation

Man must recognize that it is not easy to repent and turn away from his customary bad habits. One must battle and conquer the inclination which diverts a person from the good path. There is a great reward for the one who masters the impulse to do wrong. . . . Succeeding in this task is like the struggle of a sick person who, in order to cure his illness, must resist certain foods and tempting delicacies and take bitter and unpleasant medicine. So too, a repentant person must discipline himself and resist temptation. It is wise to emphasize the other extreme of one's passion and thus strive hard to resist the attractive but harmful deed—just as a sick person must withstand the attractions of certain food. For actually evil behavior is the greatest malady and only one who turns away from it is really healthy, as it is written, "Return, ye backsliding children, and I will heal your backslidings" (Jeremiah 3:22), and it is written, "Who (God) forgiveth all thine iniquities; who healeth all thy diseases" (Psalm 103:3).

— Menorat Hamaor

Choose Life
Bernard Mandelbaum
New York: Random House, 1968

Balance

We have to acquire a peace and balance of mind such that we can give every word of criticism its due weight, and humble ourselves before every word of praise.

— Dag Hammarskjöld

From *Markings* by Dag Hammarskjöld, trans., Leif Sjoberg & W. H. Auden. Translation copyright © 1964 by Alfred A. Knopf Inc. and Faber Ltd. Reprinted by permission of Alfred A. Knopf Inc.

Putting On Christ

Up till now, I have been trying to describe facts—what God is and what He has done. Now I want to talk about practice—what do we do next? What difference does all this theology make? It can start making a difference tonight. If you are interested enough to have read thus far, you are probably interested enough to make a shot at saying your prayers; and whatever else you say, you will probably say the Lord's Prayer.

Its very first words are *Our Father.* Do you now see what those words mean? They mean, quite frankly, that you are putting yourself in the place of a son of God. To put it bluntly, you are *dressing up as Christ.* If you like, you are pretending. Because, of course, the moment you realize what the words mean, you realize that you are not a son of God. You are not being like The Son of God, whose will and interests are at one with those of the Father: you are a bundle of self-centered fears, hopes, greeds, jealousies, and self-conceit, all doomed to death. So that, in a way, this dressing up as Christ is a piece of outrageous cheek. But the odd thing is that He has ordered us to do it.

Why? What is the good of pretending to be what you are not? Well, even on the human level, you know, there are two kinds of pretending. There is a bad kind, where the pretense is there instead of the real thing; as when a man pretends he is going to help you instead of really helping you. But there is also a good kind, where the pretense leads up to the real thing. When you are not feeling particularly friendly but know you ought to be, the best thing you can do, very often, is to put on a friendly manner and behave as if you were a nicer person than you actually are. And in a few minutes, as we have all noticed, you will be really feeling friendlier than you were. Very often the only way to get a quality in reality is to start behaving as if you had it already. That is why children's games are so important. They are always pretending to be grown-ups—playing soldiers, playing shop. But all the time, they are hardening their muscles and sharpening their wits so that the pretense of being grown up helps them to grow up in earnest.

Now the moment you realize, "Here I am, dressing up as Christ," it is extremely likely that you will see at once some way in which at that very moment the pretense could be made less of a pretense and more of a reality. You will find several things going on in your mind which would not be going on there if you were really a son of God. Well, stop them. Or you may realize that, instead of saying your prayers, you ought to be downstairs writing a letter, or helping your wife to wash up. Well, go and do it.

You see what is happening. The Christ Himself, the Son of God Who is a man (just like you) and God (just like His Father) is actually at your side and is already at that moment beginning to turn your pretense into a reality. This is not merely a fancy way of saying that your conscience is telling you what to do. If you simply ask your conscience, you get one result: if you remember that you are dressing up as Christ, you get a different one. There are lots of things which your conscience might not call definitely wrong (especially things in your mind) but which you will see at once you cannot go on doing if you are seriously trying to be like Christ. For you are no longer thinking simply about right and wrong; you are trying to catch the good infection from a Person. It is more like painting a portrait than like obeying a set of rules. And the odd thing is that while in one way it is much harder than keeping rules, in another way it is far easier.

The real Son of God is at your side. He is beginning to turn you into the same kind of thing as Himself. He is beginning, so to speak, to "inject" His kind of life and thought, His Zoé, into you;

beginning to turn the tin soldier into a live man. The part of you that does not like it is the part that is still tin.

— *C. S. Lewis*

Mere Christianity
New York: Macmillan Co., 1952

Some Or None

Temperance is moderation in the things that are good and total abstinence from the things that are foul.

— *Frances E. Willard*

Encyclopedia of Religious Quotations
Fleming H. Revell Co., 1965

Keeping Your Temper

Let your light so shine before men, that they may see your good works, and glorify your Father which is in heaven (Matthew 5:16).

If a man has not grace to keep his temper, he is not fit to work for God. If he cannot live uprightly at home, he is not fit for God's service; and the less he does the better. But he can keep his temper, he can live uprightly at home, by the grace of God.

— *Dwight L. Moody*

The D. L. Moody Year Book
Selected by Emma Moody Fitt
New York: Fleming H. Revell, 1900

Steps Toward Growth in Good Temper

First, fix it in your mind as an axiom that bad temper is self-defeating—it gets you nowhere except backward. The bad-tempered can't win, for the bad temper itself is defeat. Two bitter last words never made a sweetheart or a sweet home.

Second, cultivate good temper as a life policy. Good temper is not a luxury; it is a necessity. You can't go through life on another basis and go through. You will always be up against opposition and hate if you manifest bad temper. "A soft answer turneth away wrath: but grievous words stir up anger." If you give out anger, you will live in an angry world.

Third, remember that your keeping of your temper is the victory. You have lost if you lose your temper. No matter what temporary advantage you may have gained, you have lost your case if you lose your temper. If you control your temper, you control the situation.

Fourth, breathe a prayer for those with whom you are about to lose your temper. That prayer will be the pivot on which impending defeat will turn to victory. If one were to pick out the three greatest Christians in the New Testament, the choice would undoubtedly be Jesus (Some say: "The only Christian who ever lived!"), Paul, and Stephen. And if one were to pick out the greatest facts in their lives, the choice would be the fact that all three died with a prayer of forgiveness of their enemies upon their lips. Jesus died praying, "Father, forgive them"; Stephen died praying, "Lord, lay not this sin to their charge," and Paul writing his valedictory, said: "The first time I had to defend myself, I had no supporters; everyone deserted me. (God grant I may not be brought up against them!)" (2 Timothy 4:16 Moffatt). These were the crowning acts of their lives. Prayer for enemies, potential or real, is the crowning act of prayer. And when you pray for your enemies, it proves to be a catharsis for yourself.

Fifth, breathe a prayer for yourself when you are about to lose your good temper. For you are the center of the problem at that moment. Jesus said: "Take heed to yourselves: If thy brother trespass against thee . . . forgive him" (Luke 17:3). Take heed to yourself at a particular moment—at the moment when your brother sins against you. For your reaction to what he does to you may color and determine your whole life for good or ill. Your actions are important, but your reactions are just as important. Many are correct according to actions, but they react badly to what happens to them. They are converted in their actions, but not in their reactions.

Sixth, thicken your skin deliberately so you will no longer be a touchy individual. Many find themselves very thin-skinned. I was once one of them. On board ship going out to India forty-six years ago I would deliberately stay down in my cabin rather than walk on the deck, lest someone would say something about me. Believe it or not, I was shy. But through the years I've had to toughen my skin, so now I wonder if my skin isn't like a rhinoceros hide! I've had to thicken it to survive in a thorny, critical world.

Someone remarked, "I don't believe you know when you are insulted." And I replied, "Well, I suppose I don't. For my soul is too glad and too great to be the enemy of any man."

Seventh, have a convenient memory—a memory that easily forgets hurts and slights. Some people have long memories for slights and hurts and short ones for the blessings and good things of life. A college turned down Dr. George Washington Carver when it found he was a Negro. Years later when Dr. Carver became famous, I asked him what college it was, for he had never mentioned the name. He brushed it aside and said, "Oh, that doesn't matter." And he would not tell me! And rightly so, for if he had mentioned it, it would have fixed it more and more in his mind.

Eighth, if you are to grow in good temper, you must grow in good humor. God has given us the power of laughter not only to laugh at things, but to laugh off things. There is no good in a movement or a person where there is no good humor. For good has laughter as a corollary. There is something basically wrong with a person who doesn't know how to laugh.

— *E. Stanley Jones*

Growing Spiritually
Nashville, Tenn.: Abingdon Press

He Refused To Be Seduced

When Joseph arrived in Egypt as a captive of the Ishmaelite traders, he was purchased from them by Potiphar, a member of the personal staff of Pharaoh, the king of Egypt. Now this man Potiphar was the captain of the king's bodyguard and his chief executioner. The Lord greatly blessed Joseph there in the home of his master, so that everything he did succeeded. Potiphar noticed this and realized that the Lord was with Joseph in a very special way. So Joseph naturally became quite a favorite with him. Soon he was put in charge of the administration of Potiphar's household, and all of his business affairs. At once the Lord began blessing Potiphar for Joseph's sake. All his household affairs began to run smoothly, his crops flourished and his flocks multiplied. So Potiphar gave Joseph the complete administrative responsibility over everything he owned. He hadn't a worry in the world with Joseph there, except to decide what he wanted to eat! Joseph, by the way, was a very handsome young man.

One day at about this time Potiphar's wife began making eyes at Joseph, and suggested that he come and sleep with her.

Joseph refused. "Look" he told her, "my master trusts me with everything in the entire household; he himself has no more authority here than I have! He has held back nothing from me except you yourself because you are his wife. How can I do such a wicked thing as this? It would be a great sin against God."

But she kept on with her suggestions day after day, even though he refused to listen, and kept out of her way as much as possible. Then one day as he was in the house going about his work — as it happened, no one else was around at the time — she came and grabbed him by the sleeve demanding, "Sleep with me." He tore himself away, but as he did, his jacket slipped off and she was left holding it as he fled from the house. When she saw that she had his jacket, and that he had fled, she began screaming; and when the other men around the place came running in to see what had happened, she was crying hysterically. "My husband had to bring in this Hebrew slave to insult us!" she sobbed. "He tried to rape me, but when I screamed, he ran, and forgot to take his jacket."

She kept the jacket, and when her husband came home that night, she told him her story.

"That Hebrew slave you've had around here tried to rape me, and I was only saved by my screams. He fled, leaving his jacket behind!"

Well, when her husband heard his wife's story, he was furious. He threw Joseph into prison, where the king's prisoners were kept in chains. But the Lord was with Joseph there, too, and was kind to him by granting him favor with the chief jailer. In fact, the jailer soon handed over the entire prison administration to Joseph, so that all the other prisoners were responsible to him. The chief jailer had no more worries after that, for Joseph took care of everything, and the Lord was with him so that everything ran smoothly and well.

— *Genesis 39* (TLB)
HOLY BIBLE

The Discipline To Win

Do you not know that those who run in a race all run, but one receives the prize? Run in such a way that you may obtain it. And everyone who competes for the prize is temperate in all things. Now they do it to obtain a perishable crown, but we for an imperishable crown. Therefore I run thus: not with uncertainty. Thus I fight: not as one who beats the air. But I discipline my body and bring it into subjection, lest, when I have preached to others, I myself should become disqualified.

— *1 Corinthians 9:24-27* (NKJV)
HOLY BIBLE

Contentment

When was the last time you met someone who was truly content and at peace with the world? There are many such people! They usually got the wisdom to be that way by learning from the experiences of an active spiritual life. They discovered a sense of inner peace and contentment through their walk with God. But many folks eat their hearts out, suffering from the contagious "If Only" disease. Its germs infect every slice of life:

If only I had more money
If only I could make better grades
If only we owned a nicer home
If only we hadn't made that bad investment
If only I hadn't come from such a bad background
If only she would have stayed married to me
If only our pastor were a stronger preacher
If only my child were able to walk
If only we could have children
If only we didn't have children
If only the business could have succeeded
If only my husband hadn't died so young
If only I would've said "No" to drugs
If only they had given me a break
If only I hadn't had that accident
If only we could get back on our feet
If only he would ask me out
If only people would accept me as I am
If only my folks hadn't divorced
If only I had more friends

The list is endless. Woven through the fabric of all those words is an attitude that comes from the simple choice to see the negative side of life, the choice to be unhappy about almost everything that happens. Taken far enough, it leads to the dead-end street of self-pity—one of the most distasteful and inexcusable of all attitudes. Contentment, on the other hand, comes from another one of those simple choices, one that doesn't allow ourselves or others to listen to our list of woes. We simply choose to create a different kind of list—a positive one—for if we don't, people won't stay around us very long. Discontented souls soon become lonely souls.

— *Charles Swindoll*

Active Spirituality
Dallas: Word Publishing, 1994

Holding Your Tongue

He that covereth a transgression seeketh love; but he that repeateth a matter separateth very friends (Proverbs 17:9).

"Covering a transgression" simply means that we don't spout off about everything we know of a wrong inflicted. At times, it means "just don't bring it up at all." But there is more: God says that if we remain silent under these conditions, then He knows that we are truly seeking love. Love is far different from the tempting thrill of shocking someone with a bit of sensational news. Love covers. Love protects. Love endures the boredom, often the dullness, of just keeping still.

— *Eugenia Price*

Remain Sober To Discern and Teach

Then the Lord spoke to Aaron, saying: "Do not drink wine or intoxicating drink, you, nor your sons with you, when you go into the tabernacle of meeting, lest you die. It shall be a statute forever throughout your generations, that you may distinguish between holy and unholy, and between unclean and clean, and that you may teach the children of Israel all the statutes which the Lord has spoken to them by the hand of Moses."

— *Leviticus 10:8-11* (NKJV)
HOLY BIBLE

My Kingdom

A little kingdom I possess,
    Where thoughts and feelings dwell;
And very hard the task I find
    Of governing it well . . .
I do not ask for any crown
    But that which all may win;
Nor try to conquer any world
    Except the one within.

— *Louisa May Alcott*

From *New Quotable Woman* by Elaine Partnow.
Copyright © 1985 by Facts on File.
Reprinted with permission of Facts on File, Inc.

The Man Who Lost His Self-Control

One day Samson went to the Philistine city of Gaza and spent the night with a prostitute. Word soon spread that he had been seen in the city, so the police were alerted and many men of the city lay in wait all night at the city gate to capture him if he tried to leave.

"In the morning," they thought, "when there is enough light, we'll find him and kill him."

Samson stayed in bed with the girl until midnight, then went out to the city gates and lifted them, with the two gateposts, right out of the ground. He put them on his shoulders and carried them to the top of the mountain across from Hebron!

Later on he fell in love with a girl named Delilah over the valley of Sorek. The five heads of the Philistine nation went personally to her and demanded that she find out from Samson what made him so strong, so that they would know how to overpower and subdue him and put him in chains.

"Each of us will give you a thousand dollars for this job," they promised.

So Delilah begged Samson to tell her his secret. "Please tell me,

Samson, why you are so strong," she pleaded. "I don't think anyone could ever capture you!"

"Well," Samson replied, "if I were tied with seven raw-leather bowstrings, I would become as weak as anyone else."

So they brought her the seven bowstrings, and while he slept she tied him with them. Some men were hiding in the next room, so as soon as she had tied him up she exclaimed, "Samson! The Philistines are here!" Then he snapped the bowstrings like cotton thread, and so his secret was not discovered.

Afterward Delilah said to him, "You are making fun of me! You told me a lie! Please tell me how you can be captured!"

"Well," he said, "if I am tied with brand new ropes which have never been used, I will be as weak as other men."

So that time, as he slept, Delilah took new ropes and tied him with them. The men were hiding in the next room, as before. Again, Delilah exclaimed, "Samson! The Philistines have come to capture you!" But he broke the ropes from his arms like spiderwebs!

"You have mocked me again, and told me more lies!" Delilah complained. "Now tell me how you can really be captured."

"Well," he said, "if you weave my hair into your loom . . . !"

So while he slept, she did just that and then screamed, "The Philistines have come, Samson!" And he woke up and yanked his hair away, breaking the loom.

"How can you say you love me when you don't confide in me?" she whined. "You've made fun of me three times now, and you still haven't told me what makes you so strong!"

She nagged at him every day until he couldn't stand it any longer and finally told her his secret.

"My hair has never been cut," he confessed, "for I've been a Nazirite to God since before my birth. If my hair were cut, my strength would leave me, and I would become as weak as anyone else."

Delilah realized that he had finally told her the truth, so she sent for the five Philistine leaders.

"Come just this once more," she said, "for this time he has told me everything."

So they brought the money with them. She lulled him to sleep with *his head in her lap, and they brought in a barber and cut off his hair. Delilah began to hit him, but she could see that his strength was leaving him.*

Then she screamed, "The Philistines are here to capture you, Samson!" And he woke up and thought, "I will do as before; I'll just shake myself free." But he didn't realize that the Lord had left him. So the Philistines captured him and gouged out his eyes and took him to Gaza, where he was bound with bronze chains and made to grind grain in the prison. But before long his hair began to grow again.

The Philistine leaders declared a great festival to celebrate the capture of Samson. The people made sacrifices to their god Dagon and excitedly praised him.

"Our god has delivered our enemy Samson to us!" they gloated as they saw him there in chains. "The scourge of our nation who killed so many of us is now in our power!" Half drunk by now, the people demanded, "Bring out Samson so we can have some fun with him!"

So he was brought from the prison and made to stand at the center of the temple, between the two pillars supporting the roof. Samson said to the boy who was leading him by the hand, "Place my hands against the two pillars. I want to rest against them."

By then the temple was completely filled with people. The five Philistine leaders were there as well as three thousand people in the balconies who were watching Samson and making fun of him.

Then Samson prayed to the Lord and said, "O Lord Jehovah, remember me again—please strengthen me one more time, so that I may pay back the Philistines for the loss of at least one of my eyes."

Then Samson pushed against the pillars with all his might. "Let me die with the Philistines," he prayed.

And the temple crashed down upon the Philistine leaders and all the people. So those he killed at the moment of his death were more than those he had killed during his entire lifetime. Later, his brothers and their relatives came down to get his body, and they brought him back home and buried him between Zorah and Eshta-ol, where his father, Manoah, was buried. He had judged Israel for twenty years.

— *Judges 16* (TLB)
    HOLY BIBLE

Who Has Control?

Just as (the apostle) Paul told the church at Rome that it is not a controlled mind but a renewed mind that God seeks (see Romans 12:2), so here he informs the Christians that it is not controlled ungodliness but denied ungodliness, and not controlled lusts, but denied lusts, that are required in order to faithfully demonstrate divine holiness. All of the desires, affections, and appetites that govern the men of this world system are to be denied their controlling influence in the lives of men and women who have been made holy. Gluttony, drunkenness, anger, malice, revenge, immoderate love of riches, power, and fame must have no place in our lives. They belong in the world system; we must flee them as we would run from a poisonous serpent. They will never be content to serve us; they are bent upon ruling and ruining us.

The teaching of self-denial is never pleasant nor popular, but it is necessary. We own the controlling voice in our lives. It is we who say "yes" or "no," and the results of that choice affect the entire spectrum of our lives and ministries.

— Judson Cornwall

Cornwall, Jackson. *Let Us Be Holy*
South Plainfield, NJ: Logos International
(Bridge Publishing, Inc.) 1978, p. 112.
Used by permission.

"God" Control

I will allow that the mere effort of will . . . may add to the man's power over his lower nature; but in that very nature it is God who must rule and not the man, how very well he may mean. From a man's rule of himself in smallest opposition, however devout, to the law of his being, arises the huge danger of nourishing by the pride of self-conquest, a far worse than even the unchained animal self—the demoniac self. True victory over self is the victory of God in the man, not of the man alone. It is not subjugation that is enough, but subjugation by God. In whatever man does without God, he must fail miserably—or succeed more miserably. No portion of a man can rule another, for God, not the man, created it, and the part is greater than the whole. . . . The diseased satisfaction which some minds feel in laying burdens on themselves, is a pampering, little as they may suspect it, of the most dangerous appetite of that self which they think they are mortifying.

— *George MacDonald*

The Truth in Jesus
Unspoken Sermons, Second Series
George MacDonald, 365 Readings
Edited by C. S. Lewis
New York: Macmillan, 1947

The Right Channels

Greatness is never just strength. Hitler had strength to frighten a world and practically exterminate a race. Yet, no one would dare call him great. Nero's authority and strength remain unchallenged, but tarring Christians, lighting their still breathing bodies so his gardens might have night torches, is certainly not a display of greatness. Greatness is not just the display of strength, but also the restraint. Lincoln was great because while he had the might to crush the South, he preached and practiced "malice toward none, and charity for all." Washington could have been a dictator, but chose to restrain himself, desiring a strong democracy. Similarly, happiness is not free pursuit of our fancies, but also willful restraint of them.

Our lives are as rivers, either useful in their energies or destructive in their force. One can view the majesty of a plummeting waterfall channeled to bring electricity to a dark community or irrigation to a parched land and feel a sense of appreciation. Or, one can see a swirling undisciplined stream gushing out of its banks, eating away valuable farm land and creating havoc which years of labor cannot right, and feel frustration. The usefulness or destruction is not just in the water itself, but in how it is channeled. Similarly useful and meaningful lives can only come from the temperate hearts which have passions channeled for the greatest good. We are bundles of passions, desires, emotions, and feelings, and inherent in them all is great good or great evil. (The apostle) Paul says the Spirit-filled life is one that is channeled and disciplined for greatest good.

— Charles R. Hembree

Hembree, Charles R. *Fruits of the Spirit*, Baker Book House Company, © 1969.

I Want a Principle Within

I want a principle within of watchful, godly fear,
a sensibility of sin, a pain to feel it near.
I want the first approach to feel of pride or wrong desire,
to catch the wandering of my will, and quench the kindling fire.

From Thee that I no more may stray, no more Thy goodness grieve,
grant me the filial awe, I pray, the tender conscience give.
Quick as the apple of an eye, O God, my conscience make;
awake my soul when sin is nigh, and keep it still awake.

Almighty God of truth and love, to me Thy power impart;
the mountain from my soul remove, the hardness from my heart.
O may the least omission pain my reawakened soul,
and drive me to that blood again, which makes the wounded whole.

— Charles Wesley

Methodist Hymnal

For Consistency in the Christian Life

Lord, what is the matter with us that we are so fitful and moody, so changeful—one moment professing our love for Thee, and the next moment yielding to temptations that lure us away from Thee? One moment, cheerful, smiling, and kind, and the next, glum and surly. Lord, we do not understand ourselves! What strange creatures we are!

Yet we do not pray, our Father, that always everything should be the same, for we would get tired of unending sunshine, and long for a shower of rain.

We do not pray that our way may always be on level places, for then we would long to see a mountain.

We do not pray that always our lot might be favored with pleasant strains of music, for then we would long for the ministry of silence.

But we do pray, O Lord, that there might be some pattern of consistency in our relations with Thee. Teach us how to maintain life on an even keel, that with a balanced life of faith and trust in Thee, and kindness and love toward each other, we shall not be at one moment up in the sky and at the next at the bottom of a well.

Help us to walk with our hand in Thy hand, knowing that Thou Thyself didst come down from mountaintops to walk in the valleys.

— Peter Marshall

Peter Marshall's Sermons and Prayers
New York: Revell,

INDEX

HONOR
B O O K S

P.O. Box 55388
Tulsa, Oklahoma 74155-1388